The scripture-doctrine of atonement, first in relation to Jewish sacrifices, and then to the sacrifice of Jesus Christ, vindicated from the misrepresentations of Mr. John Taylor, of Norwich. In a letter to the author. By Philo-Biblos.

Henry Lee

The scripture-doctrine of atonement, first in relation to Jewish sacrifices, and then to the sacrifice of ... Jesus Christ, ... vindicated from the misrepresentations of Mr. John Taylor, of Norwich. In a letter to the author. By Philo-Biblos.

Lee, Henry, LL.B.
ESTCID: T172584
Reproduction from John Rylands University Library of Manchester
Philo-Biblos = Henry Lee. A reply to John Taylor's 'The scripture-doctrine of atonement examined'.
London : sold by E. Gardner, 1752.
264,[2]p. ; 8°

Eighteenth Century
Collections Online
Print Editions

Gale ECCO Print Editions

Relive history with *Eighteenth Century Collections Online*, now available in print for the independent historian and collector. This series includes the most significant English-language and foreign-language works printed in Great Britain during the eighteenth century, and is organized in seven different subject areas including literature and language; medicine, science, and technology; and religion and philosophy. The collection also includes thousands of important works from the Americas.

The eighteenth century has been called "The Age of Enlightenment." It was a period of rapid advance in print culture and publishing, in world exploration, and in the rapid growth of science and technology – all of which had a profound impact on the political and cultural landscape. At the end of the century the American Revolution, French Revolution and Industrial Revolution, perhaps three of the most significant events in modern history, set in motion developments that eventually dominated world political, economic, and social life.

In a groundbreaking effort, Gale initiated a revolution of its own: digitization of epic proportions to preserve these invaluable works in the largest online archive of its kind. Contributions from major world libraries constitute over 175,000 original printed works. Scanned images of the actual pages, rather than transcriptions, recreate the works *as they first appeared.*

Now for the first time, these high-quality digital scans of original works are available via print-on-demand, making them readily accessible to libraries, students, independent scholars, and readers of all ages.

For our initial release we have created seven robust collections to form one the world's most comprehensive catalogs of 18th century works.

Initial Gale ECCO Print Editions collections include:

History and Geography
Rich in titles on English life and social history, this collection spans the world as it was known to eighteenth-century historians and explorers. Titles include a wealth of travel accounts and diaries, histories of nations from throughout the world, and maps and charts of a world that was still being discovered. Students of the War of American Independence will find fascinating accounts from the British side of conflict.

Social Science

Delve into what it was like to live during the eighteenth century by reading the first-hand accounts of everyday people, including city dwellers and farmers, businessmen and bankers, artisans and merchants, artists and their patrons, politicians and their constituents. Original texts make the American, French, and Industrial revolutions vividly contemporary.

Medicine, Science and Technology

Medical theory and practice of the 1700s developed rapidly, as is evidenced by the extensive collection, which includes descriptions of diseases, their conditions, and treatments. Books on science and technology, agriculture, military technology, natural philosophy, even cookbooks, are all contained here.

Literature and Language

Western literary study flows out of eighteenth-century works by Alexander Pope, Daniel Defoe, Henry Fielding, Frances Burney, Denis Diderot, Johann Gottfried Herder, Johann Wolfgang von Goethe, and others. Experience the birth of the modern novel, or compare the development of language using dictionaries and grammar discourses.

Religion and Philosophy

The Age of Enlightenment profoundly enriched religious and philosophical understanding and continues to influence present-day thinking. Works collected here include masterpieces by David Hume, Immanuel Kant, and Jean-Jacques Rousseau, as well as religious sermons and moral debates on the issues of the day, such as the slave trade. The Age of Reason saw conflict between Protestantism and Catholicism transformed into one between faith and logic -- a debate that continues in the twenty-first century.

Law and Reference

This collection reveals the history of English common law and Empire law in a vastly changing world of British expansion. Dominating the legal field is the *Commentaries of the Law of England* by Sir William Blackstone, which first appeared in 1765. Reference works such as almanacs and catalogues continue to educate us by revealing the day-to-day workings of society.

Fine Arts

The eighteenth-century fascination with Greek and Roman antiquity followed the systematic excavation of the ruins at Pompeii and Herculaneum in southern Italy; and after 1750 a neoclassical style dominated all artistic fields. The titles here trace developments in mostly English-language works on painting, sculpture, architecture, music, theater, and other disciplines. Instructional works on musical instruments, catalogs of art objects, comic operas, and more are also included.

old books. new life.

The BiblioLife Network

This project was made possible in part by the BiblioLife Network (BLN), a project aimed at addressing some of the huge challenges facing book preservationists around the world. The BLN includes libraries, library networks, archives, subject matter experts, online communities and library service providers. We believe every book ever published should be available as a high-quality print reproduction; printed on-demand anywhere in the world. This insures the ongoing accessibility of the content and helps generate sustainable revenue for the libraries and organizations that work to preserve these important materials.

The following book is in the "public domain" and represents an authentic reproduction of the text as printed by the original publisher. While we have attempted to accurately maintain the integrity of the original work, there are sometimes problems with the original work or the micro-film from which the books were digitized. This can result in minor errors in reproduction. Possible imperfections include missing and blurred pages, poor pictures, markings and other reproduction issues beyond our control. Because this work is culturally important, we have made it available as part of our commitment to protecting, preserving, and promoting the world's literature.

GUIDE TO FOLD-OUTS MAPS and OVERSIZED IMAGES

The book you are reading was digitized from microfilm captured over the past thirty to forty years. Years after the creation of the original microfilm, the book was converted to digital files and made available in an online database.

In an online database, page images do not need to conform to the size restrictions found in a printed book. When converting these images back into a printed bound book, the page sizes are standardized in ways that maintain the detail of the original. For large images, such as fold-out maps, the original page image is split into two or more pages

Guidelines used to determine how to split the page image follows:

• Some images are split vertically; large images require vertical and horizontal splits.
• For horizontal splits, the content is split left to right.
• For vertical splits, the content is split from top to bottom.
• For both vertical and horizontal splits, the image is processed from top left to bottom right.

MAB

PRO CHRISTO ECCLESIA

RICHMOND COLLEGE

SURREY

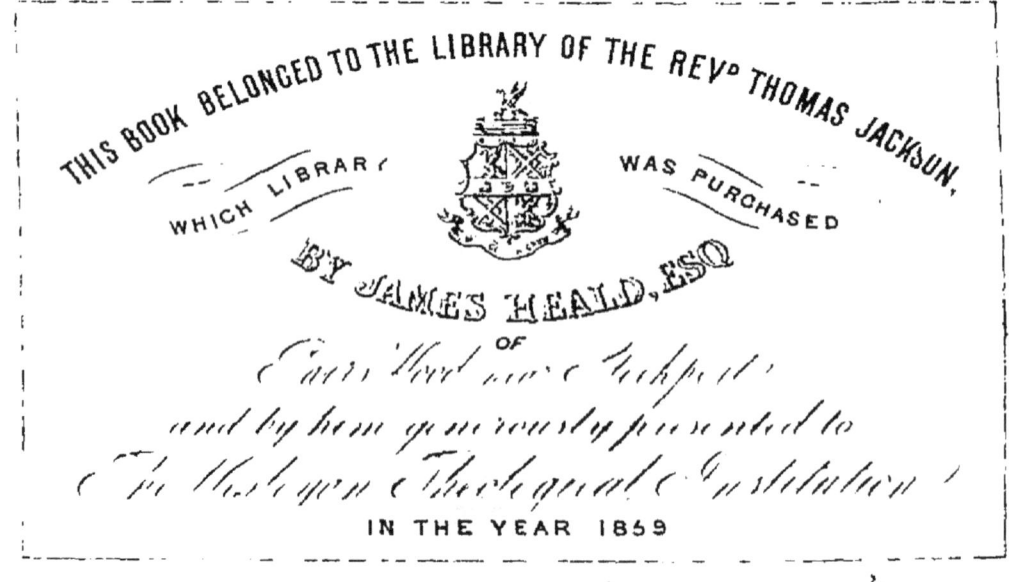

THE
Scripture-Doctrine
OF
ATONEMENT,
FIRST
In relation to *Jewish* Sacrifices,
AND THEN
To the Sacrifice of our Blessed Lord and Saviour JESUS CHRIST,

EXPLAINED,

And proved to be Vicarious, Equivalent, and Satisfactory, for S I N ; and vindicated from the Misrepresentations of Mr. JOHN TAYLOR, of *Norwich*.

In a LETTER to that AUTHOR.

By HENRY LEE, LLB.

Lecturer, and Master of the Free-Grammar School of St *Olave's, Southwark,* and Chaplain to the Rt Hon. Lord MOUNT-CHARLES.

LONDON

Printed for G KEITH, at the *Bible* and *Crown* in *Gracechurch-street.* 1756.

[Price Two Shillings sewed.]

THE

Scripture-Doctrine

OF

ATONEMENT,

FIRST

In relation to *Jewish* Sacrifices,

AND THEN

To the Sacrifice of our Blessed Lord
and Saviour Jesus Christ,

EXPLAINED,

And proved to be Vicarious, Equivalent,
and Satisfactory, for SIN, and vindicated from the Misrepresentations of
Mr. JOHN TAYLOR, of *Norwich*.

In a LETTER to the AUTHOR.

By *PHILO-BIBLOS*.

LONDON:
Sold by E. GARDNER, near the *Cross-Keys*
Inn, Gracechurch-street. 1752.

Thos Hutchins

THE

Scripture - Doctrine

OF

ATONEMENT, &c.

S I R,

 FRIEND of mine lately put into my hands your treatise on the *Scripture-doctrine of atonement*, and defired me to give him my free opinion of it. I have read it with the *caution* you recommend in your preface, being well apprized how careful a man ought to be in matters of religion, left he fhould admit a doctrine without evidence of its truth, or reject it without due examination; extremes which men are too apt to run into: I hope I have kept clear of them, for I meant to do fo.

A 2 I have

I have also read it, as you defire, without *any deference to your judgment*. Indeed, as all true *faith cometh by hearing, and hearing by the word of God*, no great names, no perfonal refpects fhould be fuffered to put any biafs upon our minds, to incline them to accept or difcard what may be propofed to them. The credentials of a doctrine ought to be examined fingly by every man; to be tried by the *word of God*; and what can be eftablifhed by fuch authority, has undoubtedly a right to our affent. I wifh all, Sir, may have read your performance with care, and, as you wifh, with little deference to your judgment, notwithftanding you have given the world great hopes of your abilities; for you poffibly may, as you fay, have miftaken the fenfe of revelation. I declare myfelf your friend, whether or no you will count me fuch I know not: but I have reafon to think you will not look on me to be your *enemy*, becaufe I here mean at leaft to *tell you the truth*, as well as to comply with my friend's requeft.

You fay, in your preface, your intention is upright; and that you heartily wifh your errors may be clearly difcovered, and candidly corrected: therefore from fuch an upright mind I may expect nothing lefs than that my endeavours, which aim to gratify your wifhes, will be acceptable. I have endeavoured to acquit myfelf with *Chriftian* candor,

candor, and that warmth only which becomes the use of *the sword of the spirit.*

To begin then with the proposition
you set out with in your first chapter,
" That the *Jewish* religion consisted very
" much in symbols, i. e. in outward mate-
" rial signs, by which *inward moral dispo-*
" *sitions* were represented." And, of a
truth, it did consist not only very much,
but, if I may believe the Apostle, *all* of
shadow or *symbols*; their very lives being
the manifestations of the *life of* Him *by the*
faith of whom they lived, *Galat.* ii. 26.
And these *symbols* were doubtless outward
material signs of *inward moral disposi-*
tions, if you mean by *moral dispositions,*
certain *dispositions of God* towards our sinful
nature, effectual to take away sin, and re-
new our title to happiness. But it is not
clear, that by moral dispositions you meant
this. If you did, then I conceive a common reader would have understood you much
better, if you had defined these symbols to
be *outward material signs of inward hea-*
venly graces, to be given to man in Jesus
Christ. But I apprehend you meant not,
or at least your words (and I hope I don't
wrest them) lead me to think you meant
not, that we should take your expression in
this sense; because you say, *p.* 6. though
without any other evidence than your own
personal judgment, " That sacrifice is some-
" times

" times offered without any fpecial reafon
" given for it." " That then it feems to
" have been an act of homage, *p.* 15. God
" who is a Spirit cannot be thus pleafed,
" (meaning with effufion of blood)." *p.* 14.
" Nor is it poffible to make any applica-
" tion of material things to His mind or
" effence, which can no ways be affected
" with them." *P.* 20. " Sacrifices were a
" fymbolical addrefs to God, intended to
" exprefs before Him the devotion, &c. of
" the heart, &c. Whatever is expreffive of a
" pious and virtuous difpofition may rightly
" be included in the notion of a facrifice."
P. 21. " The effect that facrifices had with
" God cannot well be conceived to be *any*
" *other* than that of prayer and praife, and
" other expreffions of our religious regards."
You call it " A penitent addrefs to God,"
and fay, *p.* 22. " That the prieft made
" atonement for fin, by facrificing a beaft
" only, as that was a fign and teftimony of
" the facrificer's pure and upright heart."
Whence I think I have a right notion of
your meaning, when I fay you underftand
facrifices not to have been offered as *propitiatory*, or with any reference to *Jefus, the
One offering for all.* On this account therefore, and in the defence of our *moft holy
faith*, I muft except againft your firft pro-
pofition; not becaufe you make the *Jewifh*
religion

religion to confift " very much of fymbols,"
but becaufe you make thofe fymbols to have
a reference to fomewhat in the *offerer*, and
not to *Jefus*, and to have *no other* effect
with *God* than that of prayer and praife.
For, fhould this be granted, we fhould deftroy the very *foundation* of *Chriftianity*,
and give up the faith of the Gofpel . we
fhould be obliged, with no little blafphemy, to fay, *Chrift fulfilled not the law*, nor
anfwered the end of facrifice, when he offered himfelf, for man, as the perfon without whom there was no coming to the Father, and as *the Lamb which taketh away
the fins of the world.* Now facrifice, and
the other rituals under the law, according
to you, referred not to any thing of this
fort: upon your principles, facrifice had a
view to fomewhat in man, which fhould
qualify him to be accepted : yet under
the gofpel it refpects us as perfons, who
without it *can do nothing*, John xv. 5.
How then was the law fulfilled upon
your fuppofition? Not at all. And who
dare advance fuch a horrid accufation a-
gainft the fpotlefs Lamb of God? But is
the end of the facrifice under the law different from that of the great *paffover facrificed for us ?* God forbid. I am fhocked
to think how a man can ftudy to make it
fo, much more fhocked to fee you have done
it

it in the places already cited, not without
great contradiction to yourfelf, *p.* 15. and
128. where you allow us to take our account of the defign of the law from the
Apoftles, who were infpired to give fuch
account by the fame Spirit that indited the
law. We have the authority of the Apoftle,
Galat. iii. 24. that the law was *a fchool-
mafter to bring us unto Chrift.* I muft infift then, that *attending* to the *law* was
learning Chrift; that *doing the law* was exhibiting *Chrift* before *God*; that *Chrift* was
the end of the law towards *God* and towards
man; and that the difpofition he wrought
in the Father was *good-will towards men*;
and in *man*, abhorrence of thofe fins which
coft Chrift fo dear, *repentance* or renovation
towards God; gratitude and love to *Him,
who wafhed us from our fins in his own
blood*, Rev. i. 5. If a *fchoolmafter* was to
teach the art of fortification from *models* or
maps, furely attending to him would be
learning fortification, and *doing* what he
taught would be exhibiting a *regular fortification* to another *in favour of* ourfelves.
And this appointment of the *fymbolic* law
as a *fchool-mafter*, to bring us unto *Chrift*,
was, as yourfelf does not doubt but it was,
well adapted to the genius of the people,
and to the times. I fhould fuppofe the genius of the people of the *Jews* was like that
of

of *all other* before or since, only inftructible *through the channels of fenfe.* Their religion was therefore, by *fymbolic* reprefentations, brought *under* the cognizance of their fenfe. A glafs was made, which faithfully reflected its concernments ; and herein they *faw*, though *darkly* and *in part*, and had evidence before their eyes, of the things they were to believe in, and to hope for, *1 Cor.* xiii. 12. And, as to the times, they were like the *prefent* times, wherein not only nothing lefs than this *fenfible* evidence would go down, but this alfo was frequently *overlooked* : men took upon them then as they do now, in direct oppofition to the firft and fecond commandments, to *make gods* for themfelves, and *terms* for themfelves.

2. You fay, " a great part of thefe fym-
" bols are of little ufe to us now-a-days,
" and therefore it is of no great confequence
" whether we do, or do not, underftand
" them." Yet, by your own conceffion,
" Their facrifices feem to bear fuch a rela-
" tion to the death of *Chrift,* and are fo
" frequently referred to in the writings of
" the New Teftament ; that you fay it
" feems neceffary to have juft ideas of the
" one, in order to our forming a right judg-
" ment of the other." Whereby you feem moft evidently to contradict yourfelf : facrifices *of neceffity* imply the *temple* and its

B　　　　appur-

appurtenances, and the offerers and their difpofitions; and not only the *greateft* part, but *all* the fymbols; becaufe as *Chrift*, the great facrifice, is the *end* of the law, the whole of it, fo the *Levitical* facrifice was the *typical* end of the *law*, whereto all its *commandments* or *ftatutes* referred, and wherein all its *curfes* centered: confequently then, it is abfolutely neceffary for us to know the meaning of *all* the fymbols, in order to conceive properly of the *nature* and *end* of facrifice in *every* refpect, under the law, as the right conception of this muft be previous to our forming a right judgment of Chrift's facrifice in *every* refpect. You muft furely pay but little regard to what St. *Paul* fays, *Rom.* xv. 4. *Whatfoever things were written afore-time were written for our learning, that we might have hope*, before you can juftify what you have here afferted; and I prefume your miftakes (I would hope I may call them fo) have arifen from your not attending to the *meaning* and *ufage* of the *fymbols* under the law. Be our enquiry then into the *nature* of facrifices.

3. Now, in making this enquiry, I fhall not rehearfe the feveral *occafions* of facrifice, which were *many*, and made the matter of the facrifice *different*: nor fhall I be particular about the rituals, but mention them as I need them. I fhall only here then

prove,

prove, that you have no grounds for asserting, sect. 4. " That, on general occasions," (which words, I confess, I do not understand) " there is no special reason given for " sacrificing." All *faith cometh by hearing, and hearing by the word of God.* Yet we read *Heb.* xi. 4. *By faith* Abel *offered a better or greater sacrifice than* Cain: therefore there was a *preceding word of God* to man, whereon this *faith* was grounded. Now the word of God speaks at all times *uniformly*; nor can we suppose, but that what is declared to be *the end of* sacrifice in *one* place, was *always the end* of it, Christ then being called *the end* of the law, *Rom.* x. 4. He must necessarily have been *the end* of sacrifice *under* the law, *sacrifice* being a *part* of the law · and, if Christ was *the end* of sacrifice *under* the law, according to *the word of God*, then he was, *before* the law was written, declared, by the *word of God*, to be *the end* of sacrifice *before* the law. Whence we have this instructing inference, that whenever sacrifice was *properly* offered, let the occasion have been *what* it will, *general* or *particular*, as you please to speak, it was offered with the view of *pleading* or *urging* a Christ crucified before *God*, to make prayer or praise acceptable, as we are won't to say, according to Christ's direction, through Jesus Christ. I say, it

was

was offered, when *properly* offered with this view. Indeed, *Cain* offered it, as you conceive it to have been offered, as " An *act* " *of homage* paid to God, as the Maker, " Owner, Ruler, and Preserver of all things," as if he held his inheritance from God, by *some service of his own:* for he brought not the *Lamb,* and pleaded not his title *under the right* of his Saviour. But please to remember, God *had not respect* unto him, and his offering, but *rejected* him. And, I will be bold to say, you cannot produce me one more instance of a sacrifice mentioned *before* the law, which was not offered as a tender of Christ crucified: though you seem to think, without any evidence, there may be many ranked under this head, *p.* 7.

4. Again, To give you further proof of the invalidity of your assertion, " That sacrifice " was at times offered, without any special " reason assigned for it," I must desire you to recollect, that Christ is called, *Rev.* xiii. 8. *The Lamb slain from the foundation of the world.* Now, how is this true, if he was not *slain* in his *figure.* Remember also, that the Holy Spirit, to whose determination we who believe the Scriptures are bound to submit, frequently speaks of sacrifice as a type of Christ, *our Passover, sacrificed for us.* The reasoning in the Epistle to the *Hebrews,* and 1 *Cor.* v. 7. is grounded upon

its

its being fo. *Abraham* is faid, *through
faith*, to have offered his *fon, to whom the
promife was, that in him All the nations
of the earth*, and not only his feed after the
flefh, *fhould be bleffed. Through faith* Noah
*condemned the world, and became heir of
the righteoufnefs* (of courfe fomewhat extraneous to the inheritor) *which is by faith.
Through faith* Sarah *herfelf received ftrength*
(as the Church does now). *Through faith*
Jacob *bleffed his fons*, and *Mofes kept the
Paffover* ; All before the law was written :
fo that I cannot conceive how my conclufion, That facrifice, *properly* offered, was
offered *through faith*, in the thing *fignified
by the Holy Ghoft*, Heb. ix. 8. can be
evaded, unlefs you can prove, 1. That *facrifice* means not *the fame* thing in *one* place
that it does in *another*, and was not always attended with the *fame difpofitions*
or *faith* in the offerer to make it *acceptable*. 2. That the Cherubims ferved not
the *fame* purpofe to *Adam*, that they did
to *Mofes* and *Aaron*; which purpofe St.
Paul declares to be, that of *patterns of
heavenly things, purified with facrifices*, that
were alfo *patterns of better things* than
thefe. And I hope you will not make ufe
of this evafion, for then you may go on with
an *equal fhew* of reafon to prove, that the
fame God is not underftood by the word
God

God in any *two* places in our Bible. Paſs
we on then next,

5. To *chap.* 2. in which you propoſe to
ſhew the *meaning, deſign,* and *efficacy,* of
ſacrifices.

Of a *religious* nature, as you ſay, doubtleſs they were, and had a *primary* and prin-
cipal reſpect to God. Becauſe,

6. (1) As you ſay, " The *tabernacle,* af-
" terwards the *temple,* was regarded as the
" palace and *reſidence of God upon earth,*
" where his preſence was *ſignified, &c.* and
" therefore *all* appioach to that muſt be
" ſuppoſed (I ſhould have ſaid *believed*) to
" be an *approach to God:*" And, by your
permiſſion, I muſt add, *through Jeſus Chriſt
our Lord,* of whoſe *body,* with *the fulneſs
of the Godhead dwelling in him,* the temple,
wherein the *ſymbolical preſence* of God
dwelt, is declared to be a *figure* by Chriſt
himſelf, *John* ii. 21. " And, when all the
" ſacrifices are ordered to be brought to *this*
" ſanctuary, *&c.* and the *blood, partly* to
" be ſprinkled towards the *Divine Pre-*
" *ſence,* and *partly* pouied out at the *foot*
" of the altar; no doubt can be made, but
" thoſe ſacrifices had reſpect unto God ;"
and, by your leave, unto *the body of Jeſus,*
the *great* offering to be made by the *great
High-Prieſt,* and *to the blood of ſprinkling*
in this body. *Chriſt,* as we iead in *Heb.* ix.
24.

24. went into the true *Holy* (place) *of the Holies* (or Holy Ones) to plead his blood and merits, of which this typical transaction in the *tabernacle* or *temple* was a *preluding* or *rehearsing* scene.

(2) " The priests," as you say, " were his " servants, and ministered to him in holy " things ; and therefore their solemn ac- " tions," and I must add, *every one* of their actions in the *House of God*, down *to the bearing of burdens in* the tabernacle, *Numb.* iii. and iv. " must bear relation to God, " whose ministers they were." To this account I must add a more *explicit* one from the Scriptures. These ministers or priests, which were taken *in the stead of all the first-born among the children of* Israel, *Num.* iii. 12. officiated not in their own name, but *in the Name of the Lord*, Deut. x. 8.—xviii. 19. St. *Paul* therefore calls the priesthood, which was a part of the law, *Heb.* x. 1. *A shadow of the good things to come*; *a figure for the time then present*, iv. 9. *who serve unto the example and shadow of heavenly things*, viii. 5. He stiles this ministry, a pattern of a *more excellent* ministry, viii. 6. the high-priest of an *high-priest of good things to come, by a greater and more perfect tabernacle*, ix. 11. So that what things the priests did in the *tabernacle* or *temple*, were, *in figure*, the actions of the Lord, done

done in *his body*, in *whose name* they officiated. The offerings or facrifices *in the
temple* were, *in figure*, the offerings or facrifices *of the Lord, in the temple of his
body.* And it was a Saviour they looked
at in the perfon of the prieft, *the Lord's
Chrift, taken in the ftead of all the firft-born
of the Ifrael of God,* who were all to be
holy and *clean* as the *Ifraelites* were, by
what he did in the *tabernacle of his body.*

7. Indeed, upon your own principles, this
account is true, becaufe you call the temple
the refidence of God; and this temple you
muft own, as you value your perfeverance
in the faith of the Scriptures, to be a figure
of the body of *Chrift :* I ask then, whether
every action done in this *temple*, was not, *in
figure*, the *action* of our *great High-Prieft*
in the *temple of his body.* This cannot be
denied, as the Scriptures are true, by any
who receive them ; nor by you, unlefs you
will argue againft your *own conceffions* here,
and in *p.* 128. in the note. If you want
further proofs from the Bible, that the tabernacle or temple had a reference to another
more perfect tabernacle or temple, fee them
in *Pfal.* v. 7.—xi. 4.—xxvii. 5, 6.—xlvi. 5, 6.
—lxi. 4.—lxv. 4.—lxviii. 29. — lxxviii. 67,
69.—xcii. 13. — cii. 16. — cxxii. 9.—cxxxii.
5, 8, 13, 14. and *Ifa.* iv. 5, 6. — xvi. 5. —
xxxiii.

xxiii. 20. *Amos* ix. 12. *Ezek.* xxxvii. 27. and *Mal.* iii. 1.

8. (3) Befides, " Some facrifices, you " fay, were, and fome were not, accepted." If they were offered, as God would have them offered, they were accepted, *Lev.* i 4. The facrifice in *Lev.* xxii. 2. *for a peace-offering* to the Lord (to make our peace with him) *muft be perfect*, as *Chrift*, who is *our peace*, was and is perfect. there fhall be no blemifh therein. A fpotted, blind, or difeafed offering, he cannot away with; what pleafes him muft be fpotlefs, and man muft plead this to be accepted. Why you bring *ver.* 23. as a proof that fome facrifices were *not accepted*, I know not; for it fays only, that *a bullock or lamb, that hath any thing fuperfluous or lacking in his parts, fhall be accepted, if offered,* as God would have it offered, *as a free-will offering*; but *for a vow*, or retribution to God, it fhould not be accepted. A work, offered in Chrift as this facrifice in the tabernacle, which has *additions* it ought *not* to have, or fome defects in it, fhall be accepted for a *free-will* offering of *love*, &c. but for *that* which fhould make *peace* it fhall not be accepted. No, we muft *not* plead ourfelves, but Chrift for *our peace-maker*; which fhewed the *If-raelites*, that their acceptance was not of *works* but of *grace*. The *blind* were not

C   ac-

done in *his body*, in *whose name* they officiated. The offerings or facrifices *in the
temple* were, *in figure*, the offerings or facrifices *of the Lord, in the temple of his
body*. And it was a Saviour they looked
at in the perfon of the prieft, *the Lord's
Chrift, taken in the ftead of all the firft-born
of the Ifrael of God*, who were all to be
holy and *clean* as the *Ifraelites* were, by
what he did in the *tabernacle of his body*.

7. Indeed, upon your own principles, this
account is true, becaufe you call the temple
the refidence of God; and this temple you
muft own, as you value your perfeverance
in the faith of the Scriptures, to be a figure
of the body of *Chrift :* I ask then, whether
every action done in this *temple*, was not, *in
figure*, the *action* of our *great High-Prieft*
in the *temple of his body*. This cannot be
denied, as the Scriptures are true, by any
who receive them ; nor by you, unlefs you
will argue againft your *own conceffions* here,
and in *p*. 128. in the note. If you want
further proofs from the Bible, that the tabernacle or temple had a reference to another
more perfect tabernacle or temple, fee them
in *Pfal.* v. 7.—xi. 4.—xxvii. 5, 6.—xlvi. 5, 6.
—lxi. 4.—lxv. 4.—lxviii. 29. — lxxviii. 67,
69.—xcii. 13. — cii. 16.—cxxii. 9.—cxxxii.
5, 8, 13, 14. and *Ifa.* iv. 5, 6. — xvi. 5. —
xxxiii.

xxiii. 20. *Amos* ix. 12. *Ezek.* xxxvii. 27.
and *Mal.* iii. 1.

8. (3) Besides, " Some sacrifices, you
" say, were, and some were not, accepted."
If they were offered, as God would have
them offered, they were accepted, *Lev.* 1 4.
The sacrifice in *Lev.* xxii. 2. *for a peace-
offering* to the Lord (to make our peace
with him) *must be perfect*, as *Christ*, who
is *our peace*, was and is perfect : there shall
be no blemish therein.   A spotted, blind,
or diseased offering, he cannot away with ;
what pleases him must be spotless, and man
must plead this to be accepted.   Why you
bring *ver.* 23. as a proof that some sacrifices
were *not accepted*, I know not, for it says
only, that *a bullock or lamb, that hath any
thing superfluous or lacking in his parts, shall
be accepted, if offered*, as God would have
it offered, *as a free-will offering*; but *for a
vow*, or retribution to God, it should not
be accepted.   A work, offered in Christ as
this sacrifice in the tabernacle, which has
additions it ought *not* to have, or some defects in it, shall be accepted for a *free-will*
offering of *love, &c.* but for *that* which
should make *peace* it shall not be accepted.
No, we must *not* plead ourselves, but Christ
for *our peace-maker*; which shewed the *Israelites*, that their acceptance was not of
works but of *grace.*   The *blind* were not

C   ac-

accepted, nor the *lame*, nor the *sick*, nor a *corrupt thing*, Mal. viii. 10, 13. But what is your conclusion ? " That they had re- " spect unto God's favour and approbation." True, they had ; and were appointed the spotless means to obtain it. *Psal.* xx. 1, 3. (not the Lord, as you cite this text, but) *The Name of the God of* Jacob *remember all thy offerings, and accept thy burnt sa- crifice :* so *accepting* the sacrifice was *previous* to an acceptance of the person.

9. (4) " They were offered to obtain a " blessing, or by way of thanksgiving, or " for the remission of sins ;" that is, *through the blood of Jesus Christ,* and *in Jesus Christ,* of whom the temple was a figure *wherein* the sacrifice was offered, and pleaded for the sinner : whence " these sacrifices must," not only, as you say, " have respect to God in " very important concernments," but also to our Lord *Jesus Christ* (by sect. 6.) *through whom* believers, and their services, were, as they are now, accepted.

10. (5) " Add to this, that the mind of " the offerer was to be well disposed ; other- " wise the sacrifice was not pleasing to God." What disposition this was you do not men- tion, therefore give me leave to make use of St. *Paul*'s account of it, *Heb.* iv. 2. *The word preached did not profit them, not be- ing mixed with faith in them that heard it.*
They

They apprehended not the thing signified by the word, and were not by faith united to it. For, whenever sacrifice was *not pleasing,* it must have been offered with *another* view than God intended it should be offered, and not as a *memento* of Christ crucified for men, which we have already proved, in *sect.* 3. to have been the view of God in instituting it. He then that had faith in the thing signified, must have pleased God, *whom without faith it is impossible to please.* " The offerer," you say, " was " always to lay his hand upon the head of " the sacrifice, and, though an act of the " mind is but once expressly said to attend " that sacrifical rite, *viz.* upon the day of " atonement, when *Aaron* confessed the " sins of the people, *Lev.* xvi. 21. yet, pro- " bably, this was always the case." How you could mistake the end of *putting the hand* upon *the head* of the sacrifice I know not. but I conceive it appears, from the passage referred to, that the hands were laid upon the head of the live goat, and then *confession was made* (over) *upon* (עליו) *him of all the iniquities of the children of* Israel, *and of all their transgressions in all their sins :* and, by *imposition* of hands, a sign of the *imputation* of what was *not originally* his, they were put *upon the head* of the goat ; and, in consequence of this, it is

said,

faid, he *bore upon him all their iniquities.*
The *impofition* of hands was therefore an
act expreffing the *imputation* of the fins confeffed *upon* him.   But you own, " it is pro-
" bable," (I fuppofe you mean *proveable*)
" that the laying on of hands was to be at-
" tended with the confeffion of fins :" Now,
pray, why muft not I add, *upon the facrifice*, fince it is fo in the text, and the fins
are declared *to be put upon it :* and how
fuch a confeffion of their fins upon it fuits
your opinion, that *no* fins, nor guilt of fin,
were *transferrable*, will be fhewn in its
place.   But well might they facrifice with
the voice of thankfgiving, as you cite *Jon.*
ii. 9. when their fins were thus made the
Lamb's, that *his* fufferings might be deemed *theirs,* and they be perfected by the *offering of the body of Jefus once for all.* But
what do you infer ? why, what I confefs I
never heard queftioned, that " facrifices are
" of a religious nature, and moral," if you
mean fome *morem*, or *mode*, of action, on the
part of God, in order to *reconcile us to himfelf*, " and had their effects with God *to*
" *whom*, and with the perfons *by whom*,"
and I muft add, *for whom* (fee *p.* 21, 22. of
your book) " they were offered."

   11. But, firft, as to the fignificancy and ef-
ect they had with refpect to God, you ask,
" Were they a gift or prefent ?" Yes, they
weie

were a *gift*, being each a ſhadow of the *great* ſacrifice, which was a *gift of the only-begotten Son of God, whom God gave,* and of the body *or fleſh which Chriſt gave for the life of the world,* John iii. 16.—vi. 51. *Eph.* v. 2, 25. *Galat.* i. 4. Theſe texts which follow ſpeak of them as a gift or gifts, *Num.* xviii. 11. *The heave-offering of their gift.* Ezek. xlv. 13. *This is the oblation that ye ſhall offer ; — ye ſhall give the ſixth part of an ephah of an omer of barley.* Ezek. xx. 39. *Pollute my holy Name no more with your gifts.* Exod. xxx. 12. *The ranſom-money.* Deut. xvi. 17. what they *brought before the Lord* at the feaſts. *Exod.* xxxv. their *offerings* for the tabernacle are ſaid to be *given.* Nay, in *Leviticus* throughout, what they brought to the tabernacle are called *offerings,* and *Levit.* xxvii. 9. we read, *If it be a beaſt whereof men bring an offering unto the Lord, all that any man giveth of ſuch unto the Lord ſhall be holy.* Lev. ii. 18. *The offering* is ſaid to be *preſented.*—ix. 12. *The blood* is ſaid to be *preſented* ——xvi. 7. *The two goats* are ſaid to be *preſented.* Hence *Pſal.* lxxvi. 11. *Bring preſents unto him that ought to be feared.—* lxxii 10. *The kings of* Sheba *ſhall offer gifts.* Matt. v. and xxiv. Chriſt ſays, before the law was fulfilled, *come and offer thy gift :* ſo that *offerings,* by which name all the

ſacrifices

sacrifices are called, were gifts. Further, the *priests*, as well as the *sacrifices*, were a *gift*. Numb. viii. 10. *Thou shalt bring the* Levites (which were *to bear the iniquity of the congregation*, viii. 1—23.) *before the* Lord, *and the children of* Israel *shall put their hands* (their sins by imputation) *upon the* Levites. *And* Aaron *shall offer the* Levites *before the Lord for an offering of the children of* Israel, *that they may execute the service of the Lord. And the* Levites *shall lay their hands* (sins) *upon the heads of the bullocks—and thou shalt offer the one for a sin-offering,* &c. *to make an atonement for the* Levites. — 14. *They are to be separated — to be God's.* ——15. *To be cleansed, and then offered for an offering.* — 16. *For they are wholly given unto me from among the children of* Israel, *instead of such as open every womb.* Whence we read of *Christ giving himself* in the texts before cited : and because the priests offered *gifts,* St. *Paul,* in his Epistle to the *Hebrews,* v. 1. speaks of it as being a fact well known, that *every high-priest taken from among men is ordained for* (or over) *men in things pertaining to* God, *that he may offer both gifts and sacrifices for sins.* ——viii. 3. *Every high-priest is ordained to offer gifts*—4. *Seeing that there are priests which offer gifts.* —— ix. 9. *In which were offered gifts and sacrifices :* and
it

it is on thefe grounds the Apoftle fays, *ver.*
32. *Wherefore it is of neceffity that this man
have fomewhat alfo to offer.* So that, unlefs a man queftions the authority of both
teftaments, I fee not how he can queftion
whether the *facrifices,* the *priefts,* and the
tabernacle, &c. were a *gift* or no, fince they
were but fhadows of Chrift, who is in *himfelf* the *facrifice,* the *high-prieft,* and the
tabernacle, and has told us he *gave himfelf.*

12. You, in this paragraph, next ask,
" Was the burning of fat or flefh a grateful
" fmell to him?" And I muft anfwer it was,
when it was offered with that view with
which God intended it fhould be offered;
elfe what mean thefe texts, *Gen.* viii. 21.
The Lord fmelled a fweet favour, when
Noah offered burnt-offerings on the altar,
Lev. ii. 12.—iii. 16, *&c.* *Ezek.* xx. 41. *I
will accept you with your fweet favour,* and
Ifa. xliii. 23, 24. *Ye brought me no fweet
cane.* Eph. v. 2. *Chrift was the fweet fmelling favour,* re-offered and pleaded in the
fign of it.

13. To the third queftion you put, " Was
" he pleafed with the effufion of blood, and
" the death of his creatures?" I muft anfwer, Yes; he was pleafed with them, as
being *the blood of the covenant of Jefus,* and
the death of his Lamb: elfe, why is *blood*
said

faid to *make atonement for the foul?* **Why**
is the facrifice called *a facrifice for fin?* **If**
God was not pleafed with them, he never
would have ordered them, never remitted
fin on thefe accounts. But St. *Paul* fays,
they were figures and *fhadows*; and indeed
it is unreafonable to fuppofe God forgiving
fins on thefe accounts, otherwife than as
thefe things had, and were offered as having, a connection with the blood of *the
Lamb of God*; and in this light they were
as acceptable to God, as our pleading Chrift
offered *once for all.*

14. You fay, " The *Jewifh* writings ftre-
" nuoufly enter their proteft againft this
" notion of them ," and you conclude,
" God, who is a Spirit, cannot be thus
" pleafed ; nor is it poffible to make any
" application of material things to his mind
" or effence, which can no ways be affected
" with them." Now, Sir, to fpeak my
mind freely, you have miftaken the matter
toto cœlo : for, however the *Jewifh* writings
urge the ability of their legal facrifices to
take away fin by fome *fuppofed* merit in
men's works, the infpired Prophets, inftead
of protefting againft the efficacy of the *Levitical* facrifices to take away fin, or to excite an approving pleafure in God, proteft
only againft their being qualified, as mere
gifts and fervices of *men,* to draw down the
favour

favour of the Moft High. God wants not *men*'s gifts nor *men*'s fervices to juftify them, for thefe cannot avail to this end and the Pfalmift would intimate to us, that it is not in man's power to give to God *any* confideration for his mercy, *Pfal.* l. 1. *Offer unto God thankfgiving — Call upon me.* This is all man has to do, God has done the reft; and it is to what God *in* Chrift was to do which the legal fervices referred : *Confider this*, he goes on, *ye that forget God*, what he was engaged to do, by promifing to be *their God. Whofo offereth praife* (for his fpiritual creation) *honoureth me, and to him who ordereth* (his) *way aright, will I fhew the falvation of God.* But here is not a word about God's not being pleafed with the *facrifice*, as the facrifice of his *Jefus* or *Lamb*, or with the *burning of fat* or *flefh*, as the mortifying of lufts, and the deftroying of the body of the fins of the flefh, *by the circumcifion of Chrift*, or with the effufion of blood, as the *blood of Chrift*, or with the death of the facrifice, as the *death of Chrift.* No fuch things his foul delighted in. This figurative accomplifhment of his will, which Chrift fays, *Pfal.* xl 6. cited in *Heb.* x. 7. *He came to do*, he could not but be pleafed with, as it ftood and was offered, as it ftood connected with the real completion of it. For, though he was not

D   pleafed

pleafed with them becaufe of *any* ability in the things *themfelves* to raife his pleafure, yet he was pleafed with them as being the things which in the faithful officer fhewed and pleaded *the Lord's death till he came.* It is on this account the *Lord had refpect unto* Abel, *and to his offering,* Gen. iv. 4. It is hence the burnt-offerings are called, in thirty-four places in Scripture, if I am right in my calculation, *a fweet fmelling favour unto the Lord;* becaufe they reprefented Chrift's offering himfelf *a facrifice to God for a fweet fmelling favour,* Eph. v. 2; fo that you feemingly have determined too haftily, that God " cannot be thus pleafed nor " affected with material things." On your fuppofition I may fafely fay, the actions of our bodies cannot affect him. But you cannot fay this is true : then material things, *by their connection with* fpiritual things, as the body with the foul, may affect him. *Faith* indeed was the thing which *made* the union, and confequently *made* the facrifices have an effect with God, as it is that mean by which *alone* the human and divine nature can be allied. Pray, then, confider this, and recal this peremptory fentence of yours, which would fuperfede the counfel of the Moft High : for confider, you arraign, I hope unwittingly, all the *Apoftles* and *Prophets,* nay, the *Great God of Heaven,* befides

fides all the rational deductions of *common
fenfe*, when you fay, " God cannot be af-
" fected with *any* application of material
" things." Nay you, by this, condemn *all*
forts of worfhip, becaufe you take away the
only motive which can *produce* or *preferve*
it, namely, *its being agreeable or pleafing to
God*, for it is with the *tongue* we praife and
pray, it is from *matters of fenfe* we have
all our ideas whereon our *faith* is founded.
And the conclufion, from your premifles,
muft neceffarily be this, That *none* of thefe
fervices, as being *applications of material
things*, can any ways affect God. Alas,
Sir! why are we bid *to believe?* Why is
he that hath *faith* faid to *pleafe God*, and
God faid to *love him?* Are thefe mere
words, or are they not declarations of matters of fact. This I know, God has fpoken
them, and God *cannot lie.* Wonder not
then I diffent from you in this matter, as
the difference between *God's* teftimony and
your's is *infinite:* and befides this, I have
the teftimony of common fenfe; for *he that
comes to God muft believe that he is.* Now
faith fuppofes *evidence*, and *evidence* can
only fubfift in *vifible* matters, and thefe *vifible* matters offered in *faith* muft be pleafing,
becaufe *faith* is fo pleafing, that *without
faith it is impoffible to pleafe God ·* but *facrifice* is a *vifible* matter; its defign, you

D 2   own,

own, was to reprefent the *death of Chrift*, and man was to plead it as having body and foul · this *fenfible evidencing* fcene muft then be accompanied with *faith* in that which is evidenced; and an act like our nature, *mixed with faith*, muft of neceffity be acceptable to God, and excite him to perform thofe promifes which he has made throughout the Scriptures, to them *only* who *believe in the Lord God.*

15 But, (in 19.) after faying, " They " could not affect God," you fay, " The " *Levitical* law fupplies no anfwer to this " queftion, namely, In what manner facri- " fices had refpect to God." Now, not to dwell on the *inconfiftency* of making this en- quiry, after you have determined " no ap- " plication of them can make them to affect " God;" I apprehend you have overlooked the *fenfe* of the *Levitical* law, as you have overlooked the end of the *Levitical* facri- fices. For, in truth, I cannot but charita- bly believe, before you could venture to publifh fuch a doctrine, that you did not confider the *Levitical* law was given by God, and that you was fuppofing God to have given a law to his people, whofe mean- ing they were ftrangers to. For, on fuch a fuppofition, what will become of the wifdom, or of the goodnefs, or of the juftice, of God? What *blame* could be laid on the *Ifraelites*, for

for not performing ordinances which they did not underſtand? And what *puniſhment* be in juſtice inflicted upon tranſgreſſors, through an involuntary and neceſſary ignorance? I hope, therefore, when you ſee theſe conſequences of your aſſertion, which I believe you will not chuſe to juſtify, that they may induce you to correct your judgment on this head, by taking it for granted amongſt all men, that what brings on ſuch ſhocking concluſions, can never be a true account of the divine law. However, at leaſt excuſe me for juſtifying the faith for which I muſt anſwer at the great tribunal of Heaven, and which is, that God talked intelligibly to his people, and gave them a law, whoſe meaning they were well acquainted with, and for tranſgreſſing of which they are, as all muſt be, ſaid to be *inexcuſeable*. I can produce you abundant evidence for this; but, to wave it at preſent, let us reaſon upon your own principles.

16. I will, with you, take it for granted, " That, to conſult the ſenſe of the Pro-
" phets and Apoſtles, who had a clear and
" full knowledge of the nature and ends of
" the divine inſtitutions, is a juſt and au-
" thentic method of diſcovering and aſcer-
" taining the truth." But, in order to ſtrengthen their evidence, I do not ſuppoſe the Fathers knew not the meaning of their rites,

rites, as for instance, of *circumcision* : for I believe, because it is to be proved, that this was known by them to be *a token of a covenant confirmed before of God in Christ.* *Circumcision* had " a relation to the heart," you say, " and signified the putting off of " the body of the sins of the flesh." But pray say, whether by the person circumcised, or by another whom the circumcised and circumcising person represented? If you say, It was done by the person circumcised, I must insist upon it, that no mere man of *himself* ever put them off, or had his heart *thus* circumcised. If you say, It was done by *another* whom the parties doing and suffering this act represented, then I must join issue with you. *Abraham* was a type of the *Father of the Faithful, our Lord,* and being circumcised did, by your allowed evidence from *Coloss.* ii. 11. represent Christ circumcised, *in whom also ye are circumcised with the circumcision made without hands, in putting off the body of the sins of the flesh by the circumcision of Christ* ; and the parties circumcised knew they were *not* to circumcise themselves, but to *suffer a circumcision* by and in *another,* of which *circumcision* was known to be only a *token :* and every considerate person (to use your own words) will allow this account to be so far satisfactory. But if it is, how tallies this

estimation

eftimation of fuffering a circumcifion in Chrift, *in whom ye are circumcifed*, with your affertion, That there was *no* transfer of fin and guilt made to Chrift? For what can be plainer, than that if we are circumcifed in Chrift, we were deemed to be collectively in him, as we all were in the loins of *Adam, who was the figure of him that was to come*, Rom. v. 14. If *in* him we *put off the body of the fins of the flefh* by the circumcifion of him, then *his* body was held to be the reprefentative *body of the fins of the flefh*, which was circumcifed, cut off, or put off. But more of this by and by: I muft now confider the fenfe of the *Levitical* inftitutions, as gathered from the Prophets and Apoftles.

17. "The temple," you fay, *fect.* 20. "is " called the *houfe of prayer*, Ifa. lvi 7. and " with relation too to the facrifices there of-" fered." True, it is called *a houfe of prayer*, but remember it is the *temple of the body of Chrift*, and the refidence of God, by your own conceffions, *fect.* 13. Now let us hear the text. *All the fons of the ftranger that* (join themfelves) *are joined* (נלוים) *to* (upon, על) *the Lord* (and do not depend upon themfelves, nor detach themfelves from their interefts in this Lord, but are one with him) *to ferve him* (and not the vanity of their own minds) *and to love*
                                                                    the

Name of the Lord (which is given to Jesus Christ, and is *above every name*, and besides which *none other name under Heaven is given unto men,* whereby they may be saved) *to be his servants; every one that keepeth the sabbath from polluting it, and taketh hold of my covenant; even them will I bring to my holy mountain, and make them joyful in my house of prayer; their burnt-offerings and their sacrifices shall be accepted upon mine altar; for mine house shall be called an house of prayer for all people,* namely, Christ, wherein *the fullness of the Godhead dwelleth bodily (for the Most High dwelleth not in temples made with hands,* Acts v.) *in whom ye, who sometimes were far off, are made nigh by the blood of Christ,* Eph. ii. 13, *in whom neither circumcision availeth any thing, nor uncircumcision,* Gal. vi. 15; *where there is neither* Greek *nor* Jew, *circumcision nor uncircumcision,* Barbarian, Scythian, *bond or free, but Christ is all, and in all,* Coloss. iii. 11; *for through him (the temple not made with hands) we both have access by one Spirit unto the Father,* Eph. ii. 18. " Here prayer," you say, " or solemn address to God, and sacri-" fices, are terms *equipollent.*" On what grounds I know not: I confess I see not any such equivalence. *Prayer* seems to me to be *one* thing, and *sacrifice* to be *another.* But

But it is promised, their *sacrifices shall be accepted*, and the *temple* is called *a house of prayer* (though indeed the *Jewish* temple is not called so in this text) and therefore the terms are equipollent, that is, equivalent. Surely, Sir, you are not desirous to urge this matter home upon any considerations. It is a *Prophet* to whom you are ascribing your sense of his words, and therefore you should thank a person that would prevent your speaking of him what he *never* meant to say. And indeed, what weak premisses have you chose to ground your conclusion upon. *Sacrifice*, in its primitive meaning, from *sacrum & facio*, as *making* persons *holy* who were not holy *before* they were made so, seems to be a thing you do not relish; and therefore this meaning of it is to be explained away, because the temple, wherein sacrifices were offered, is supposed to be called a *house of prayer*; though should it be called so, it would not prove that sacrifice and prayer was one and the same thing. The text, Sir, speaks of the Christian dispensation: it speaks of Christ as the *house of God*, of the sacrifice offered in him, and pleaded by us in prayer, of us, as accepted on account of it, and of Christ as the *house of prayer*, in consequence of this sacrifice, *for all*, not for the *Jews only*, but for *all* people. It speaks of those who, according

E   to

to the law, were *far off*, as *brought nigh* by a connection and union with the Lord *in the temple of his body*; and it holds forth Chrift as the perfon *in* whom, and *through* whom, they fhould pray to God and the Father. So, in 2 *Chron.* vii. 12. the temple is called *a houfe of facrifice*, reprefenting the body of Chrift, in whom the great facrifice was to be made *once for all.* " Incenfe," you fay, " was an emblem of prayer;" of what prayer? of man's prayer, unqualified with the weight of *any* merit? No; incenfe was not the prayer of man, a *mere* man had *no* bufinefs in the temple where the incenfe was fumed, none but the *prieft* fumed it. Incenfe then, that fweet-fmelling favour, was, in figure, the merits of our great *High-Prieft*, offered up by him for us *in the temple of his body, by* and *through the eternal Spirit*. We are to plead thefe merits in prayer, being *a Royal Priefthood built up in Chrift*, the true temple of God, 1 *Pet.* ii. 9.—and *made priefts unto God*, Rev. i. 5. to offer up facrifices by and in Chrift Jefus, the temple *not made with hands*; and accordingly, inftead of its appearing, from *Luke* i. 10. that incenfe was an emblem of *prayer*, which you have referred to as a *proof* of it, we read only that *the whole multitude of the people were praying without at the time of incenfe.* Now, how you

could

could conclude from hence, that " incenfe
" was an emblem of prayer," I know not;
this would have been offering fhadow and
fubftance together: befides, we read this
incenfe was what was fumed *in* the *temple*,
and they played *without*. As incenfe then
was offered when the facrifice was flain,
that is, as the fweet-fmelling favour of the
merits of Chrift afcended upon the death of
Chrift, which was the *greateft* act of obedience for us, the purport of their prayers
was, as it is of *the Chriftians now*, to plead
thefe merits in their favour. This is clear
from St. *Paul*'s calling Chrift's death *a
fweet-fmelling facrifice*, and his blood *precious*, &c. Neither is it plain from *Rev.*
viii. 3, 4. that incenfe was an emblem of
prayer, though you cite them to prove it:
*Another Angel came, and ftood at the al-
tar, having a golden cenfer; and there was
given unto him much incenfe, that he fhould
add to the prayers of all faints upon the
golden altar which was before the throne:
And the fmoke of the incenfe, with the prayers
of the Saints, afcended up before God out
of the Angels hands.* So here was incenfe,
meritorioufnefs, and weight or agreeablenefs,
added to the prayers, to make them acceptable, fomewhat that was *extraneous to* the
prayers, that was *given* to the Angel: moreover, not the people but the Angel was to

E 2 offer

offer them *with* the incense; but not a word of its being an emblem of *prayer*. Indeed *Rev.* v. 8 would, in appearance, have suited your purpose better, had we not already seen what incense was; because here we read of *golden vials full of odors or incense, which are the prayers of Saints*; but they are prayers clothed with a *meritorious incense*, with the *addition* made to the prayers by the Angel in the above citation: they are prayers offered *in the name*, and through the sweet-smelling merits, of our Lord and Saviour Jesus Christ; for so Christ directs us to pray, *John* xv. 16.——xvi. 23. As to *Psal.* cxli. 2. *David* (representing Christ, as all the Prophets did) says, *Let my prayer be set forth before thee as the incense* (incense therefore made prayer acceptable) *and the lifting up of my hands as the evening sacrifice.* Whence we can infer only, that the prayer of a meritorious Christ for man was to be as agreeable *as the incense,* and the *intercession* of Christ, in virtue of his sacrifice, available in God's eye *as the evening sacrifice.* Incense, sacrifice, and *prayer,* are three distinct things; the two first made the third acceptable. Pass we on,

18. To consider, 1 *Sam.* xiii. 12. *I have not made my supplication to the Lord: I forced myself therefore, and offered a burnt-offering.*

offering. And from hence too we can gather
nothing but the *neceffity* of pleading the
merits of a facrifice, the burnt-offering, in
order to make prayer acceptable. *Prayer*
formerly was accompanied with facrifice ;
this only averted fin, and its confequences,
though *modern fchemifts* vote *all merit* to
their prayers, and to themfelves, exclufive
of *any* facrifice · they preach *themfelves*,
and not Chrift Jefus our Lord. But let
fuch remember, *Saul* was rejected for his
daring prefumption, not for *praying*, but
for offering a meritorious confideration or
facrifice *himfelf*, inftead of going to *the
high-prieft of his profeffion* to do it *for*
him.

19. Before I go on any further, *it is* neceffary to make an obfervation, which you
feem not to have had an eye to, namely,
that facrifice fometimes relates to the great
fin-offering, peace-offering, and *burnt-offering Jefus Chrift*, and at other times to the
free-will offerings which we offer in Chrift,
as the *Ifraelites* in the *temple* or *tabernacle*,
Lev. xxii. 3. For throughout the Scriptures, Chrift is the *foundation* on whom,
and the *temple* in whom, we muft offer, and
through whom we muft go to God ; and
we, as members of his body, are faid to
facrifice various things. *Sacrifices of righteoufnefs*, or juftification, related to their
offering

offering Chriſt, the juſtifier, in arreſt of
judgment upon themſelves, *Pſal.* l. 14. We
read of ſacrificing *thankſgiving*, 23.——
Praiſe, li. 17.—*A broken Spirit*, being *crucified, dead*, and *buried* with him, *Rom.* vi.
4—6. *Eph.* ii. 5. *Col.* ii. 12. *Gal.* ii. 20.
Spiritual ſacrifices: *Praiſe unto God continually, that is, the fruit of our lips giving
thanks unto his Name*, which *Name* is the
Lord God manifeſt in the fleſh, the *Name*
of Jeſus, *Pſal.* xx. 1. and *Phil.* ii. 9. The
labours, expences, and perſons of Chriſtians,
are called *ſacrifices*; but in what ſenſe?
Every ſacrifice ſuppoſes a temple, ſomewhat
extraneous to ourſelves, wherein to ſacrifice; and this *temple*, under the Chriſtian
œconomy of grace, is Chriſt's body; and he
who is ſaid to offer or ſacrifice aught, muſt
of neceſſity be underſtood to do it in Chriſt,
the *true tabernacle* or *temple*: for we are
only *reconciled*, and *holy*, and *without blame,
before God* in *him*, Eph. i. 4; and our ſer-
vices are only accepted *for his temple's ſake
at* Jeruſalem, *where his Name dwelleth*,
i. e. for the ſake of him in whoſe *Name*
we are bid to do *all whatever we do*, Pſal.
lii. 8.—cxxii. 9. *Col.* iii. 17. For our High-
Prieſt muſt take our offerings, and, through
the *additional* incenſe of *his* merits, obtain
them admittance. Hence we read in *Iſa.*
lxvi. 20. (which you cite *ſect.* 20.) *They ſhall
bring*

*bring all your brethren for an offering unto
the Lord:* But where were they to bring
them for an offering unto the Lord? *To my
holy mountain* Jerufalem, *faith the Lord,
and I will also take of them for Priefts and*
Levites (and make them *Priefts unto God,*
Rev. i. 5.) *Ifa.* lx. 10. further explains
this; where fpeaking of the manifeftation
of the glory of the Lord by the birth of
Chrift, the Lord fays, *They fhall come up
with acceptance on mine altar, and I will
glorify the houfe of my glory; the fons of
ftrangers fhall build up thy walls* (be built
up *a fpiritual houfe,* Eph. ii. 21, 22) *Thy
gates fhall be open continually* (Chrift is the
door) *that they may bring the forces of the*
Gentiles *unto thee: The city of the Lord,*
where the *Lord is,* the *everlafting Light
and God, thy glory.* So that the dedication
was to be of themfelves, and their fervices
to the Lord *in Chrift,* who was to be the
door by which they fhould *enter in,* and be
faved, *John* x. 9. *Blood* (meaning of men)
fpilt in God's fervice is alfo called *a facrifice,* as you obferve, *Phil.* ii. 17.) but to
whom was it offered, through *whom* was it
acceptable, and for *what* was it offered?
It was offered to God, and it muft be offered as all offerings were, *in* a temple:
but the blood of a mere man could not be
offered by him for the remiffion of his fins:
the Chriftian *Philippians* knew better; and
St.

St. *Paul* has taught them otherwife in *Phi-*
lip. ii. and iii. However, you fay, " agree-
" ably to this, the fouls of them who were
" flain for the word of God, are reprefent-
" ed to be under the altar, *Rev.* vi. 9, 10.
" the very place where the blood or foul of
" the facrifice was poured out, *Lev.* iv. 7.
" —xviii. 25, 30." It is true indeed, that
the fouls are faid to be *under* the altar;
it is true, the blood was poured at the bottom of the altar · but what doth all this denote? You fay, " The readinefs of the per-
" fon who offered the facrifice to lay down
" his life in adherence to God." On what
grounds do you fay this? I confefs I fee not.
It at firft view appears to denote rather the
actual fhedding of blood, and laying down
of life, than " the readinefs" to do it. But
your allegory, in my eye, feems far fetch-
ed ; becaufe this blood, under the law, was
the blood of *the Lamb of God,* and the
bottom of the altar, which was *without* the
veil, and therefore not the place covered
with the mercy-feat, the *foundation,* than
which we muft not prefume to lay *any other,*
even Jefus Chrift. Pouring therefore the
blood on this, denoted the *purifying* or *wafh-*
ing of the pattern of heavenly things, called
reconciling the holy place, Lev. xv. 20. the
figure of the body of Chrift, *who wafhed*
us, and confequently himfelf, in his *own*
blood

blood from our sins, and himself purged our sins, Rev. i. 5. Heb. i. 3. This was the cleansing of our blessed surety, the ground and bottom whereon we stand, and the souls in *Rev.* vi. 9. were seen in their proper place, built upon this *foundation,* and purified and sanctified by *the blood of the everlasting Covenant,* and having *their robes washed white in the blood of the Lamb. Blood,* in the sacrifical style, is not, as you say it is, *life*; neither doth it stand for the *life* of the soul, if you mean that the terms are equivalent. But if you mean, that, by the *blood of the Lamb,* we have our *life,* as *without shedding of blood there is no remission of sins,* I join issue with you; though you must, by this concession, retract what you have said, that it sanctifies as an example *only.* But what then? Was it the blood of the martyrs, or the *blood of Jesus,* that was *poured out at the bottom of the altar?* Surely, this is not to be made a Question of. The Law, the Prophets, and the Apostles, all assert it was, in figure, the *blood of Jesus,* with which *those patterns of heavenly things* were *purified*; nor can *any* come but *through Christ,* or be *presented faultless* but *through his blood. I am the door, by me if any man enter in he shall be saved,* John x. 9. So that St. *John,* and the rest of the Apostles and Prophets, *could*

F not,

not, and *did* not, call this, with you, " the
" fouls facrificed in the caufe of religion."
All therefore that he does is, to place thofe
who were flain for the *word of God under
the altar, under* Chrift's covering, *under*
his fhelter, and *in the temple of his body,
wafhed in his blood fhed therein.*

21. Confider, Sir, you are treating of the
things of Heaven, when you make the rituals of the law your fubject. Nay, you
own " the temple to be the refidence of
" God, and all approach to it an approach
" to God." Can then, or cannot, man come
to God, *without* a facrifice? The Apoftle
fays, *without fhedding of blood there is no
remiffion.* Now what facrifice muft this be?
If you fay, of man, pleafe to recollect, it
was fomewhat *extraneous* to the offerer, and
was offered in a place where *none* but the
Priefts came. If you fay, of aught that
is man's, I muft be pardoned if I fay, this
is fuppofing man of *himfelf,* and by fome
perfonal fervices of his *own,* is accepted of
God: but remember the Holy Spirit fays,
it is *by the blood of Chrift we are brought
nigh,* Eph. ii. Befides, God was to be ap-
proached to *through* the *temple,* and the
temple could not be entered into but through
the *door;* and the *temple* is the *body* of
Chrift, and the *door* is Chrift, and therefore
the *facrifice* offered, and the *blood* fhed,
herein,

herein, muft needs have relation to the *fa-crifice of Chrift* ; *how* then was man con-cerned ? He was indeed *concerned*, but you fee it was at *fecond* hand : here is no imme-diate approach for man; all they had, like all we have, is through a μεσιτης, *a media-tor*, a bleffed *medium* of availing mercy, de-termined on in the council of the Moft High; for we read, *the people ftood without*, Luke i. 10. But if this is the true ftate of the cafe, I entreat you, by your integrity, to reflect ferioufly how the exhibition of this mediation under the law, witneffed by the Apoftles and Prophets to be made there, is fruftrated by your reference of the facrifice, and of the blood of it, to fome moral dif-pofitions in the offerer, and not to Chrift, *the facrifice to God*, Eph. v. 2. Heb. ix. 14. According to you, " Our Lord was himfelf " both the facrifice and facrificer, and is " ftiled a Lamb without fpot and blemifh, " to denote his perfect holinefs and purity : " this fuggefts to us, that the facrifice's be- " ing without fpot and blemifh denotes, " that the facrificer ought to perform the " fervice, or to lead his whole life with the " utmoft fincerity and fanctity of heart." Pleafe to explain to us *how* this could be done ? that is, How Chrift could *live* in this world with fanctity of heart, &c. which you fay facrifice denoted, when he *died* by

being

being a facrifice? I cannot conceive this to be agreeable at all to that common fenfe by which we muft try opinions. What! have I lived to hear the wonderful things of thy law, O God, *explained away* : forgive my zeal. How fhocking is it to a Chriftian to hear a *new* purpofe, a *new* end of the law, infifted upon, by *one* that profeffes himfelf a friend to Chriftianity ? Can any thing be more obvious than the fenfe of thefe words, *Chrift is our Paffover facrificed for us,* 1 Cor. v 7. *A better facrifice,* Heb. ix. 23. *Sacrifices were figures,* ix. 9.—*offered for fin,* vii. 27.—ix. 7. *Things pertaining to God* (ordained) *to make reconciliation for the fins of the people,* ii. 17.

Laying *all* this together with a cool and candid mind, can *any* thing be *more* clear than that facrifices had a reference to fome better and more perfect offering, and that Chrift was the offering, *the Lamb of God that taketh away the fins of the world.* Can *any* thing be *plainer*, than that they were not " a fymbolical addrefs," confifting in I know not what, to God, but *figures* of the *price* paid to God the Father, *for the redemption* of captive finners, *figures* of the fpotlefs *Lamb of God*, which was not an unmeaning addrefs, but a *vicarious, fatisfactory,* and *meritorious* offering, whofe *obedience* and *fufferings* are pleaded in *our*
behalf

*behalf by the High-Prieſt of our profeſſion,
in the temple of his body.*

24. You ask, " to what did they avail?"
Did *what* avail, the prayers of a *righteous*
man? *Not* to his juſtification; the text ſuppoſes him juſtified *already*, and calls him
righteous, putting up the prayer of *faith*,
James v. 16. So that theſe his prayers and
praiſe only proved his gratitude for mercy
received and *obtained*; *more* ſanctifying
grace, as Chriſt promiſes to us. See *James*
i. 6. *John* xvi. 24. *Jude* 20. *Phil.* iv. 6.

25. But if you ask, What *did* the *Levitical ſacrifices* avail the perſon by whom
they were offered? the anſwer *the ſcriptures*
ſupply us with is, *That* they were effectual
to obtain that *peace*, or *remiſſion of ſins*,
which God ordeied, and promiſed to be conveyed to them *through this* channel; for it
is repeated in *Leviticus*, chap. iv. v. vi. *The
Prieſt ſhall make atonement for him*, or
them, or *their ſin, and it ſhall be forgiven.*
On *what* account, I pray? On account of
the ſacrifice's being " a penitent addreſs to
" God?" or, On account of the *blood* of
the *ſacrifice?* Doubtleſs, on account of *the
Lamb of God*, and *his* blood exhibited and
pleaded in a *figure:* for the ſacrifice was a
figure of Jeſus, and its blood of the *blood*
of Jeſus, and there is *none other name under
Heaven given to man whereby he may be ſaved:* all poſſibility and probability of it is
taken

taken away. Why hear we then of *other* mediums, or *other* methods of salvation or acceptance? The law ordained *sacrifices for sin*, and thefe are offered *for sin* as fymbols of Jefus, the great facrifice. But you feem inclined to deftroy *this* their meaning and ufage : you fuppofe they were offered only as they were each " a fign of the facrificer's " pure heart;" and you make *repentance* in man the account on which fin is forgiven; though *repentance* can only come by *grace,* and *grace and truth,* as you own, *fect.* 120. come *by Jefus Chrift.* I pity you with all my heart, if you have been *undefignedly* guilty of this miftake. But I fee not how I can call it a miftake in the cafe before us : *Sacrifice* is offered for *fin,* the *fin* is forgiven, and yet it is denied to be forgiven for the fake of the *facrifice,* though the *facrifice* is declared to be a *figure* of Jefus; and it is alfo declared, there is *no other name* given under Heaven for a *mediator,* or *means* of forgivenefs, or of remiffion of fins. Again, you cannot but fee, it is not the *party* but the *Prieft* who made *atonement for fin*; and therefore you muft alfo fee the *facrifice* was *only* effectual when it was offered by the *Prieft* for an atonement *for fin.* Indeed you fay, that only *in the fight of God, and with regard to his acceptance,* the Prieft made atonement; which I

take

take to be the reason of your diftinguifhing
thofe expreffions by printing them in *Italics*.
But, if he did make atonement *in the fight
of God*, then I conceive *man* had nothing
to fear from *any other quarter*, and that
there was not *any* thing left to be done by
man with refpect to God, but to plead it as
he did by offering it. Why? Becaufe the
atonement is exprefsly faid to be made *by
the Prieft*. Now this Prieft was plainly
not the party offending, and yet you fee it
was laid *upon* him, to make atonement *for*
the offences of *others*; and this atonement
was made with a *fuffering facrifice*. But
the *Prieft* was a *type* of Chrift, and acted
not in his *own* name, but in the *Name of
the Lord*, and the *fuffering* facrifice was a
fhadow of the *Lamb of God*; therefore I
conclude, *that under the Law, as well as
under the Gofpel*, atonement *was underftood, as it is exprefly declared, to be made
by the Lord himfelf, and by his offering a
fuffering facrifice in the temple of his body* :
but he who *fuffers* muft fuffer *juftly*; the
facrifice then, which was a *type* of Chrift,
fuffered *juftly*, but for whom did it *fuffer?*
Not for its *own* offences : it was, by your
own confeffion (*fect.* 31.) incapable of *any*;
yet a goat was a *proper* emblem of the *lufts
of the flefh crucified*, and as fuch fuffered *for*
the fins of the people, that is, what was
due

due for thofe fins; and accordingly this is faid to be the atonement *for* fin exprefsly faid to be *in another*, and called the fin of the *other*; but guilt and fin muſt, fome how or other, be *juſtly* chargeable to a party, before it can with *juſtice* fuffer for *ſuch* fin or guilt: *fin* and *guilt* therefore was and muſt be confidered as *in* the facrifice; but here it was not *actively*, therefore it muſt have been by *imputation*. Say then, Sir, whether or no it is not, on the faireſt evidence, to be again concluded, *That atonement was known to be made by a facrifice, which was prefigurative of the Meſſiah, and which, like him, was to ſuffer what was due for offences not his own, in juſtice on the part of God, and of courfe as bearing man's fin and guilt by the imputation or transfer of it to himſelf.*

26. But you think *differently* upon this ſubject. You except (*ch.* iii.) *againſt* the notion of atonement, by a *ſubſtituted* or *vicarious* facrifice, fuffering the wrath of God *for* us, and *in our ſtead*. Your reafons, if I collect them aright, are thefe following:

I. Becaufe there is not any facrifice faid to have fin *put upon it*, or *to bear fin*, and of courfe that we have neither *inſtance* nor *argument* to juſtify, in *any* fenfe, the fentiment

ment of *transferring* fin, excepting *Lev.* xvi. 21. which you deem inconclufive (*fect.* 31.)

II. Becaufe, upon an examination of the fcriptural notion of *bearing fin* or *iniquity,* you think it means *no more* than God's *taking it,* or *carrying it, away*; and fay, *no* proof can be drawn from *Scripture,* that *bearing fin* includes the notion of *tranf-ferring* of guilt from the nocent to the inno-cent (*fect.* 33 to 53.)

III. Becaufe the victim is *never* faid to be offered, or to die, *in the ftead* of the fin-ner (*fect.* 53.)

IV. Becaufe there can be *no* vicarious guilt, and of courfe *no* vicarious punifhment (*fect.* 56.)

V. Becaufe a vicarious punifhment, as an *equivalent* to divine juftice, is *not* included in the notion of atonement (*fect.* 57.)

VI. Becaufe the *means* of making atone-ment *for* fin are *not* uniform, but *any means,* whereby finners are reformed, the judgments of God averted, *atone,* or make atonement, for fins; fuch as the *fole goodnefs of God, the prayers of good men, repentance, difci-plinary vifitations, fignal acts of virtue and juftice* (*fect.* 112.)

VII. Becaufe *transferring* of guilt doth *not* belong to the fenfe of atonement (*fect.* 114.)

G   Thefe,

Thefe, I fay, are your reafons, if I collect them aright. By your leave then I will
confider them in order, and the arguments
with which you think to fupport them.

27. *Firft*, You fay, " There is not *any*
" facrifice faid to have fin *put upon it*, or
" *to bear fin.*" I anfwer, That *a fin-offering* or offering for fin, and *all* facrifices
on which *the hands* were *laid, are* faid to
have fin *put upon them*, and *to bear fin.*
For we read in *Lev* xvi. 5. *He* (the High-
Prieft) *fhall take two kids of the goats for
a fin-offering ; one* of which was to die, as
being a type of the *human* and *mortal* nature ; and the *other* to live, as being a type
of the *divine* and *immortal* nature in the
complicated offering *for fin :* And of thefe
two goats, which were taken to be *a fin-
offering*, and were both brought before the
Lord, *one* was *chofen by lot for the Lord,*
and the *other by lot for a fcape-goat :* then
the *goat* upon which the Lord's *lot* fell, reprefenting *him* whofe *portion* was and *is the
Lord* (Pfal. xvi. 5. — lxxiii. 26. — cxix. 57.)
was to be offered a fin-offering ; but the
other, reprefenting the *divinity* in *him* who
liveth and abideth for ever, was to be pre-
fented *alive* (עמד fubfifts) *before the Lord,*
to make atonement *upon* him (עליו) not
with him, for it is tranflated *upon,* ver. 8.
Now,

Now, *how* the atonement was made *upon*
him we read in the following verses · — 15.
*He shall kill the goat of the sin-offering
which is for the people, and bring his blood
within the veil*—16. *and make an atonement* (or *covering* as you would have it) *for*
(or on *account of*) *the holy place, from* (מ)
the uncleanness of the children of Israel, *and
from their transgressions in all their sins,*
and so shall *he do for the tabernacle of the
congregation that remaineth* (or, as it stands
in the margin, *dwelleth among them*) *in the
midst of their uncleanness—and he shall go
out unto the altar before the Lord, and make
an atonement for it,* 18. —— and (וטהר)
hallow (*purge* or *cleanse*) *it from the uncleanness of the children of* Israel, 19.——
*And when he hath made an end of recon-
ciling* (or atoning for) *the holy place,* and
the tabernacle of the congregation, and *the
altar, he shall bring the live goat* (this *joint*
partner in the sin-offering, whose *other* partner was slain, and whose blood cleansed)
20. *and* Aaron (the type of Christ, as bearing the iniquity of the congregation, and
the judgment of the people) *shall* (סמך)

lay, or *stay,* or *lean,* or *establish* (so *Leigh*
in his *Crit. Sac. Montan. Buxtorf*) *both his
hands* upon *the head of the live goat* (the
head of Christ is God, *Cast thy burthen upon*

                                        the

the Lord, and he shall sustain thee, Psal.
lv. 22.) and confess (עליו) upon *him all
the iniquities of the children of* Israel, *and
all their transgressions in all their sins, putting them upon the head of the goat*; *and
shall send him by the hand of a fit man into
the wilderness*, 21.——*And the goat shall bear
upon him all their iniquities unto a land of
separation*, 22. representing that *separate*
estate to which the *divinity* of Christ, by
bearing sin, submitted himself to *after the
death* of the human nature, and during its
continuance in the grave : and all this is
said to be done, that they *might be clean
from all* their *sins before the Lord*, ver. 30.
One kid of the goats a sin-offering, *besides*
the sin-offering of atonement, and the con-
tinual burnt-offering, and the meat-offering,
and the drink-offerings, were to be offered
this day, Numb. xxix. 11. to keep up the
expectancy of that *joint* complicated person,
mortal and *immortal*, who, by an *extra-
ordinary* sin-offering, was to cleanse their
sins by *bearing them*, having them first *put
upon him* by our *confession* of them *upon* him,
in order to make an atonement *for* them.
And excuse me if I say, that you have not
considered this great transaction in its several parts ; if you had, you must have seen
imputed sin, vicarious guilt and *vicarious
punish-*

punishment, and *substituted offering*: for your
saying, this goat was *not* slain, will not
avail you; because it is sufficient for our
purpose, that it is called *a sin-offering*, and
said to *make atonement*. For you can only
argue thus against it, " What represented
" the Godhead of Christ, our complicated
" Mediator, though it had sin *put upon it*,
" did not die, because he whom it repre-
" sented was not to die, and therefore it is
" not true, that a sacrifice is said to bear
" sin, or to have sin put upon it ." and, by
the same way of reasoning, you may deny
the *blood of Christ* to be the *blood of Christ*,
which yet it is most expresly called, *Acts*
xx. 28; because God, the Divine nature,
did not die: nay, you may go on, and say,
the Divine nature of Christ was *not sacrificed*, because he *died* not · which is contrary
to the whole tenor of the Scriptures. But
you will not surely build such conclusions
upon such premisses : because you object to
the *vicariousness* of this offering, merely because it suffered *not* what the party it represented could *not*, from the *immortal* nature of him, be liable to; therefore this does
not *at all* affect the matter in debate: for
was, or was not, *sin put upon* the scape-
goat, is he, or is he not, said to *bear sin
upon him*, sin *imputed to* him, sin *imposed*
on him? which imposition was denoted by
the

the impofition of hands. You cannot deny *this*, without denying what the Scripture pofitively afferts : and is he not, becaufe of this, called a *fin-offering* ? But *fin-offerings* and *burnt-offering* were flain ; not *always*, Lev. v. 11. It is *always* ordained, that offerings fuffer, or be dealt with, according to their *nature*, or to the *nature* of the party whom they *reprefented*. The *Prieft*, though a gift and offering unto the Lord, who *bore fin*, and made atonement *for fin*, *died not* ; becaufe he was a type of the Lord, in whofe name he acted ; though that facrifice, which was *given to him to bear the iniquity of the congregation*, Lev. x. 17. *died*, by the application of the blood of which he made atonement *for others*. But, on *this* day, here was to be a rehearfal of what Chrift, both *God* and *Man*, both *mortal* and *immortal*, was to do and fuffer, in his *two* natures, to make an atonement for *men*, that they might, in virtue of it, be *clean* before the Lord : and therefore, not only *the death* of Chrift was exhibited, by whofe blood they were cleanfed, but alfo the *fhare* which the Divine nature had in their reconciliation ; therefore the reprefentative goat *dies* not. But does not he fuffer ? I believe you have not confidered either the live goat, as *joined with* the Lord's lot, the *other* goat ; or that he *fuffered* for man : for, if

you

you will allow me to call it fo, this *furvi-ving*, and, with refpect to this facrifice, *immortal offering*, fuffered the imputation of the fins of all *Ifrael*, by the impofition of hands *upon* him; and fuffered a feparation from his *former* paftures, as God in Chrift, from a life of glory to a life of humiliation, *bearing* the reproach of fin. But why fhould I prefs this any further, when you own " it " is probable, the laying on of hands upon " all piacular facrifices was attended with " this confeffion of fins;" and I muft add, as I before obferved, what the text autho-rifes me to fay, and you own (*fect.* 11.) *upon* them. And indeed it admits of proof, that this was the cafe, if we are to gather the *end* of facrificing with a certain rite in one place, from the account of this rite in an-other: for this is a moft juftifiable method of reafoning, efpecially when the writings of the Holy Spirit, who *always*, by the *fame* words, means the *fame* things, are treated of. Sacrifices then, Sir, whatever their fufferings are, according to the nature of the things facrificed, are exprefsly faid to *bear fin*, and to have fin *put upon them*. If you need to be referred to inftances, pleafe to confult *Leviticus* throughout, where you will find *arguments* and *inftances* enough to juftify, in the Chriftian fenfe, our fentiment of *transferring* fin, and enough to confute

your

your dangerous and deadly affertion of the
contrary : where you will find *fin* became
transferred to the holy place, that it required to be cleanfed on *this* account, *Lev.*
xvi. 16; that every one, who *touched* or *eat*
of the facrifice *for fin*, became holy by *imputation* and *transfer* of its figurative holinefs, *Lev.* vi. 18—27. becaufe the facrifice was *moft holy*, Lev. vi. 17—29. Befides, we know, that *iniquity*, mifchief, in-
juftice, wrong, violence, are faid to be in
the hands, *Pfal.* xxvi. 10—lviii. 2. *Job* xi.
14. *If iniquity be in thine hand, put it far
away*, Job xvi. 17. 1 Chron xii. 17. Jonah
iii. 8. *Putting* then, or *laying* on of hands
upon the head of the facrifice, was *putting*
or *laying the iniquity in* their hands *on* fuch
facrifice, and *becoming*, as they are faid to
be in virtue of this, *clean from all their
fins before the Lord*, Lev xvi. 30. and to
have *clean hands*, Job xvii. 9. Pfal. xxiv. 4.
And accordingly the *Jews* have this faying
amongft them, That on *this* day they are as
innocent as *Adam* in Paradife, when he was
firft created (fee *Burkett* on *Hebr.*
where this faying is mentioned). So that
we affert not the *imputation* or *transfer* of
fin, as far as I can fee, without the *greateft*
reafon ; becaufe it is fo *plainly* and *literally*
expreffed throughout this great tranfaction,
which was nothing lefs than an acting before-
hand

hand of that wonderful scheme of things, *by* which we have *redemption* from our sins, and *righteousness* unto life; nor have you advanced the shadow of an argument against it · all, I think, you have done is, not without some boldness, to assert, against the face of the *plainest* letter of Scripture, that *no sacrifice is said to* have *sin put upon* it, or to *bear sin*; because the scape-goat was, as it is called, *a sin-offering*, that is, *a sacrifice*, though it was *not* slain, because its partner in this complicated offering was slain; and it is said to have sin *put upon it*, and to *bear sin*. Nay, what is *more* remarkable in the text you unluckily point out, and whose sense you would evade, *Lev.* x. 11. to 17. we find the *goat referred to*, which was also *the sin-offering* (jointly with the live goat) *Lev.* ix. 15. And it is said, *ch.* x. 16, 17. Moses *diligently sought out the goat of the sin-offering, and behold it was burnt; wherefore have ye not eaten the sin-offering in the holy place, seeing it is most holy, and* (God) *hath given it to you to bear the iniquity of the congregation, and to make atonement for them before the Lord.* Now, if the goat, which was slain *for* the people, *ch.* ix. 15, is said to *bear* the iniquity of the congregation, then surely it had sin *put upon it* previously to its *bearing* it, which makes your assertion a downright *contradiction* to Holy
H   Writ.

Writ. And, as to *uncleanness* being contracted by the *touch* of the things, *Lev.* xi.
23, &c. you say, certainly *no guilt* was
transferred · if you mean, becaufe *no* guilt
could be predicated of *thofe* things they could
not transfer *guilt*, I agree with you ; but if
you mean, *no uncleannefs was transferred*,
I muft, upon the authority of the Scriptures, infift, that it was *transferred*. If
liquid colours will leave their tinge on any
thing that is capable of it, it is true, that
things deemed *unclean* in the eye of God,
for very good and wife ends, moft certainly
transfer their uncleannefs to *every* fubject
that is connected with them. How, elfe,
was a *veffel of wood*, or *raiment*, or, &c.
unclean by the falling of their *dead* carcafes
upon them ? Here is a *transfer* of uncleannefs exprefsly mentioned. You may foon
find the reafon of this, when you confider
the law in its *typical* view, and the *quali-
ties* of the things held unclean : fo that you
cannot evade the proof from hence of the
transfer of fin and uncleannefs from *one* fubject to *another*, which had it not otherwife
than by this *transfer* of it. Thefe Scriptures plainly affert it; and, if you chufe to
difpute it againft them, I am ready to con-
tend with this *fword of the Spirit* againft
all your oppofition.

28. Yet

28. Yet you ask, " How was the fin put " upon the facrifice?" I anfwer, If fins were put *upon* the goat, then it was by the *imputation* of them to him, denoted by the *impofition* of hands. You fay, they could not *really* be transferred ' now, if they were transferred at all, then they were *really* transferred by a proper and full imputation of them to the facrifice ; but if you mean, they were not his *perfonal* offences, I know none that will affirm it ; becaufe fin *imputed* and transferred can never be *perfonal* offence : this is to fuppofe the offerer actually to become the goat, and the goat the offerer ; when the true account is, that their natures were the fame as we are, and muft be the fame by nature ; but the eftimation of the two parties were different. The fin-offering bore the *imputation* or *impofition* of the fins of the people, and they, on the *account of it*, were efteemed *clean* and *holy*, Lev. xvi. 30. As to any *capacity of fin* in the brute, we affirm it not, no more there was in Chrift : but what hinders, that a fubject, in itfelf innocent, and incapable of fin, may, as a facrifice *for* fin, and if he confents to bear it, have the fin of *another* imputed to him ?

29. We muft therefore conceive, that fin was put *upon* the facrifice as a *figure*, to denote its being put *upon* Chrift. Its effects

H 2   were

were with God and Man. But I wonder to hear you ask, What effect it could have with him, that the guilt of any person was to be considered as if it was *put upon a brute?* For who says it was *put upon a brute,* considered as a brute? What the Scripture authorises us to say is, that sin and guilt were put *upon* the sacrifice as a *figure* of Christ, and consequently put *upon the Lamb slain from the foundation of the world.* And what *effect* this had with God, hear from God's *own* mouth · *This is my beloved Son, in whom I am well pleased,* Mat. iii. 17. *I will defer mine anger for my Names's sake,* Isa. xlviii. 9.—*for mine own sake,* xxxvii. 35. The *effects* it had with man were, the remission of his sins, and peace and joy in the Holy Ghost, in believing in the thing signified and pleaded.

30. II. Your second reason which you give for excepting *against* the notion of atonement, by a transfer of our guilt and sin, is grounded upon a supposition, that to *bear sin,* in the scriptural notion of it, means *no more* than God's *taking it,* or *carrying it away.* I thank you for your collection of the passages, where mention is made of *bearing* sin; I shall use a *few* of them, as I might all, to shew, that *bearing sin,* when applied to *God,* to our *Lord Jesus Christ,* to the

Angel

Angel of the Lord, to the *Priests and* Levites, means *imputed sin.*

31. I. First, The *Lord God,* this *fearful* and *glorious Name,* for whose sake God so often promises forgiveness, is said to *bear sin,* Exod. xxxiv. 7, &c. It were blasphemy to say it was *any* but the sin of his people which *he* bare ; and we know God was *in* Christ, and that it is *he,* who, in the Scriptures, especially in *Exodus,* and the rest of the Pentateuch, is denoted by this attribute ; for God would not go with them, *Exod.* xxiii. 21.—xxxiii. 3. As to God's bearing a place or people, it is never said in all your citations, *Gen.* xviii. 24—26. *Numb.* xiv. 19. *Psal.* xcix. 8. *Isa.* ii. 9. that he bears a place or people, but-*for* (ל) a place or people, which you seem to have overlooked : נשא is applied to bearing and supporting his people from *Egypt,* even until now, *Isa.* xlvi. 4. —lxiii. 9. *he* being one who carried them as on eagles wings, *Exod.* xix. 4. (as משא a burden upon him) and took sin upon him for their sakes.   For the connection of his people with him cannot be better expressed, nor the consequences of it better described, than by these phrases, *he bare them as a nurse beareth her sucking child, in his bosom,* Isa. xl. 11.   If a person may be said with propriety to *bear* a thing when he has it in his *bosom,* or on his *wings,* then,

then, I conceive, I shall have the permission of all sensible people to say, that this Holy Person *bore* sin, for that he *bore* sin, when he *bore* man in his bosom, needs not to be proved, though it was not *his* but *man*'s sin and offence. To this, unless I mistake the application of it, belongs *Psal.* lxxxix. 50. *I bear in my bosom the all of many people——wherewith they have reproached thee.* I have given it you literally as it stands.

II. Our *Lord Jesus Christ* is said to bear sins, *Isa.* liii. 11. *He shall bear their iniquities,* as a burden borne upon a man's shoulder, *Isa.* xlvi. 4. So that if a *burden* may safely be said to be *upon* the shoulder of him who *bears* it, we may surely with as much truth affirm, that our iniquities were *upon* our blessed Saviour *Jesus Christ.*

III. Of the *Angel* God promised to send before the *Israelites,* Exod xxiii. 21. it is said, *He will not bear your sins.* A terrible declaration! because if he did not in whom that *Name* was, whereby *alone* they could be saved, they must *die in their sins,* for this *Angel* or *Agent* was *Jehovah,* afterwards incarnate.

IV. The *Priests* and *Levites* are said to *bear sin,* yes, and the *judgment* of sin, *Exod.* xxviii. 29, 30. *And* Aaron (type of Christ) *shall bear the names of the children of Israel in the breast-plate of judgment as a memorial.*

morial.—And Aaron *shall bear the judgment of the children of* Israel, 36.—*Holiness to the Lord—and thou shall put it upon a blue lace, and it shall be upon* Aaron's *forehead, that* Aaron *may bear the iniquity of the holy things.* The Levites *shall do the service of the congregation, and bear their iniquity,* Num xviii. 23. Now, if *Aaron bore* the names of the children of *Israel upon* the breaſt-plate, then he *bore* (for the original word is the ſame) *the iniquity of the congregation,* as did alſo the *Levites,* denoting Chriſt in their perſons *bearing* the ſins of *his Israel.*

V. They who have been offended are required to bear ſuch offence of others. True, we are to *bear* one another, as our bleſſed Lord has *bore* us, and, if there was no conſideration of this ſort, our *bearing* ſin and offence would in juſtice draw down the puniſhment due to ſuch ſin *upon* us, for forgiveneſs of enemies is not juſtifiable upon any *other* grounds. As to 1 *Sam.* xv. 25. *Saul* was addreſſing *Samuel* (and in his perſon Chriſt) *to bear his ſin.*

VI. The criminals are ſaid to *bear* iniquities, *Lev.* vii. 18.

VII. The children of the *Israelites bare* the iniquities of their parents in the wilderneſs, *Num.* xiv. 33: and they complain of
this

this in the *Babylonish* captivity, *Lamentat.*
v. 7.

VIII. The Prophet *Ezekiel bare* the iniquity of the house of *Israel*, Exek. iv. 4, 5, 6.

32. (1) Now *all* Levitical *piacular* facrifices are faid to *bear fin*, becaufe *all* had the *hands laid upon* them, according to your own conceffion (17), and this I have proved was laying the fin *in*.the hands *upon* the facrifice, *fect.* 27. for uncleannefs was *transferred* by touch, *fect.* 27 ; and the fcape-goat is faid to *bear* fin which fuffered, though it was not flain, and its partner, which was flain, is faid to *bear* iniquity, *Lev.* x. 17.

(2) The glorious *God and Saviour* is faid to *bear* as a burden, or a child in arms, the people, and the *fins* of the people. Indeed you fay, the common and current fenfe of the word is, to carry, or take away. Now fetting afide, that this fenfe of yours will *not* agree with many places, as you may fee if you will try *Ezek.* iv. 4, 5, 6. *Lam.* v. 6. *Lev.* vii. 18. and many more texts; be it fo, with all my heart, that it is the fenfe of it in the texts where God is faid to *bear* fin; for *carrying* or *taking away*, in God or Man, can only be done by *bearing* : whoever *takes* away, or *carries* a thing, muft of neceffity previoufly *bear* it, or have it,

upon

upon him; call it *remove* if you will; the remover muft *lay hold* of it before it can be *removed*: and, as to סבל grant it fignifies to *carry off*, you get no fort of countenance from this its meaning; for *carrying off* neceffarily fuppofes the *taking upon* us the thing to be carried off.

(3) And in the fame fenfe our *bleffed Lord*, as well as the *Jewifh High-Priefts and* Levites, bore fin *upon* them, and what is more, the *judgment* of fin, becaufe they acted in *the Name of the Lord*: hence what they *bore* is faid to be the *iniquity* of the congregation, and of the holy things. As to the *figurative* way of expreffing this removal of guilt, I conceive, that the good things of Heaven muft be revealed to our underftanding by *allufions* or *figures*, and that according to thefe figures we muft model our ideas: fo that if *taking* away, or *carrying* away, or *bearing*, or *removing*, do fuggeft to us an *affumption* of the thing to be *taken* or *carried* away, *bore* or *removed*, then we muft conceive, and firmly hold faft, our holy faith, *That God, the Angel of the Lord, Jefus Chrift, both God and Man, our great High-Prieft, took our guilt and fin* on himfelf, *the* true *holy place and tabernacle which God pitched, and* our *fins* were transferred *to him by his* taking *them away* from *us*.

I   (4) Men

(4) Men might *bear* the fin of others if they could give a reafon for it; otherwife, if juftice required it to be punifhed, and they then bore with it, and ftood mediators, they muft have fuffered the ftroke of avenging juftice. But juftice, the ftricteft juftice, then required them, as it now does us, to *bear* fuch offence for Chrift's *fake*, even as he *bore* our fins. And you may obferve, that when we *bear* the fin of others, or their offence, fuch offence is, in fact, *bore* by Chrift, who *bears* us, that bear fuch fin of others. He mercifully, by his fatisfying fufferings, has made that a *virtue* which had otherwife *not* been allowable, and has enabled us to fhew *love* to *one another*, even as he *hath loved us*; though before he could thus enable us, he muft fuffer for the confequences of fuch forbearance, and purchafe it for us. In vain then do we pretend to love from *other* motives: we but break in upon the fcheme of God, contract *frefh* iniquities, and make ourfelves liable to a heavier judgment. *Love*, that is *not bought* and *paid for*, and not fhewn for *Chrift's fake*, is a trefpafs of a very deep dye, and ferves but to heighten a man's condemnation.

(5) God in Chrift might *bear* fin *for* a place; he does now, otherwife our fins, and the ftrange antifcriptural, *independent*, prefuming way of thinking, which the men of our

our days have run into, calls for judgment.
But his *bearing* us neceffarily connects our
guilt with him, as much as my *bearing* a
ftaff in my hand, a burden *on* my fhoulder,
or a child *in* my arms, connect thofe fubjects
with me. See how every fin of ours extends
to the bleffed Jefus: fee how his mercy
makes them *his*; that mercy which made
him content to fuffer *for* them, that we
might be faved.

(6) You own the word denotes to *bear* a
burden; hence then take your idea. No,
you except againft it; but why? Becaufe,
when the innocent muft *unavoidably* fuffer
with the criminals, in this cafe the innocent
are faid to bear the fin of the guilty; which
you think *not* the cafe with Chrift and Man.
Now, firft, by your own conceffion, the
doctrine of imputed fin is not a doctrine *contrary* to Scripture, becaufe, to mention no
other places, it is here exprefsly afferted.
Num. xiv. 33. *Lam.* v. 7. Secondly, Chrift
was moft folemnly engaged to bear man,
and to redeem him before man was made
Tit. i. 2. 2 *Tim.* i. 9. and *fect.* 40. Man
then by *falling* unavoidably brought the
confequences of his fin *upon* Chrift, the *juft*,
that *fuffered for the unjuft*, 1 Pet. iii. 18
But you evade the natural conclufion from
thefe texts, in favour of imputed fin you
fay. " they are faid to *bear* the fin of the

" guilty, as they fhared in their fufferings."
Surely, this is a flip of your pen, and the
correcteft writer is at times liable to it. The
text fays, they *bore* the *whoredom* of their
fathers; and *bearing* of fufferings is not
bearing of another's fin, nor can we conclude
that they *bore another*'s fin becaufe they
fuffered, they might fuffer for their *own*
fin. But be it, that they *bore* the fufferings
of their fathers, and taking it for granted,
that it is fenfe to fay, they *bore* the fufferings of their fathers, yet fin they muft have
before they can *juftly* fuffer, and if they
fuffered *for* their fathers, they muft have
the *fin of their fathers* by fome means or
other. But how could they have it? *Not
actually* or originally *in* them; becaufe it
was their *father's whoredom*, therefore they
muft have it by *imputation*: they muft
bear it *upon* them by eftimation, as criminals *bore* their fins actually *upon* them, and
in their natures. Let me intreat you ferioufly to confider this paffage, and to remember, that fome perfons were to *bear
their* fins, and others were to have their
iniquity *born for* them, and you muft own,
I think, a tranfer of *man*'s fin to *another*
to be the doctrine of Scripture.

(7) How the Prophet *Ezekiel bare* the
iniquities of the children of *Ifrael*, is not fo
uncertain as you think it to be: for they
were

were *upon* his fides, and it is very obfervable, that he himfelf was to put them *upon* his fides. Now *Ezekiel* was a Prophet that perfonated the *great* Prophet; his name is, in plain *Englifh*, *God will hold faft : None can pluck them out of my hand*, fays Chrift; *the Son of Man, who bore the fins of his* Ifrael *in his own body*, 1 Pet. ii. 24. and took them voluntarily *upon* him. A common reader of the Bible cannot overlook the connection this facred account has with Chrift, when he fees *One*, by the name of *the Son of Man*, bearing the fins of the people *upon* himfelf. Patiently indeed he did it, that is, he was *paffive* of them, *recipient* of them, as none can be patient of a thing which is not fome how or other *upon* him, and affects him not. As to *for bearing* their punifhment, here is not a word about it; unlefs you may fay, by bearing their fin he *forbare* their punifhment, *bare* it *for* them.

Upon the whole I muft confefs, that, as your fuppofition, " no guilt is *ever* tranf-" ferred from the nocent to the innocent," was never entertained by any but an unbeliever, fo it has no warrant of *Scripture* to fupport it; the contrary of which is fo abundantly evident from the *exprefs* words of Holy Writ.

33. I come then to enquire into the grounds of your third reafon, which has led

you to think, that *all* the Chriſtian churches
ever ſince Chriſt have *miſtaken* the doctrine
of atonement. " The victim," you ſay,
" is *never* ſaid to be offered, or to die, *in*
" *the ſtead* of the ſinner." To make your
aſſertion appear the more feaſible, you wave
conſidering the caſe of *Abraham's* offering
up his ſon *Iſaac*, Gen. xxii. 13. You tell
us, " every-body knows this is foreign to
" the preſent purpoſe :" But, I confeſs, I
am an exception to your imagined number ;
and I could name you many more of high
rank and learning, and a *little* reaſoning will
vindicate them from exceptions : for, as it
has ſeemed to them, ſo it ſeems to me to be
ſo far from being *foreign* to the preſent purpoſe, that I cannot but think it concluſive
enough to induce me, and every impartial
examiner of it, to determine againſt you.

34. I take it for granted, that *Abraham*
knew the Goſpel, as ſaith St. *Paul*, Gal. iii. 8.
and conſequently that Chriſt was to *ſuffer*.
Abraham had received the promiſe, that in
his ſon *all* nations, and conſequently himſelf,
and all the *Gentile* world, *ſhould be bleſſed:*
ſoon after God bids him offer up this ſon to
him *for* a burnt-offering. *Abraham* therefore
it is plain knew this bleſſed ſon, whenever
he came, ſhould *ſuffer* the fiery wrath : ſee
ſect. 42. He goes to the very place where
the

the *Son* was afterwards offered —The Lord prevents him, because *Isaac* was but a mere man like himself—And *Abraham* offers up a *ram*, a type of the Saviour of the world, *in the stead of* Isaac. From which transaction we have these plain inferences, 1. That if *Abraham* offered up the ram *instead* of *Isaac*, then a victim *is said* to be offered up, and to die in *the stead of the sinner*, of *Isaac*, who, because he was a man, was a sinner: 2. That inasmuch as it was offered expresly *in the stead* of the seed of *Abraham*, it was offered *in the stead of us*, who are of the *seed*; if so be we are *of the faith*, *of* Abraham, *Rom*. iv. 16. 3. That this ram died, and, as a *figure*, was offered up *for all* who were, with *Abraham*, *heirs of the promise made unto* Abraham, *Gal*. iii. 9. 4. That as we are to consider these things by the express directions of Holy Writ, as an *allegory*, here is a positive assurance that Christ should be offered up and die, as was the case, upon this very mount, *for* and *instead of all* the children of *Abraham*. See *Gal*. iv. 24—iv. 31.

You may be convinced how strongly this word חתת imports a *substituted* or *vicarious* person, if you consider *Genes*. xxx. 2. *Am* I (חתת) *in God's stead*, or *in* the stead of God?—l. 19. *I am in the place of God*.

God. Outr. de Sac. p. 337, 349. was right then, when he afferted the *Mofaic* facrifices were *furrogates*, reprefentatives of Chrift, the great *Surety*, dying *for* finners.

35. See your citation from *Deut.* xxi. 1— 10. confidered, *fect.* 50. IV.

36. But you object (54) " That the fins " for which facrifices were generally offered " were fins of ignorance, and ceremonial " uncleannefs, which were not capital by " law. The victim therefore could not die " in the offender's ftead, when his offence " was not punifhable with death." Now granting that facrifices were *generally* offered on thefe accounts, though I make no doubt the *Jews*, as all men, finned often *wilfully*, and might be pardoned ; yet thefe fins deferved death, if it is true that death *entered into the world by fin.* And we read in *Jam.* i. 15. *Sin when finifhed bringeth forth death* (*eternal*, if unatoned for) *Ezek.* xviii. 4. *The foul that finneth it fhall die.* And indeed, if we confider the law of God as *not* ordaining facrifices for fin, every fin againft this law deferved *death :* but God in his mercy provided figurative facrifices, that they might be exempt from the *curfes* of fin, and from death eternal : fo that none under the law was punifhable with death, deprived of the *benefit* of the facrifice, or cut off from this *common-wealth*

wealth of God, but he who did not apply God's means for his cleanfing ; as none are cut off from God's *Ifrael*, but he who accepts not the *blood* and *merits of Chrift*. It is faid, in *Exod.* xxx. 20. *They fhall wafh that they die not*, Deut. xvii. 12. *The man that will not hearken unto the Prieft fhall die.—Curfed is every one who confirmeth not (all) the words of this law*, Deut. xxvii. 26. *The blood of the Paffover was fhed that they died not*, Exod. xii.—*which if a man do he fhall live in them*, Lev. xviii. 5. So that the figurative rituals and facrifices were appointed that men might *not* die, and of courfe the facrifice *died* that the officer might *not* die, *Deut.* iv. 1. but live : that he might *not* bear the curfes which *any* tranfgreffion of the law made him liable to. It were ftrange reafoning if I fhould fay, that a debt was *not* paid for me, becaufe there were means given me by which I might plead fuch payment, and efcape a gaol, and becaufe I was *not* excluded the benefit of fuch payment. Yet ftrange as it is, your objection is grounded upon it : for you fay, " The victim could not die inftead " of the offender, when his offence was not " capital by law, nor punifhable with death." But why was it not capital ? becaufe there remained unto the finner *a facrifice for fin ?* Alas, Sir ! had there been *no* vicarious facri-

K   fice,

fice, the *Ifraelites* had been moft miferable ;
for the curfes of the law were his portion
who kept not all the law, *Deut.* xxvii.
26. *Gal.* iii. 10. and God muft inflict the
penalty he has denounced : But when they
put *their* fins, they knew they put the *curfes*
due by the law to fuch fins, *upon* the head
of the facrifice ; and confequently the victim was *fubftituted* to *bear the wages of fin,*
which are death, in their ftead : the law
therefore was a *figurative* difplay of God's
dealings with men. Some fins, whofe *wages*
were *death*, were atoneable ; others were
not, becaufe there remained *no more facrifice
for fin.* When this was the cafe, they were
what you call *capital,* fuch as deprived
them of the benefit of the facrifice. But
was not death due to other fin ? Doubt-
lefs, for *the wages of fin are death,* though
it was not inflicted *upon* them, becaufe they
pleaded *a facrifice for fin,* fomewhat ordained of God, and *dying,* though without perfonal fin, and only bearing *their* fin, that
they might *not* die. Hence the facrifice,
and its *blood,* is faid to make *atonement for
the life :* but for what life ? not for this life
merely ; they foon died, therefore it was for
another life, which was before forfeited, and
to efcape *another* death, that the atonement
was made by the *Prieft,* and not by themfelves.

37. Again,

37. Again, confider, that the law of *Mofes* was *life for life, eye for eye, tooth for tooth, hand for hand, foot for foot*, Deut. xix. 21. Nothing *lefs* could fatisfy under this divine adminiftration of juftice, wifdom, and mercy. If man therefore finned, and by fin incurred *death*, as a finner moft certainly does, *nothing* but death could fatisfy or atone. This is the voice of his own law, according to which, I fuppofe, you will allow God to act. Death then there muft be, death of the offender, or death of his lawful furety (fee *fect.* 40, 99.) but it was the *facrifice* died; and it is with *this* the Prieft is faid to *make atonement*, and the party is *difcharged* on account of it. The facrifice then, as perfonating Chrift, was offered as a *retaliation* and *fatisfaction for and in the ftead of the parties* death and fuffering, and *its* death pleaded in the room of his.

38. Nor was the effect, as you fay it was, " the fame by whomfoever a facrifice was " offered." The *Prieft* muft offer it for them, and it muft be offered through *faith* in the thing *fignified* by the Holy Ghoft. (See *Heb.* xi. 6.) So that the objection you from hence take occafion to make is very trifling : you might as well fay, the word of God is a *light* to all that take it into their *hands*, and never take it into their

K 2 *hearts*

hearts by a full affurance of faith in its contents.

39. " The victim," you own, " might " reprefent the perfon who offered it." If it did, pray whether is it more rational to fay, that it did fo, to fhew him that he ought to " kill the brute in himfelf," as you would have it, which is its fecondary view? or, That it did fo in its primary meaning, to fhew the *Lamb of God* dying *for* him, and himfelf *dying together* with him? efpecially when this is the fcriptural meaning, and the fcriptural application, of facrifice, namely, to *fhew the Lord's death till he* fhould *come.* But your account, as you own, is very remote from the victim's fuffering in the offerer's ftead the death he deferved ; and it is *equally* remote from Scripture, and the reafon of the thing : the poor offerer wanted not to know, that he had got the brute *in* him, and ought to flay it. Any retrofpect into himfelf would fhew him thefe things : but he wanted to be pardoned for having acted the brute, and to know by what means he might be enabled to put off this *old man* of fin, never to act the brute again, and to become *a new creature :* and let the Scriptures determine what thefe means are, and the nature of thefe means: let them fpeak *why* the facrifices were inftituted ; and do you tell me what *other* connection

nection can be found by the moſt ſubtle un-
derſtanding, between ſlaying a harmleſs in-
offenſive creature, and the *remiſſion of ſins,*
than that reference which the Scriptures
make of it to the oblation of Chriſt, the
ſpotleſs *Lamb of God,* once offered *for* and
in the ſtead of all? Indeed you are pleaſed
mighty modeſtly to call it a contradiction in
terms to ſay, " that the ſacrifice ſuffered a
" vicarious puniſhment;" but I confeſs I
would have read my Bible over and over,
before I would have ſaid ſo; and you ſee
if you had done it, you would have found
this as *expreſs* a doctrine of the Scriptures
as that our *ſouls* are *immortal,* or that there
is a *God:* and ſurely you will not argue
againſt aught revealed *in them,* as involving
a contradiction. But be it you think ſo;
produce your cauſe, and bring forth your
ſtrong reaſons.

40. You ſay, " as there cannot be a vi-
" carious guilt, or as no one can be guilty
" in the ſtead of another, ſo there cannot
" be a vicarious puniſhment, or no one can
" be puniſhed in the ſtead of another; be-
" cauſe puniſhment, in its very nature, con-
" notes guilt in the ſubject which bears it."
This is your reaſon; but on what do you
ground it? upon an unwarranted aſſertion,
" that there cannot be a vicarious guilt,"
for by vicarious I underſtand one who con-
ſents,

fents, and is, upon his confent, accepted, to be deemed and treated *vice alterius*, *in the ftead or room of another*; one to whom the concerns of another are transferred, as *viceroy*; and in the cafe before us, one who is looked upon not as he is *in himfelf*, but as he is by being *a proxy* or furety, refponfible for *our* fins, and obliged to make reftitution : and will you fay, an obligation, or the penalty of an obligation, is not tranfferrable? What would become of you or me if we were fureties, and he fhould fail whofe fureties we were? Should not we be *lawfully* called upon? Perhaps you fay, this is done in confequence of a *covenant* or *bond*. True, and fo was *our furety* affected by the covenant; it was *this* transferred the obligation to him on man's bankruptcy : for guilt is nothing but a failure, and contracting an obligation to fuffer, by a tranfgreffion of the terms of a covenant. There may then be a *vicarious* guilt, or a *vicarious* imputation of failure : a tranfgreffion may be deemed *mine* at fecond-hand, and fatisfaction for fuch failure required from a *furety*. To deny this is to deny the juftice and lawfulnefs of the proceedings we find amongft the *beft* of men in *all* ages : it is to deny there can be a *vice-man*; it is to deny the failures, like the *authority* of one perfon, cannot become thofe of *another*.

But

But you may fay, they are not his obligations, nor his failures, originally : no, they
are not his originally, but they *are*, and
you fee in juftice *may* be, his by imputation, with his confent, by covenant; and,
becaufe they are thus his, he is juftly liable
to the pain or penalty.

41. Again, by your own reafoning, " pu-
" nifhment or fuffering connotes guilt in the
" fubject that bears it." The facrifice evidently fuffered the knife and the fire, therefore it *bore* fin and guilt; the innocent fuffered, therefore they *bore* guilt; but guilt
was not *actually* in them you ftile " inno-
" cent, or incapable of fin," therefore they
muft be only by *imputation*, or *vicarioufly*
guilty, and the facrifice was an acquittance
for or *in the ftead* of man. I am glad to find
you agree not with yourfelf in your treating of
this fubject, becaufe I have the greater hopes
you will drop a fcheme, which neceffarily
leads you into fo many contradictions. But
thefe are not the only reafons which you
have adopted without any grounds. For,

42. V. You fay, " That a vicarious pu-
" nifhment, as an equivalent to divine juftice,
" is *not* included in the notion of atonement."
And what grounds you have for thus peremp-
torily determining in the negative I cannot
find : for atonement was made with the piacular facrifices, which were flain, and paid
death

death for death. And, though it was alfo made with the fcape-goat, which was *not* flain, yet it was not made with him *alone*, but in conjunction with the *other* goat in this complicated fin-offering, which was *flain*, and *bore iniquity:* and in this it cor-refponded with the manner in which the *great* atonement was made by the divine natuie, not by himfelf alone, but in con-junction with the *human* and *mortal* nature, the Lamb that *was flain*, and who *jointly* made up the *one* great offering for the fins of all. Add to this what I before obferved, that this fcape-goat fuffered the *imputation of fin*, the *reproach of fin*, and a *deprivation* of his *former* eftate, even as God emptied himfelf of his glory, while the *other* goat, like the human nature, died, and paid *life for life.* The turtle-doves and pigeons, for a fin-offering, were killed; the handful of fine flour underwent *the fire* for a fin-offer-ing, and with this the Prieft made atone-ment. And what could the offerer think of thefe things, when he knew they made atonement foi him, but that the facrifice whereon his fins were laid died for him? that the dove or pigeon died for him? that the floui fuffered the fire for him? For *fire* de-notes the wrath of God, witnefs thefe texts, *Deut.* iv. 24. *The Lord thy God is a con-fuming fire.* Dan. vii. 10. *A fiery ftream issued*

issued from before him, noting the speedy execution of his judgments. *Psal.* xviii. 8. *A fire devoured.* —— lxxxiii. 14. *As the fire burneth the wood, so persecute them.* Isa. xlvii. 14. *The fire shall burn them.* Jer. iv. 4. *Lest my fury come forth like fire.* — xxi. 12. Lam. ii. 4. Neh. i. 6. Deut. xxxii. 22. *For a fire is kindled in mine anger*, & al. And it is pretty remarkable, the sacrifices which made atonement are said to be *sacrifices*, Lev. x. 13. Numb. vi. 2, 28. *Offerings*, Lev. 2. 3. —4. 35, &c. *made by fire unto the Lord*, made by a fire which was appointed *by* the Lord, and not by *strange fire*, and which they were to keep burning *for ever*. It seems, from *Lev.* ix. 24. to have been a miraculous fire, *There came a fire out from before the Lord, and consumed upon the altar the burnt-offering.* However, the Priests were to feed it with *their* sacrifices, *for* or *instead* of the people, as Christ satisfied the wrath of God by a sacrifice *for us*, Lev. vi. 12, 13. When then the sacrifices of animate things, or, if the party could not procure them, of inanimate things, underwent this *fire*, expressly said to be *fire from the Lord*, Lev. ix. 24. and all this to make atonement for him, the offerer saw in part what he deserved to suffer, and that these were offerings *substituted, instituted*, and *ordained*, not of

L   himself,

himself, but of God *for* him : so that even the burning of the *flour*, contrary to what you affert, fuggefted to him the idea of a *vicarious fatisfying*, burning or fuffering *for* him. The *flour* was not punifhed indeed, but it was put to an ufe it had *never* been put to but *upon* man's account, and *for* man, for it was burnt ; it fuffered the fire *for* him, and it was *his* fins which brought this *burning* upon it, as well as *upon* the other facrifices, becaufe they are called of-ferings *for* fin. But how could this, or any other offering, have made atonement, unlefs there had been another offering in view ? Not at all ; for this would be to attribute to them what the Scriptures proteft againft. They were offered then as types of a *better* facrifice, the *Lamb of God* ; and the *flour* as a type of the *flour* of Heaven, of the *bread of life*, which *cometh down from Hea-ven*. It was offered as a figure of that holy *leaven* to which our bleffed Lord compares the *kingdom of God*: therefore I muft be al-lowed to conclude, notwithftanding what you have faid, that a finner's offering aught unto the Lord, by the hands of his me-diator, the High-Prieft of his profeffion, was to make a *fatisfying*, that is, an *equi-valent* atonement. For it muft, in the na-ture of the thing, be confidered not only as a *vicarious* and *fubftituted*, but as an *equi-valent*

valent offering, in itself not deserving thus to be treated, but brought to this by the transgression of the party, because as a type of the Lamb of God, who was *God* and *Man*. And who dare to be so forgetful of his soul's good, as to deny it to be *equivalent*? For in this light it was the sacrifice of an *infinitely* valuable God in the flesh; and this would assist the offerer's meditations; this would give him comfort when, knowing that he was *dead in sin*, he saw the death and burning of an offering ordained of God in *his stead.* For he could rejoice in a full assurance of faith, in what was thus evidenced to him, namely, that he had life, because his surety died in *sacrifice to God for* him; as it is written, *He died that we might live unto him that died for us*, 2 Cor. v. 15. But how the burning of *flour* could *otherwise* assist the offerer's meditations, unless by suggesting the idea of a vicarious offering, I confess I cannot conceive, and must desire you to inform me. Again, you say,

43. " Nor did the shedding of blood," my blood chills whilst I repeat your assertion, " in itself imply atonement by vica-" rious punishment." Alas, Sir! you indeed mistake the strength of your arguments, when you bring them to support such absurd and unscriptural doctrines. For you object that it is never said, " that atone-

L 2   " ment

" ment was made for fin by peace-offerings,
" confequently we have no ground to fup-
" pofe vicarious punifhment in fuch facri-
" fices, though blood was fhed and fprin-
" kled in them, as well as in fin-offerings."
Now obferve,

44. (1) Sins were confeffed *upon* it by
the impofition of hands, as in the cafe of
Aaron, to *fanctify* him, and to *make him
holy*, Lev. iii. 8.

(2) It is called an *offering made by fire*
of a *fweet fmelling favour unto the Lord*,
ver. 3.

(3) It was to be offered *in* the courts of
the tabernacle or temple, Chrift's body,
Exod. xx. 24.

(4) The *blood* of it was *fprinkled on the
people*, xxiv. 8. of which St. *Paul* fays, *it
fanctifieth to the purifying of the flefh.*

(5) This is faid, *Levit.* viii. 31. jointly
with the others, to make *atonement for*
Aaron, ix. 7. jointly with the *fin-offering*,
ver. 18. *for the people*, Ezek. xlv. 15. *to
make reconciliation for the houfe of* Ifrael.

45. From hence then I conclude,

(1) That the *peace-offerings* were of the
number of the *facrifices for fin* which St.
Paul recounts, *Heb.* v. 1.

(2) That they had fins put *upon* them as
a figure of Chrift.

(3) That

(3) That they were offered by *fire* a *sweet smelling savour unto the Lord*, as the things whereon the *chastisement of* their *peace* was in figure, and which were in figures their *peace*, and reconciled them by their *blood*.

(4) That therefore their *blood* was shed, as they are said to make atonement *for*, or *instead of*, the people.

Hence it is evident, you have misrepresented the Scripture account of these offerings for *peace*, which should obtain it *instead* of us, for our souls: you have denied that effect to be attributed to them which Holy Writ plainly assigns them.

46. Indeed, *Lev.* xvii. 11. seems to be somewhat in your way: the words are, *Ye shall not eat blood, for it is blood that maketh atonement for the soul.* But you ask, " How, by way of vicarious punishment? " not a word of that." And yet I own for my part, that I see not how any conclusion can be better suited to its premisses than this, namely, that blood atoned by way of vicarious punishment, because *blood* is said to make *atonement for the soul*: for say, *Why* was it shed? *What* made the creature suffer? If you answer, God ordained this; then I must take God's account of his appointment; and he says, the blood of this suffering sacrifice *maketh atonement for the soul.*

soul. It is then the *soul* of man which occasions the sacrifice; and for what? For its *sins.* Now assign what meaning you please to this particle *for*; call it *on account*, or *in favour, of*; it is plain it did *for* man, or the soul, what they could not do *for* themselves, because it was *for* him, *Heb.* ix. 7. Its sufferings therefore, and its *death*, and, what we are now considering, its *blood*, was all *for* him; and, tho' not *his* blood nor sufferings, yet charged to his account, if pleaded in payment of his great debt to God. The allegory you would draw out of it is shewn, *sect.* 20. to be made without reason: so that " a reverend regard to religious so-" lemnities" was not the thing to be wrought in them, as being the final cause of these rites: no, it was the regard to the things signified by them, namely, the grace of God in Christ Jesus, that this blood was intended to keep up. And please to remember what effect the putting of this blood as *a token*, upon their perishable houses, had *with God* and the *Israelites*, when he made a *rehearsal* of his final judgment on *Egypt*. God, because he saw this *memorial* blood, passed over the *Israelites*, and they, by virtue of it, had deliverance, liberty, life, and rest, from their labours.

47. But it seems to you, that the sense of atonement hitherto hath rather been taken

for

for granted than underftood: however, you are willing to let the Scriptures determine it, fo am I.

48. The word *atonement*, you fay, is always rendered from fome formation of the root כפר *caphar*, as a noun or a verb; and to *pitch*, or *fmear with pitch*, feems to you to be the natural and original fenfe of the word, and the fenfe, when it fignifieth the mercy-feat and *atonement* feems to be transferred, from covering or fecuring with pitch, to things of a different nature. Be it fo: let us then examine the texts where *atonement* is fpoken of without *any* relation (you fay, but without *any* reafon as to moft of them) to *Levitical* facrifices, that we may be able to judge what it means when applied to them: and let us fee what effect fuch atonement wrought, and what were the means by which atonement was made.

(1) Exod xxx 15, 16 *The rich fhall not give more, nor the poor lefs, than half a fhekel, when they give an offering unto the Lord, to make an atonement for their fouls or lives, that it may be a memorial for or to the children of* Ifrael *before the Lord, to make atonement for their fouls or lives*

EFFECT. That there be *no plague amongft them when thou numbereft them*, ver. 12.

MEAN. Half a fhekel given, by *every one* that was numbered, *to the fervice of the tabernacle*; acknowledging, that they were

were bought, and pleading the price of their redemption from evil, which was put to the ufe or account of Chriſt, the *true* tabernacle.

EFFECT. That they were not cut off.

MEAN. The prayer of *Moſes*, as the figure of Chriſt, *into whom they were baptized.*

EFFECT. The ſtaying of the plague.

MEAN. *Aaron*, as a type of Chriſt, ſtanding mediatoi in *the midſt of the congregation, between the dead and the living*, with a cenſer of holy fire, and of *incenſe*, the ſymbol of the ſweet ſmelling ſavour of the merits of Chriſt crucified, in his hands, *Revel.* viii. 3.

EFFECT. Stopping the plague.

MEAN. The Prieſt doing juſtice upon two criminals, *Zimri* and *Comri*, and zeal for,

(2) Exod xxxii. 30 Moſes *ſaid, Peradventure I ſhall make an atonement for your ſin*

(3) Numb xvi 46, 47. *Take a cenſer, and put fire therein from off the altar; and put on incenſe, and make atonement for them; and he put on incenſe, and made atonement for the beople*

(4) Numb xxv. 13. *And he* [Eleazar, i e. God will help] *ſhall have it, and his ſeed after him, the covenant of an unchangeable Prieſthood, becauſe he*

*was zealous for his God,
and made an* atonement
for the children of Israel

(5) Numb xxxi 50
*We have brought an ob-
lation for the Lord, to
make an* atonement *for
our souls.*

(6) 2 Sam xxi 3.
David *said unto the*
Gibeonites, *wherewith
shall I make the* atone-
ment, *that ye may bless
the inheritance of the*
Lord

for, and confequently faith in, God.

EFFECT. You fay it was uncertain; but you fee it was to fave them from the plague upon their being numbered, *ver.* 49.

MEAN. An offering out of the fpoils of every man given to (Chrift) *the ta-bernacle of the congrega-tion, for a memorial be-fore the Lord* of the price of their redemption, and of their title to be *numbered* among the *Ifrael of God.* See No. 1. and *fect.* 55.

EFFECT. You fay it was fatisfaction to the injured *Gibeonites;* I add, from *ver.* 1, 14. the ceafing of the *famine.*

MEAN. An act of juftice upon *Saul's* bloody houfe, determined by the *Gibeo-nites,* at *David's* requeft, but intimated by the Lord, *ver.* 1. who requires equi-valent recompenfe, *life for life.*

M   EFFECT.

(7) Deut xxi 8 *Be merciful unto* [atone] *thy people whom thou haft redeemed, and the blood* fhall be forgiven [atoned to] *them*

EFFECT. Exemption from the judgments of God.

MEAN. The flaying of an heifer that had not *drawn yoke*, wafhing *their hands in innocency* over it, *upon* it, and a proteftation of their ignorance of the murder (like our taking of the Sacrament upon a thing) *that their hands had not been upon the flain.*

(8) Deut xxxii 43. *Rejoice, O ye nations, with his people, for he* [God] *will be merciful to* [atone] *his land, and his people*

EFFECT. Redemption from evil unto life.

MEAN. *God* himfelf doing what the *High-Prieft* did, and being the *Mean* or *Mediator.*

EFFECT. Difcharge from the evil of another's perfonal fin.

(9) Numb xxxv. 33 *The land cannot be clean* fed [atoned for] *of the blood that is fhed therein, but by the blood of him that fhed it*

MEAN. The death of the murderer.

EFFECT. Clearance from, and not only non-punifhment of, fin.

(10) Pfal lxv 3 *Iniquities prevail againft me; as for our tranfgreffions thou fhalt* purge them away [atone them]

MEAN. Same as No. 8. *God*'s being the *atonement.*

EFFECT. Clearance from fin.

(11) Pfal lxxix 9 Purge away [atone for] *our fins for thy Name's fake*

MEAN. His *Name, Jefus.*

EFFECT.

(12) Prov xvi 6 *By mercy and truth iniquity is* purged [atoned for]

EFFECT. Clearance from sin.

MEAN. *Mercy* and *Truth* (Chrift; fee *Pfal.* lxxxv. 10. — lvii. 3. *Luke* i. 76) not a word of human mercy and truth.

(13) Ifa vi 7. *Thine iniquity is taken away, and thy fin is* purged [atoned for]

EFFECT. Pardon, or bearing of fin, or purification.

MEAN. The *live coal*, not a fign of pardon, but of the mean which wrought the effect, and *took away* his fin, namely, the wrath of God. See *fect.* 42.

(14) Ifaiah xxii 14 *Surely this iniquity fhall not be* purged *from you* [atoned to you] *till ye die*

EFFECT. Of non-atonement, death *in* their fins.

MEAN. *God*'s accepting no atonement, becaufe they had rejected *his.*

(15) Ifa xxvii 9 *By this fhall the iniquity of* Jacob *be* purged.

EFFECT. Purification fiom fin, and a right to Heaven.

MEAN. The death of a *perfon*, at a time when he fhould make *all the ftones of the altar as chalk ftones that are beaten in funder :* the deftruction of *Jerufalem*, when *one* ftone was

not

not left upon *another*. See *Mat.* xxiv. 2.

EFFECT. The making up of their accounts, *finishing of* man's *transgressions, by bringing in of everlasting righteousness.*

MEAN. The *transfer* of the sin to Christ by *impression,* imposition, or imputation, *upon* him, and the *Messiah's* being *cut off, but not for himself.*

(16) Dan. ix 24. *Seventy weeks are determined [for their discharge] on account of thy people, and on account of thy holy city, to finish the transgressions [of men] and to make [an end of, ‏לחתם‎ a transfer sin [to Christ, as by impression the signature or seal is transferred, witness de Dieu on John.* vi 27 who says, the *Syriac* and *Arabic* there use this *Hebrew* word to denote this signature transferred by impression from the seal to the wax] *and to make [atonement] reconciliation for iniquity* [thus transferred to, or stamped or sealed *upon, him from another subject] and to bring in everlasting righteousness ———* and *———the Messiah shall be cut off, but not for himself*

(17) Gen. xxxii 40. *For he [Jacob] said, I will* appease [atone] *him [Esau] with the present that goeth before me*

(18) Prov. xvi 14 *A wise man will* pacify [atone] *it.*

EFFECT. The calming or *satisfying* of *Esau.*

MEAN. A present or offering *for* acceptance.

EFFECT. Escape of the resentment of the king.

MEAN. Wife and prudent to *satisfy* or *pacify* it.

EFFECT.

(19) Ezek. xvi 60, 63 *I will remember my covenant——I will establish with thee an everlasting covenant, that thou mayest remember and be confounded, and never open thy mouth, because of thy shame, when I* [have atoned] *am pacified towards thee for all that thou hast done, saith the Lord*

(20) Isa xlvii. 11 *Therefore* [speaking of *Babylon*] *shall evil come upon thee—thou shalt not be able to* put it off [to atone it]

(21) Deut xxi 8 See above No 7

(22) 2 Chr xxx 18. *The good Lord* pardon [atone] *every one*

(23) Psal lxxviii 38 *He being full of compas-*

EFFECT. *Knowledge* of the *Lord,* and all his grace; *confusion* of themselves; *submission* and *silence* before God; *remission* of sins; and on earth *peace and good-will towards men.*

MEAN. God's *remembering his covenant.*

EFFECT. That evil would come upon her; *her nakedness should be uncovered, her shame seen,* ver. 3.

MEAN. None that she should use, because she had trusted in herself, *ver.* 10. therefore God would *take vengeance* upon her, *ver.* 3.

EFFECT. Acceptance, though not *Levitically* purified, and deliverance from some bodily disease; for it is said, *ver.* 20. *That the Lord healed the people.*

MEAN. Pleading of *God's atonement,* and praying him to atone.

EFFECT. *Remission* of sins.

MEAN.

sion forgave [atoned for] them their iniquities.

(24) Jer xviii 23 Forgive not [atone not for] their iniquities

(25) Isa xxviii 18. Your covenant with death shall be disannulled [atoned]

(26) Exod xxi 29, 30 If there be laid on him a sum of money [atonement money] then he shall give for the ransom of his life whatever is laid upon him

(27) Exod xxx 12 When thou takest the sum of the children of Israel, then shall they give every man a ransom [an atonement] for his soul

(28) Job xxxiii 24 Deliver him from going down into the pit, I have found a ransom [atonement] for him.

MEAN. The *atonement* of *God*.

EFFECT. Overthrow, and death in sin.

MEAN. *God's* not atoneing.

EFFECT. Their being *troden down with the overflowing scourge*, ver. 18.

MEAN. The " atoning, " blotting out, smearing " over," covering, and so " cancelling of their cove- " nant;" its not being attended to.

EFFECT. Exemption from death.

MEAN. A ransom or price paid.

EFFECT. See No. 1. that there be *no plague amongst them*.

MEAN. The *price* paid for an atonement.

EFFECT. Being *saved* from death temporal and eternal, and restored to life, *ver.* 25—27.

MEAN. The *interpreter*, the *manifester* of his *own* righteouf-

righteoufnefs to man, being *mediator*, and finding what man could not, a ranfom *for* him ; for *godlinefs* has the *promife of the life which now is*, as well as of that which is to come, 1 *Tim.* iv. 8.　The *Apocryphal* Scripture you cite, or Dr. *Patrick's* expofition of the text, cannot be admitted in evidence, when they *con-tradict* the plain letter of *Canonical* Scripture.　*I have found* (not repentance but) *a ranfom*, therefore *deliver him*, cannot be con-ftrued aught but redemp-tion of *one* party by the payment of *another*.

EFFECT. Death.
MEAN. No atonement.

(29) Job xxxvi 18 *Becaufe there is wrath beware—then the great* ranfom [atonement] *cannot deliver thee.*

EFFECT. Being fubject to his refentment.
MEAN. His not accept-ing *any* fatisfaction.
EFFECT. Redemption.
MEAN. A fum of money given.

(30) Prov vi 35 *He* [the jealous man] *will not regard any* ranfom [atonement].

(31) Prov. xiii. 8 *The* ranfom[atonement] *of a man's life are his riches.*

EFFECT.

(32) Prov xxi 18 *The wicked fhall be a ranfom [atonement] for the righteous [juftified] and the tranfgreffor for the upright*

(33) Ifa xliii 3 *I am the Lord thy God, I gave* Egypt *for thy ranfom [atonement]* Ethiopia *and* Seba *for thee*

(34) Pfal xlix 7 *None of them can by any means redeem his brother, nor give to God a ranfom [atonement] for him*

(35) Num xxxv 31 *Ye fhall take no fatisfaction [atonement] for the life of the murtherer, which is guilty of death, but he fhall furely be put to death—ver 32 And ye fhall take no fatisfaction [atonement] for him that is fled to the city of his refuge, that*

EFFECT. Deliverance of the *juftified* perfon from evil.

MEAN. The fufferings of the wicked. He who is juftified fhall be delivered at the expence of the wicked. A *fubftituted vicarious* means; where *one* fuffers, and *another* is faved by it.

EFFECT. Redemption of *Ifrael.*

MEAN. The punifhment and fufferings of *other* nations; the gift of *Egypt, Ethiopia,* and *Seba, for* him.

EFFECT. Death, if they trufted in *fuch* redemption.

MEANS. Ineffectual application.

EFFECT. In the firft cafe, death; in the fecond, no releafe nor redemption till *the death of the Prieft* (Chrift in figure).

MEAN. In one cafe *no* fatisfaction; in the other, *the death of the Prieft* (Chrift

(Chrift in figure) which you have overlooked.

EFFECT. Deviation from ftrict juftice.

MEAN. A premium, valuable *confideration* or *fatisfaction* given.

le fhould come again to duell in the land, until the death of the Prieft

(36) 1 Sam xii 3 *Of whofe hands have I received any* bribe [atonement]

(37) Amos v 12 *They afflict the juft, they take a* bribe [atonement]

49. Before we pafs a judgment upon thefe texts, I muft fort them as you have done, abating fome little differences concerning the cafes to which they feverally belong.

1. Then obferve, that in all thefe cafes, firft negatively, that *no* perfons made atonement for themfelves; for that mean by which the atonement is made is fomewhat *extraneous* to, and *diftinct* from, the party who applies it; wherefore it is a downright contradiction to fay, as you do (107), " that in fome cafes perfons made atone- " ment for themfelves;" when it is not the *perfons* that atone, but *that* which they apply or ufe: and if it is thought reafon good enough to conclude fo, becaufe the parties applied or ufed thefe outward means, I fee not why we may not with as much reafon impioufly conclude, that falvation belongeth to man, though it is faid to belong *unto the Lord*, Pfal. iii. 8. becaufe man muft accept i, and open his heart to its powerful in-

N   fluence:

fluence: whence, secondly and positively, it was always somewhat extraneous to, and distinct from, the party which atoned.

2. Some places relate to the Messiah, No. 8, 10, 11, 12, 13, 15, 16, 19, 22, 23, 24, 28. from whence I shall draw proper conclusions in their place.

3 One to the disannulling or covering of an agreement from the eye or sight, so that it should not be attended to. No. 25.

4. Six relate to the dealings of one man with another, No. 17, 18, 30, 31, 36, 37. In these cases one person is represented to be obnoxious to the resentment of *another*, and the atonement or ransom is made by giving or doing somewhat to *content*, appease, I add, to *satisfy*, pacify and reconcile, the offended party. For he who remits his anger is *satisfied* and pacified, and that which induces him to remit it, is the ransom, which is therefore the *satisfaction*, as it is justly rendered, No. 35; and, because it is the *satisfaction*, it is the *equivalent*.

5. " Three," you say, " seem to be mix-" ed cases, because they relate partly to " God, and partly to Man:" and, by the same rule, I may call all of them mixed cases, excepting the six last mentioned. No. 6. indeed more explicitly sheweth the effects of atonement, *peace with God*, and
con-

consequently satisfaction and restitution made. No. 26. shews, that God would accept of an atonement, or vicarious satisfaction, in *one* case, instead of the death of the murtherer No. 35. of none in another case *till the death of the Priest*, Christ in figure, on whose death he had a right to a portion in the inheritance of the *Israelites*.

6. The remaining fifteen are cases between the Most High God and *Judge* of the whole earth, and the *criminal* Man, and relate to his reconciliation of them to himself, or to his display of vengeance upon them, brought upon them on account of their pleading, or not pleading, his atonement, what you call " atonement or non-atonement." You say, " in two of those cases sin is neither expres- " sed nor implied, No. 32, 33." But if it is implied when a man is said to be *justified* or acquitted, then it is implied in No. 32. And in No. 33. if *Saviour* implies a subject to be *saved* from evil, and if *evil* can only arise to man from *sin*; or if *ransom* implies slavery, and slavery a subjection of the party to an enemy; then here also *sin* is most emphatically implied · and accordingly when we look into the context, *Isa.* xlii. 24, 25. we find, though *Israel* was *beloved* of his *Maker*, yet it was *a back-sliding people*, which had been guilty of sin, and needed a *Saviour*, who would, as it is expressed,

N 2

for

for his *own fake*, and not for the fake of a man, or a man's merits, *blot out* their *fins*. We may now then pafs our judgment on the effect and means of atonement.

50. I. The effect is the pardon of fin varioufly expreffed, becaufe the confequences of being pardoned are various; but peace, fanctification, or any bleffing, neceffarily befpeaks *pardon*, and pardon *juftification*, and this a *previous* atonement, and you fee the effect is certain, where you fuppofe it not to be fo, No. 5.

II. The means by which atonement was made, are fuch as God affords and appoints, and you fay, " or fuch as men devife." 1. Such as God affords and appoints, (I) *God* himfelf, the great and *infinitely* valuable atonement, No. 8, 10, 11, 13, 14, 19, 22, 23, 24, 28. (II) The interceffion of *Mofes*, the *Vice-God*, and type of Chrift in his human nature, and confequently the interceffion of Chrift, No. 2. [No. 3. has no place here]. (III) The heifer, that had *never* drawn yoke; Chrift the propitiation, *who knew no fin*, and never drew in fubjection to the yoke of fin, by *Heb.* ix. 1. pleaded and offered through faith. (IV) The Interpreter or Mediator between *God and Man*, who *fheweth* or manifefteth *unto man his righteoufnefs*, bringeth *in everlafting righteoufnefs*, Dan. ix. Ifa. xlvi. 13. and faith, *Deliver*

liver him, for *I have found a ransom*, No. 28. (V) The Priest, as Christ, paying *life for life* forfeited, and satisfying God with doing justice on the criminals, No. 4. (VI) Punishment of sin, No. 4. (VII) Plenary, and adequate satisfaction, No. 9. (VIII) The Divine *Mercy and Truth*, Christ, who is the truth, *John* xiv. 6. and the mercy performed, *Luke* i. 72. No. 12. (IX) The disciplinary visitations you speak of from No. 15. are no other than the sufferings of Christ, on whom this *chastisement of our peace* was. (X) " An offering," you say, " to the service of religion:" but it is in fact the price paid for their souls, which were *numbered in* Israel, No. 1, 5. See *sect.* 55 and 56. below. (XI) You say, " Sufferings of some for others," No. 32, 33. Now No 32. speaks nothing of atonement for sin: Why? Because the man, for whom is the *caphar* כפר is already said to be justified · what it means I shall endeavour to shew below. And, as to No. 33. it speaks of the price of their redemption, with No. 1 and 5.

51. II. You say, " such as men devise, " as counsels, riches, forces, or any shifts " they use to preserve or secure themselves," No. 20, 29, 34. Now, first, as to No. 20. *Isa.* xlvii. 11. *God* says (to *Babylon*) *Mischief shall come upon thee; thou shalt not be*
able

able to atone it. But what, shall I conclude, because God says, *Thou shalt not
atone it*, therefore there are human atonements? On these principles you may say
again, " Salvation is of man, because it is
" said, *Thou shalt not save thyself.*" And
this would have been no concern to *Babylon*
to be told; they could not thus *atone* the
evil, because there was still an atonement to
plead: but here they are told, that this
shall not avert the evil. And supposing
men had, as they do now too frequently,
applied *human* atonements, this is not saying they were in fact *atonements*, or effectual to remove evil, by satisfying the wrath
of God. Secondly, as to No. 29. it is said,
*A great ransom cannot deliver thee: will
he esteem thy riches?* But what shall we infer from hence? Why; not that there are
human atonements, which are available to
our acceptance with God; but that, when
a man sins against God, and rejects Christ,
which is the (אל) spoke of so *particu-
larly* in the book of *Job*, the great atonement will not deliver him, not his riches,
nor *any* thing that man has. Lastly, as to
No. 34. *None of them can, by any means,
redeem his brother, nor give to God a ransom*, or atonement, *for him.* Surely, any
one may see, that here *human* atonements
are so *far* from being spoken of as *available*
to

to our acceptance with God, that it is declared, *No man can redeem his brother*, do what he will; and of courfe it is *a fortiori* declared, that no merits of a man fhall fave a man, becaufe his works cannot be fo precious as the life of another. But obferve further, that what atones for a brother is not the brother himfelf, but *another* perfon; which may ferve to confirm what I have faid concerning a vicarious punifhment and transfer of guilt, and to confute what you have alledged againft it. In No. 36, 37. which you have not made your reflections upon, the means are plainly a *valuable confideration* or *fatisfaction*, given for the diverting of vindictive juftice from the perfon of the guilty, rightly rendered a *bribe*, if underftood as it is faid, *Exod.* xxiii. 8. *Deut.* xvi. 19. 1 *Sam.* xii. 3. to *blind the eyes of the wife*. but thefe were forbidden to be ufed by man for reafons very obvious.

52. You need not then, Sir, have ranked your means under two heads, 1. *Divine*, 2. *Human*, when you was treating of an atonement to *God*, for this you fee was never to be made but by *God* or *Chrift*, for he was *God manifeft in the flefh*, or by fome *reprefentative* of this great facrifice or price. But you feem to me to have argued thus: That the word which we render *atonement*,

is

is applied to *human* meafures, which *fatif-fy*, redeem, or divert from evil, and therefore the means of atonement to God are fometimes fuch as *man* devifes ; which you cannot call reafoning, becaufe there is no fort of connection between your premiffes and your conclufions : you had as well affirm *Levitical* facrifices to be naturally, and in themfelves effectual to obtain remiffion of fins, becaufe they are called by the name of the Chriftian *Paffover :* what then may we certainly conclude from the whole ?

53. (1) That forgivenefs of fin is exemption from the evil of fin, and beftowing of bleffings.

(2) That the means of obtaining this forgivenefs, or atoning for fin, are not far from being uniform, as you affert, in direct oppofition to the plain fenfe of the Scriptures, and of the articles of the Church of *England* (fee artic. 6.) for hence it appears that they are uniform, with refpect to the *thing fignified*; though this is fpoken of at *fundry times*, and *in divers manners*, to give mankind an idea of the nature and efficacy of the *one* great atonement, *Jefus Chrift* : wherefore we read above of atonement made by the Lord, who was manifeft in the flefh, by *his* prayer in the perfon of *Mofes*, as his human nature, *Vice-God*, Exod. xxi. and *heir of all things*,—by the facrifice of himfelf

ſelf in his *figure*, the *heifer, goat,* &c.—
by him as an Interpreter or Mediator between God and Man, *who* found the *ranſom*—by his puniſhing of ſin, and our criminal nature, in the perſon of *Eleazar*—by
his *plenary* ſatisfaction—by his bearing the
chaſtiſement of our peace upon him—by him
as the *price* of their redemption—by that
which *skreens* another, as the wicked, in *Prov.*
xxi. 18. by ſuffering, skreens the juſtified or
righteous perſon, they, as the *Jews,* unwittingly doing what may ſecure and protect the righteous— by giving to God a *ranſom* for a brother—by a *valuable* conſideration, and *adequate* ſatisfaction, to divert the
execution of juſtice upon the parties that are
perſonally guilty.—No " ſole goodneſs of
" God" without a valuable conſideration or
ſatisfaction, no " prayers of men" without
this, no " repentance" without this ; no
" diſciplinary viſitations," no jeſuitical
ſcourges or " ſufferings," from an avenging
providence, without this, no " ſignal acts,"
of the greateſt rectitude in moral life, whether " of virtue or juſtice," without this,
ever *did, can,* or *ſhall* atone.

54 (3) The *giving an equivalent to God*
is naturally, and, according to the Scripture
ſenſe of it, included in the notion of atonement : it is in this light the Patriarchs, and
Faithful *Iſrael,* offered it ; and all the

Churches,

Churches, and I, proud to be the least of Christ's members, have pleaded it. But, according to your account of this matter, we have all been in the dark: "The "giving an equivalent to God is no ways," you say, "included in the notion of atone- "ment, however it may bear that sense "with regard to men, among whom alone "equivalents, in case of injuries, I pre- "sume, can have any place." An oppo- sition of this kind, one would think, should have some sort of countenance, either from Scripture or Reason, before you could be persuaded to make it: and if it has, what an unreasonable faith have I, and all Chris- tians, held; therefore I could not but wish that you had mistaken the matter; and, ac- cording to my expectation, I find there is all the room in the world to say you are mistaken, because we have nothing but *your* word for it against the express assertions of thousands of thousands: therefore pardon me, if I say you have supported a mere conjecture by mere suppositions, and that I find no reason, from what you advance, to induce me to think as you would have me. But how, Sir, can I think thus with secu- rity? I should fear to look at that *great God and Saviour*, who suffered so much for my soul, when I will not allow *his* atone- ment to be of *infinite* value, that is, to be

an

an *equivalent to any* demands from the Father : for, with what shadow of a reason should I believe this offering not to be *equivalent*, when it is the offering of a *God in the flesh?* or, Would you have me to deny *Jesus* to be both the supreme *Lord* and supreme *God,* or to deny that *God* is infinite? For this I must do, before I can presume to hold his sacrifice was *not* equal, or *not* proportioned, to the demands of justice. But neither Scripture, nor the reason of the thing, will allow me to deny any of these truths. The light in which all of them appear is so considerable, that I cannot but boldly assert their reality, and because *Jesus* is *Lord* and *Christ,* his offering must needs be *equivalent,* as it is *infinite* in its nature : and the texts you cite in No. 1, 5. are so far from discountenancing, that they abundantly confirm to us this notion of atonement.

55. As in the first, *Exod.* xxx. 14. *God, the King of* Israel (the Gospel calls Christ *the King of* Israel) *requireth half a shekel of every one above twenty for the service of the tabernacle,* which is called *ransom,* atonement money, for their souls, you suppose, " as it was a testimony of their obligations " to God, and of their willingness to sup- " port his worship; which he so far ac- " cepted as to spare their lives, forfeited by

" their

" their transgressions." But, to suppose *nothing* of ourselves, pray what says the text? It says, That the *Priest* was to take it, and apply it for the service of the *taber-nacle, that it might be for a memorial unto the children of* Israel *before the Lord.* Now this being a *shadow* of the good things to come, represented somewhat which they were to attribute to the *High-Priest* of their pro-fession, and what *he* was to offer, because they could not offer any thing as the price of their redemption from evil : and read we not of the price of our redemption, that we are *bought with a price,* 1 Cor. vi. 20 ? Does not St. *Peter* allude to this, 1 *Ep.* i. 18. when he says. *Ye were not redeemed with corruptible things, silver and gold, but with the precious blood of Christ ?* Does not *Isa.* xliii. 24. allude to this, *Ye have bought me no sweet cane with money,* and St. *John, the gold tried in the fire,* Rev. v. 18 ? Add to *this,* that the *rich shall not give more,* and *the poor shall not give less :* and say, whether these allusions to *price,* and *silver and gold,* and *money,* and this observable fixing of the price to the poor and rich for their atonement money, have not a direct tendency to set before us the *price* or purchase money of our redemp-tion, the blood of Christ and of God, *Acts* xxix. 28 ? More than which the *richest* in endow-

endowments, or worst, must not presume to offer for their acceptance, and less than which God will not be satisfied with from a man of the *meanest* qualifications: and, in the settlement of the price to *few* as half a shekel, is not the price of their redemption set forth to them as *easy* to be come at, and to be pleaded with *little* labour, in the Lord? Yes, doubtless, and *the Gospel was preached unto them as well as unto us:* they therefore knew they were *bought with a price*, and must likewise have known from this remarkable statute or appointment, that the price they attributed to the *Priest* to offer for them when they were numbered was, since it is expressly said to be so, a *memorial* of the price paid and offered, as here, by *the High-Priest of their profession*, i. e. by the Lord, in whose Name he ministered for them, who were to be *numbered* amongst the *Israel of God* To suppose otherwise, is to suppose the *Jews* were unable to draw a *common* parallel, make an *ordinary* comparison, or trace an *obvious* likeness. It was their unhappy case when they were rejected; it is their case now; and I wish I was not forced to add, that it is the case of many now-a-days, who are for taking the Scriptures in a temporal view, and for precluding the *spiritual* import of the Law and the Prophets. If it was not, they

they could not avoid feeing the doctrine here denoted : for what is plainer, if you confider this Scripture in this view, than that a price denoted a *spiritual* price, which every one allotted to a *spiritual* High-Prieft, that he might offer it, and make atonement with it *for* them ; and that this valuable confideration offered by the Prieft, when allotted him by the *rich*, was owning they had nothing *more* to give for their *peace*, and, when affigned him by the poor, was owning nothing *lefs* would fave them ? What is plainer than that the ftipulating this figurative price fo low as *half a fhekel*, was reprefenting how eafy a thing it was to plead Chrift the *gold tried in the fire ?* What is plainer than that, when they paid the one to be numbered amongft the *Ifrael after the flefh*, they in faith paid the other in *the High-Prieft of their profeffion*, that they might be numbered with the true *Ifrael of God*, as defcribed in the *Rev.* vii. 4. and efcape a total excifion *from the prefence of the Lord*, 2 Theff. i. 9? And if this is fo, then here is a *price* fixed for the redemption of their fouls ; a *fatisfaction* and an *equivalent* given to God by the *High-Prieft* for them ; for it is a price paid, and money given, for *life*. But you fay, " no man " can judge this was given by way of equi- " valent." Why not? God could not in

justice

juftice accept, in exchange for *life*, what was *not* equivalent. To fuppofe this, a man muft firft ftrangely mifconceive of God's wifdom: and this price, this offering, was offered as a figure of the *price* of their redemption by our *great High-Prieft* ; and his price muft needs be an *equivalent*, if *Chrift* is *God*, and *God* is infinite : for the price was a *Chrift crucified, gold tried in the fire*, Rev. iii. 18.

56. Now let me freely expoftulate with you. Does not a price imply fomewhat to be bought? And would it be doing *juftice* to one's felf, or acting *wifely*, to take for it *lefs* than the thing is worth? Again ; Is not the thing transferred into *another*'s hands for the fake, and on account, of this price, or *valuable* confideration? Becaufe, if thefe queries cannot be anfwered any otherwife than in the affirmative, it is true, that giving of an *equivalent* to God is included in the notion of atonement. Nay, to drop all other proofs, the very words, *price* and *bought*, 1 Cor. vi. 20. neceffarily convey to us the idea of a fatisfactory equivalent : wherefore, when you prefume equivalents, in cafe of injuries, can have place only amongft men, it really, to fpeak my mind freely, is a mere prefumption ; becaufe to juftify it you muft impioufly fuppofe, that *God* exifts not in *three* perfons, *any* of whom,

as

as *God*, can *satisfy* the demands of God; and that Chrift is *not* God, and, by *not* being God, *not* qualified to give an equivalent to God · for otherwife God may be *offended*, and God may *recompenfe* and *satisfy* for fuch offence. But I would hope you believe the coeffential and coequally *supreme divinity* of Chrift. Remember what he fays in anfwer to *Philip* defiring him to fhew him the *Father*, John xiv. 9, 10. *Have I been fo long time with you, and yet haft thou not known Me*, Philip? *He that hath feen Me hath feen the Father. And how fayeft thou (then) fhew us the Father? Believeft thou not that I am in the Father, and the Father in Me? The words that I fpeak unto you I fpeak not of Myfelf, but the Father that dwelleth in Me, he doth the works.* After this I am perfuaded every one, who believes his Bible, will believe it If you do not, we have *light* greater than the Sun's at midday, and like that which fhone around *Paul*, to illuftrate it. When he then paid a *price* it muft be *infinite*, and therefore be an equivalent given to God, to whom he *gave* himfelf a facrifice; his life, his blood, for a ranfom for us. See *John* vi. 51. *Galat.* 1. 4. 1 *Tim.* ii. 6. Again,

(2) As to No. 5. *Numb.* xxxi. 50. there needs little to be faid about it, becaufe the occafion upon which the *Ifraelites* made the

offering

offering was the fame, namely, upon their being *numbered*. The offering indeed was different; it was out of the *spoils* of their enemies, the rebel *Canaanites*, whofe manfions they were to inherit: and herein they in figure tendered the *price* of their redemption, confifting of the fpoils of the fpiritual enemies—fpoils which were to be affigned to the *Prieft*, for him to put them *for a memorial*, and to *make atonement*—fpoils which were won for us by Jefus, and (if we fight under his banner) our *righteoufnefs*, and *cloathing of gold*, in fhort, every thing we were deprived of *in juftice* by God, ond *in malice* by the Devils. Hence we read, *Jofh.* x. 14. *The Lord fought for* Ifrael. John xvi. 33. *I have* overcome *the world.* 1 Sam. xvii. 47. *The* battle *is the Lord's.* Pfal. xviii. 39. *Thou haft guided me with ftrength to the* battle.—xxiv. 8. *The King of Glory, the Lord, mighty in* battle.—lxxvi. 3. *There* (where? *in* Salem, *in his tabernacle, in his dwelling-place,* Chrift) *brake he* the arrow of the bow, the fhield, and the fword, and the battle. *Selah:* He conquered *all* oppofition from an avenging God on the *one* hand, and from Men and Devils on the *other*, being *made of twain one new man, and fo making* peace. *Ifa.* liii. 12. *He fhall divide the* fpoil *with the ftrong.* So *Chrift* fpoiled the goods of the *ftrong Man*, the

P

Devil,

Devil, in the parable, *Mat.* xii. 29.—and *Col.* ii. 15. *Having* spoiled *principalities and powers—he sat down at the right-hand of God—led captivity captive, and took as a picy gifts for men,* Psal lxviii. 18 Whence you see, the people attributed *victory,* and *salvation unto the Lord,* in the person of the *Priest* (see *Deut.* xviii. 5.) to whom they gave the spoils, and pleaded his real spoils of their *spiritual* enemies, which he should by his *own* arm win for them, as the means of their salvation, for him *to make atonement* to God, and as a *reason why they should* be numbered with *his* victorious *Israel,* with them that *overcome.* Yes; it was Christ triumphant over Death and Hell, and all things, which they pleaded, that, because *he overcame* and *lived,* they also might *overcome* and *live,* and *sit down with him* on his throne; see *Rev.* iii. 21 *. We may also learn from hence what made *Saul's* crime in not killing *Agag,* and the concealment of the *accursed thing,* so notorious,

namely,

---

* Hence, doubtless, the *Romans* had their *spolia optima* For, when the *Roman* general had, in any engagement, killed. the chief commander of the enemy with his *own* hands, then the arms of the slain captain were carried before the victor, decently hanging on the stock of an oak, and so composing a trophy In this manner the procession went on to the temple of *Jupiter Feretrius,* so called *a ferendo* from striking or slaying, and the general, making a formal dedication of his spoils, hung them up in the temple. [See *Kennet's Rom. Antiq* 227] Hence the hanging trophies in churches

nameiy, an inclination to let the *rebel* fpirits and lufts be in us *unmortified*, not to be crucified together with Chrift. Now do not you own, Sir, that you are very much out in the choice of your proofs? For, in both thefe cafes here is a *valuable* confideration or *equivalent* pleaded for an *atonement*; tho' you are pleafed to fay, "none "of our texts look this way," becaufe *fpoils* and *money*, tho' corruptible things, are *valuable* confiderations, and being in fymbols the *price* paid, and the fpoils won, by Chrift, muft needs be *equivalent*, for *Chrift* is *God*.

57. Neither are thefe the *only* texts which look this way. For do not No 9, 10, 11, 12, 13, 14, 15, 16, 18, 23, 28, 29, 33, 35. as fpeaking of the *purging* and *clearing of fin*, imply a *fatisfaction* or *equivalent*? *for without fhedding of blood there is no remiffion:* but *blood* was not to be fhed by the tenor of the *Levitical* law, but *for blood*, therefore fhedding of blood was by way of *fatisfaction* or *equivalent*. No. 31, 36, 37. plainly fpeak of *atonement* by way of *plenary* fatisfaction. No. 26 fpeaks of an equivalent for *life*, forfeit by law *for life*, to be admitted in fome cafes; in others, 35, not till the *death of the Prieft*, in confideration of whofe *fatisfying* death all were *intentionally* releafed, and

P 2   had

had a right by law to the land, *the inheritance of the Saints*, and *seed of* Abraham.

58. Besides, do not we read, *Isa.* xxxv. 4. *Be strong, fear not—God*, a recompense (for *with* is an addition) *will come and save you; and it shall be said, Behold your God:* and, if you are desirous to know what *recompense* means, consult *Prov.* xii. 4. *Isa.* xl. 10.—lix. 18. *Joel* iii. 7. *Psal.* xviii. 20.—cxxxvii. 8. where you will find it to be *equal retaliation*, a *just* recompense. Again, we read in *Isa.* xxxiii. 13. *Now will I rise, saith the Lord: Hear ye*, &c. *acknowledge my might; who* for us *shall dwell* (sojourn) *in* everlasting *burnings?* And do these speak nothing of an equivalent? Is not an *infinite* person's (in the flesh) sojourning for them in *everlasting* burnings an equivalent? Yes; they assert it as expressly, as *any* doctrine is asserted in the Scriptures. But further; Is not the law conducted all along upon the footing of *equivalent* retribution, *&c?* Can I think then, that God has required man to make *retribution* to man, and yet not required *retribution* to himself, where the injury is of infinite more consequence to God and society, and when we cannot do better than to be renewed *after the image of him that created us*, and to live the life of God? I conclude then from all this, and from this latter observation *a fortiori*, that atonement *necessarily* includes in it the notion

tion of an *equivalent, recompenfe*, and the like, given to God.

59. Your fourth conclufion, which is another of your reafons why you except againft our notion of atonement, is, " that the " transferring of guilt doth not belong to " the fenfe of atonement." To juftify this you fay, " in the greateft part of thefe texts " there is not the leaft fuggeftion of a vica- " rious punifhment of one man's guilt being " laid upon another, and that other's being " punifhed or fuffering for it." I hope, Sir, for your own fake, your examination of thofe texts has been very curfory ; then you have fome excufe for your miftake : and, in this matter, pardon my faying, you are moft certainly under a miftake ; for, in No. 1, 2, 3, 4, 5, 6, 7, 8, 9, 10, 11, 12, 13, 14, 15, 16, 17, 19, 21, 22, 23, 27, 28, 31, 34, 35, 36, 37. we have *plain* fuggeftions, that there is a *transfer* of guilt, or obligations to *fatisfy*, which is all one ; for, in No. 1, 2, 27. there is a *valuable* confideration given, and the parties are, as we fay, *bought off.* Now I conceive, that where a *price* is paid for *any* thing or perfon, there muft be a *transfer* of the thing or perfon to *him* who buys them ; for a *price* is evidently that which is *fubftituted* for, or inftead of, the thing ; and whatever quali- fications the thing has which is to be pur- chafed, he who purchafes becomes poffeffed

of

of them; and becaufe he is defirous to be poffeffed of them, pays the price or pur- chafe money: and I cannot but think the *Ifraelites* underftood the nature of a com- mon bargain of fale. But if they did, they moft certainly knew that he who *bought* them *took* them, and their feveral fins and failings, to himfelf, as an *eagle* beareth her young upon her wings, *Exod.* xix. 4. *Deut.* xxxii. 11. and, for this reafon, became fub- ject to pay the *price* of their fouls. No. 31. *The ranfom of a man's life are his riches,* proves it: for *riches* are the medium or means of his ranfom. confequently there is an *exchange* or *transfer* to the party ran- foming. he takes the party to be ranfomed to himfelf, with all his qualifications, and pays the *ranfom.* God is faid to be the (כפר) *atonement* in No. 7, 8, 10, 11, 12, 13, 19, 22, 23, 28, 29. and we have proved *he bore fin* (60). Indeed, as the word includes in it the notion of an *equivalent,* as I have fhewn; and, as an equivalent can neither be demanded *in juftice* of any, nor paid by any from whom it is not *in juftice* due, and as it is not *in juftice* due from him, who is under *no* obligations to pay it; and he is *not* under obligations to pay it for fin, who is *no* way guilty of fin; fo whatever is faid to be a כפר *atonement for fin,* muft have had *fin :* but they had it not *actually,* and

therefore

therefore they muſt have had it *by imputa-tion.* This may ſerve for a general proof, though it might be proved to be ſuggeſted in each of the texts. See a further proof of it from your own ſenſe of the word, *ſect.* 66. I ſhall therefore wave conſidering any more of them, but theſe two following.

(1) In No. 15. *Iſa.* xxvii. 9. we read, *By this ſhall the* iniquity *of* Jacob be purged, and *this is* all *the fruit to* take away *his ſin.* By *what?* By the *ſmiting* of a perſon. Of whom? Of Chriſt it is plain from *ch.* ii. 6, 19.——xxv. 9. For it is all ſpoke of *one* day, *in that day,* in the day of Chriſtianity : but how ſhall it be *purged,* by his ſufferings, or by his *extra-ordinary* ſlaughter? It cannot be *purged* from off the perſon on whom it *never* was. But it is ſaid, It ſhall be *purged,* therefore it was *on* Chriſt, who *himſelf purged our ſins,* Heb. i. 5. But how was it upon him? Not *actually,* therefore it muſt be by *tranſ-fer* of it to him, by *imputation,* which, to-gether with a *vicarious* puniſhment, by death, the wages of ſin, are here expreſsly mentioned. As to No. 32. I urge it not, though I might, and with reaſon too. To conſider then,

(2) No. 33. *Iſa.* xliii. 3. *I gave* Egypt *for thy ranſom,* Ethiopia *and* Seba *for thee.* You ſay, the Prophet doth *not,* but I cannot

not but infift he did, fpeak of *atoning* their fins, xlii. 24. *Who gave* Jacob for a fpoil, *and* Ifrael to the robbers ? *Did not the Lord, he againft whom we have* finned ? *For they would not walk in* his *ways, neither were they obedient unto* his *law ; therefore hath he poured* upon *him his fury.* But, *&c.* to 3. Now I would ask, firft, What this tranfition from *them* to *him* means, but a *tranffer* of the guilt of the nation to *one Ifrael* or *Jacob*, as is *plainly* to be feen by any one who *reads* this prophecy ? Secondly, I would ask, Whether or no God doth not encourage his people to look for *him* who fhould *bear* their fins. For, faith he, *I once* (figuring out to thee, and in divers manners fhewing thee, my ways, *Pfal.* ciii. 7.) *gave* Egypt *thy ranfom*, Ethiopia *and* Seba *for thee ; therefore* (referring forward to the great deliverance) *will I give an* Adam *for* (תחת inftead of) *thee, and* People *for thy life* ; for in this laft verfe you find this תחת ufed as in *Gen.* xxx. 2. *inftead of* ; whence it is plain, that here it is declared *one* fhould fuffer *for* them, and *inftead of* them, as *Egypt* once did bear *all* the *plagues of the Lord ; one* fubftituted and ordained of God, *on* whom the *iniquities fhould be laid*, and *from* whom it fhould be *purged* ; and obferve, it is an *Adam* who was to be *fubftituted* for them, and yet

people

people two natures twain. Now this is the very language of St. *Paul*, Ephef. ii 15. *Made of twain* one new *Man* (and *new* he muft be to be an *Adam*) 1 Cor. xv. 45, 47. The *fecond* Man and *laft* Adam. If you feek proof, why I thus interpret *people* of the two natures of Chrift, pleafe to confult *Pfal* xx —xl. 5 — xliv. 9.— lxxx.—lxxxv. —lxxxvii. 5. which proves it beyond doubt, and St. *John* iii. 11, &c. You muft allow me then to conclude, that here is a pofitive declaration of a *vicarious fubftituted* offering, who *for us*, or in *our ftead*, fhould fuffer, and by which *vicarious* offering they fhould have *life*. How you can make this fignify " happinefs," or any thing *lefs* than *life eternal*, I know not; becaufe they to whom this promife was made died, and never enjoyed the benefit of it, and *never* will, unlefs they rife again.

61. Again, you fay, " in *all* thofe 37
" places, efpecially in No. 25. the word
" רפכ *caphar* feems to retain fomething
" of that which I take to be its natu-
" ral and original fenfe, *viz.* to cover or
" fmear over, as *Gen.* vi. 14 the only place
" where it is evidently fo ufed, which, ac-
" cording to our method of ftating the
" other texts, will ftand thus:

Make thee an ark of Gopher *wood, and thou shalt* (caphar) pitch (atone) *it within and without with* pitch (atonement).

EFFECT. The water was kept out of the *ark*, that *Noah* and his family might not perish in the flood.

MEAN. *The ark's being smeared,* and all its chinks stopped with pitch.

Be it so: for the Lexicons render it a *covering* (tegmen) a (*covered*) *cup* or *vessel*, *redemption, price, propitiation, expiation:* the *propitiatory* or *mercy-seat,* because it *covered* the ark, says *R. Sal*, little suburbs, or *out-places,* which *covered* the city; *hoarfrost,* which *covers* the ground; the shady *covering* cypress; a lion, that sits or is in *cover,* and lurketh in his den for prey. See *Psal.* xvii. 12. The *Septuagint* also render it εισφορας, somewhat induced, or *brought in, upon* their souls (על נפשתיכם) *Exod.* xxx. 16. περικαθαρμα, what cleanses *all round about,* Prov. xxi. 18. The *Chaldee* paraphrast renders it a *covering;* hence, as a verb, they use it with the *Syriac* and *Arabic* (*cafar*) for to *dissemble,* or to *cover* the truth; hence too, I presume, the *Latins* had their *caper, capra* (goat), from the use of them in sacrifices for a כפר *caphar;*

hence

hence our *English* word to *cover* : and it is obſervable, in *Exod.* xxix. 33.— xxix. 36.— xxix. 37.—xxx. 10, 15, 16. *Lev.* i. 4. and indeed in almoſt all the 109 places where it is uſed for to *atone*, or *atonement*, that the prepoſition עַל *upon*, follows the word, which naturally leads us to conſtrue it *covering* : a few places will convince us, that this muſt be the meaning. *Ezek.* xlv. 25. *Ye ſhall offer one lamb*, &c. *for a covering* (עַל *over or*) upon *them*, *ſaith the Lord.* *Lev.* i. 4. *And it ſhall be accepted for him for a covering* upon *him.* Numb. xxxv. 33. *And to the land there ſhall not be a covering* for blood. *Jer.* xviii. 23. *Be not a cover over their iniquity, neither blot out their ſin from thy ſight.*

62. Let us argue then upon this footing. " Atonement for ſin will therefore be the " *covering* of ſin, or the ſecuring from pu- " niſhment, and thus, when ſin is pardon- " ed, or calamity removed, the ſin or per- " ſon may be ſaid to be covered, made ſafe " or atoned, or, *&c.*" " Accordingly we " find the Scripture ſometimes expreſsly " calls the pardon of ſin, or removing of " ſuffering, the covering of ſin, as *Neh.* iv. " 4, 5. *Cover not their iniquities, and let* " *not their ſin be blotted out from before* " *thee* [compare this with *Jer.* xviii. 23.]

" Pſal.

" Pſal xxxii. 1. *Bleſſed is the man whoſe*
" *ſin is covered.* Pſal. lxxxv. 2. *Thou haſt*
" *covered all their ſin*, Jam v. 20." But
why muſt we not purſue the notion of
atonement, to which this ſenſe of the word
would lead us? For if it be to *cover*, then
in No. 7, 8, 10, 11, 12, 13, 15, 19, 22, 23,
28, 29. the *glorious* and *fearful* Name, the
Lord God, is ſaid to *cover*, or to be the
cover Now a *cover* implies ſomewhat to
be *covered*, and ſomewhat to be *covered*
from, ſo that the *cover* is neceſſarily in the
middle between them; and when a thing is
covered, it is *in* the *cover* : as for inſtance,
Noah was *in* the ark, and therefore all the
ſtorms that would otherwiſe fall upon the
thing covered, neceſſarily fall upon the *cover*.
Theſe are truths ſo ſelf-evident, that to
deny them muſt be to contradict the evidence of common ſenſe. A ſpiritual *coverer* or
cover then, wherever we find it uſed, beſpeaks
ſomewhat to be *covered*, and ſomewhat to
be *covered from*. That which is to be *covered* is, we find, the ſin of man, that
which it is to be *covered from*, the Scriptures as frequently declare to be the wrath
of God . whence we may as well ſee how
fully the Bible ſets forth the divinity of
Chriſt, by ſaying the *coverer* is *God*, as
how neceſſarily he, by thus interpoſing as
a *cover*, becomes the *middle* party, or an
active

active efficacious Mediator; and men and their fins that are *covered* muft be *in* the cover, this *Mediator*, as *Noah* in the ark; and all the terrible difplays of judgment which finful men deferve, muft fall *upon him out cover*, for I have proved before this is what we are *covered* from. So all the exemption you and I dare plead is *through him, in him, and by him*, as the exemption *Noah* enjoyed was *through, in,* and *by*, the ark, that fuftained the ftorm, bore him on the fwelling billows, and ftood a mediator between him and the devouring tempeft. From your own principles you fee, Sir, with how fair and firm an argument you fupply us againft your own unfcriptural conclufions. For, in the firft place, you muft difavow your own principles, and then I muft fear your faith in the Scripture; or otherwife you muft own atonement *neceffarily* includes in it the notion of a *mediating* fubject *covering* fin, or having fin under his *cover*, which he had not originally, but by impofition or imputation in his body. Secondly, you muft deny what the Scriptures moft exprefsly affert, that the ark fuftained the impetuous rain and billows, or otherwife you muft own, that atonement befpeaks a *Mediator*, like the ark *fuffering* what man, as *Noah*, would otherwife have fuffered, and confequently
for,

for, or *in the stead* of, man, by and through his *vicarious* punishment acquitting and us protecting (*a protego*). As to the imputation of his *merits*, which is as plainly to be inferred from hence, I shall urge it in its place. It is enough for my present purpose that these particulars are true; for then you must not say the means of atonement are *not* uniform, nor *vicarious* : you must yet reverence this Scripture, there is *One Mediator between God and Man, the Man Christ Jesus* (both God and Man) and pray God to lift up the *light of his countenance*, his resplendent *cover, upon* you, who once for you and your sins bore so much; for to this you have been hitherto a stranger. but as we read of the *shadow of his wings*, and of his *hiding* us therein, *Psal.* xvii. 8. in his *pavilion*, in *the secret of* his *tabernacle* (Christ) xxvii. 4.———xxxi. 20. so we read, *John* vi. 37. him *that cometh to me I will in no wise cast out*. May you therefore, following the *Light* and *Truth* which he hath sent, be led into his *holy tabernacle* (Christ).

63. And surely you must be inclined to take in this notion of the bearing of sin by *imputation* of sin, and of a *vicarious* punishment for sin, into your idea of atonement, as the *essential* parts of it, when the Scriptures every-where declare, that without

out *faith* it is impoffible to pleafe God, *i. e.* without the Chriftian faith preached unto them as well as unto us; and when they hold forth God as our *Shield*, our *Defence*, *Tower*, *Fortrefs*, and *Sun*, in whom we are *covered*, and fenced from evil, when they affure us, that *fome* facrifices, though of his own ordering, and however pompous, had *no* effect with God, becaufe they trufted not in *the Lord* for all things, and that others were to him as tenders of Jefus, a *fweet fmelling favour*, effectual to excite him to mercy. For nothing could make them difagreeable to him who ordained them, but not doing *juftice* upon themfelves and others; not *loving* the *mercy*—not *walking humbly with their God*—not by faith looking up to *Jefus*, the perfon *on* whom *juftice* was done *for* fin, and the *fheltering* mercy offered to Man. In fhort, not owning that the Scriptures unanimoufly agree, that *Salvation*, whether covering of, or fatisfying for, or clearance from, fin, *belongeth unto the Lord*, and muft be pleaded in *facramental* means of communion, before *we can at any time partake of its efficacy.*

64. But we muft not difmifs this fubject: *Why?* Becaufe you fay we muft obferve, " That the *Levitical* law, confidered apart " from the *Abrahamic* covenant, made no- " thing perfect." Now, Sir, I fhould be glad to know what right either you or I have

have to confider the law in this light. It is plain, the law is built *upon* the *Abrahamic* covenant, and its *chiefeſt* beauty *that* for which it was given, and we are to admire it; is its reference to the *purport* of this covenant; its diſcovery of the *face* of the things which, by the tenor of this covenant, *belong unto our peace*, under a ſhadowing *veil* of likeneſſes. It was given therefore to keep up a *ſenſe* of God's promiſes to *Abraham*, *Iſaac*, and *Jacob*, that he *might perform his oath and his promiſe* which he made *before the world began*, Luke 1. 72. Titus 1. 2. The ord'nances are delivered unto the people by him, under the name of the *God of* Abraham, *the God of* Iſaac, and *the God of* Jacob, how then ſhall we confider the law *apart?* You might, I think, as well confider the ſeas apart from *America* which alone lead to it. But this is not a natural way of confidering things: we ſhould confider them as God would have us; but you have diſcovered to our eye as ſtrange a polity as ever man could imagine in his greateſt ignorance; a ſtate, governed by laws which it was impoſſible for the people to obſerve *perfectly*; which afforded *no* relief for offending members; which extended *not* to the world to come; gave *no* proſpect of a reſurrection, and left them *in their ſins*, and under the

curſes

curfes of the law : and of this polity, with little credit to your judgment, you make God the head. But then I am glad you overturn the whole, by owning the *Jews* knew eternal *life*, and grace in *Chrift Jefus* (*fect.* 122.) and indeed it was a *fchoolmafter* that taught Chriftianity, *Gal.* iii. 24. But it *made nothing perfect !* no, becaufe it was, as it is called *Heb.* vii. 19. the *bringing in of a better hope*, and a fhadow of the fub-ftance, and not the *fubftance*, the *very* image of the *things* themfelves, *Heb.* x. 1. But was I to reafon from your *conceffion* here, that the facrifices related to the facrifice of Chrift, I muft neither believe what you fay about the nature of facrifice, *chap.* 2. nor what you fo *pofitively* affirm in the note upon *fect.* 190. in direct oppofition to what you *here* allow ; for then every facrifice was a tender of a Chrift crucified to God. Be-fides, you own *eternal life* to be, as it is called, *Rom.* vi. 23. *the gift of God, in Chrift Jefus our Lord.* Now if it be a *gift*, it muft be *accepted* to enjoy it, but before they could accept it, it muft needs have been *propofed* to them. If then the *Jews* were *called* unto life ; if God defign-ed they fhould *have* it ; then they had it *propofed* to them, and knew of the *offer.*

65 Again, St. *Paul* never confiders either facrifices, or the ceremonial law, *apart* from

R   the

the *Abrahamic* covenant, as you affert.
Heb. viii. 7. refers *not* to the *Abrahamic*
covenant, but to a *covenant* which was *confirmed before* of God to Chrift, which was
promifed to the reprefentative *Abraham*,
and performed to Chrift : for this covenant
is a *new* one, and called the *fecond*, ver. 7.
The *firft*, the *commandment going before* (*to*
Adam, Abraham, *or* Mofes) being *difan-
nulled for the weaknefs and unprofitablenefs
thereof*, vii. 18. The *types* of which the firft
manifeftations or adumbrations of God's purpofes confifted were *done away*, ix. 1 ; the
fhadow flew away, the day broke, viii. 13.
Neither doth *Heb.* x. 17 or 18. refer to this,
as any reader may fee.   From vi. 18. it is
plain, the heirs of the promife, that is, the
faithful *Ifraelites*, reaped the fame benefit,
*through faith and patience inheriting the
promifes* ; xii. 7 and 19. refer to the *Melchi-
zedekian* inftitution, after the *power of an
endlefs life*, ver. 16. which was only brought
to light in *Jefus Chrift*, *in* whom was life,
becaufe *in* him was the *living God :* an inftitution which was exhibited to *Abraham*
before-hand, and in the *faith* of which, as
fignified to them, he and the *Jews* lived.
They were to live *in* them it is true, but
it was *by faith* in them ; fee *Habbakuk* ii. 4.
For they, though not *by*, yet *under*, the
law, were *coheirs* of the promife, and could
not

not be confidered otherwife than as difciples
of the *Schoolmafter* which taught Chrift.
However, the *Levitical* facrifices, you fay,
" might difcharge a perfon from political
" penalties." Now, in the firft place, you
here own the facrifices to be a fatisfaction,
and deferved *fomewhat* for the man; and, in
the next place, thefe did not, and could not,
upon your *own* principles, take away offences; for God was their head, tranfgreffion of his law was a tranfgreffion of the
divine law, and this deferved *eternal* death.
But fuppofing it only deferved temporal
death, the facrifices in themfelves could not,
according to your affertion, *fect*. 53. fatisfy
for it, becaufe they died not *in the ftead* of
the finner, and were not an equivalent,
fect. 113. fo that they were ftill fubject to
the penalties But, thirdly, the facrifices
did not *thus* fatisfy; for it is the exprefs account of Holy Writ, that Chrift died for
*the redemption of the tranfgreffions that were
under the firft teftament*, Heb. ix. 15; that
it is not *poffible the blood of bulls and goats
fhould take away fins*; and, if this had been
the cafe, the facrifices *would have ceafed
to have been offered*, Heb. x. 2. Befides,
it is pofitively faid, *Sacrifice and burnt-
offerings for fin thou wouldeft not—which
are offered by the law*, ver. 8. For *Man*
made thefe neceffary, that he might have

figns

figns of what he fhould truft to ; and God
inftituted them for this very end, and *not*
becaufe he had *any* pleafure in mere *Levitical* fervices : fo that not only your *own* pofitive affertions, but *Scripture* alfo, are here
againft you.

66. Then, as to the effect of *Mofaical*
facrifices, you fay, " they extended no far-
" ther than the particular cafe in which
" they were offered. No facrifice, nor any
" number of facrifices, was any foundation
" of a general pardon ; then, and at all
" times, upon repentance." As types of
Chrift, as our Lord's *body and blood*, they
were available to the remiffion not only of
one, but of *more* fins, and a foundation of
a general pardon then through Chrift accepted and offered by faith ; for then they
were tenders of Chrift, who *died for all*
And as to your faying, " they were no ge-
" neral affurance that God would hereafter
" forgive, without a repetition of fuch fa-
" crifices," this is only faying, that a *frefh*
fin requires a *frefh* application of the blood
of the Lamb, as a frefh wound requires a
re-application of the medicine to heal it,
under the Law as well as under the
Gofpel. But as they were figns, *viz.*
Chrift in *figure*, of courfe they were the
ground of an affurance, that God would
forgive their fins upon the merits of the *One*
facrifice

thus re-applied occasionally to their persons. And they were ordered to be repeated to keep this in their mind, that they should apply Christ for their *daily* infirmities, and should trust, *not* in these significative offerings, no more than we in our sacramental figures, but in One *great offering*, thus pleaded for the remission of our sins.

67. For our Lord *Jesus Christ, by One offering of himself, hath perfected for ever them that are sanctified*, Heb. x. 14. Now observe, first, men are here spoken of as patient receivers of the grace of God in Christ Jesus, as perfected and sanctified by another. Next, we must receive him as he hath tendered himself to us in *signs*, frequently applied, by reason that we fall off; for it is no reason that I should not satisfy the wants of my person with the same precious bread *to-morrow*, because I have contented my cravings *to-day*: so that I apprehend you mistake the antithesis between Christ and the *Levitical* sacrifices, for *these* were shadows, *he* was the substance, *they* were perishable, *he* abideth for ever; *they* were ineffectual of themselves, Christ was able of himself to work out our salvation. But you have, though not without evident contradiction of yourself, laboured to distinguish them by other marks than the Scriptures point out. You come next,

68 To

68. To take a view of the only text which remains unconsidered in your collection of the paffages relating to atonement: but, as I have ranked it in its place, I need not ftate it again, but fhall refer you to it.

69. You fay, however, " the effects men- " tioned are rightly affigned to the death " of Chrift." To this all Chriftians have given their affent, and I alfo believe it on the exprefs words of Holy Writ. We may indeed, as you would have us, go to *other* Scriptures to have a further confirmation of the truths here infifted upon; but, are not the nature of the effects very fully *expreffed*, or very clearly *deducible*, from this pro- phecy alone? Let us fee. The general truths are,

(1) Firft, The finifhing of tranfgreffion. And this befpeaks tranfgreffion in *fome* fub- ject, and an application of fomewhat to this fubject, which fhould finifh this tranfgref- fion. But the application was to be to Chrift, and not to us: *he* was to be *cut off*, *but not for himfelf*, and tranfgreffion to be thereby finifhed. Tranfgreffion muft there- fore be *in* him; but it was not *actually* in him, for he was *cut off*, *but not for himfelf* —it was for *others* then, and fin was *impu- tatively* upon the *Meffiah*.

(2) *The*

(2) *The making an end*, as we render it, or to *transfer* fins, befpeaks fins previoufly exifting in one fubject to be conveyed, and bore away, to another, and that one to be cleanfed of it by fuch *transfer* of it, as of the impreffion of a feal, to this other.

(2) *The making reconciliation* (atonement) according to your own conftruction of the word, a *covering for iniquity*, befpeaks men finners, naked, defencelefs, and expofed to the ftorm of God's wrath, and beautifully, as it naturally defcribes the *Meffiah's inter- pofing* to cover this iniquity of man, to take him and his fins *under* his cover, and there- fore to bear fin *in* him, as the *ark* covered and bore *Noah*, and to intercept the blow due to man.

(4) *The bringing in everlafting righteouf- nefs* befpeaks a man *without* it, for if he had it *before*, it evidently was not *now brought in*. And again, its being *now* brought in as plain as words or facts can do it, fhews it to be *not* our perfonal or inhe- rent righteoufnefs, but an adventitious ac- ceffory, extraneous, fubftituted, imputed, inftituted or impofed, call it what you will, but your *own* righteoufnefs. Befides, *Abel*, *Abraham*, and the *Fathers*, had it (though the unbelieving *Jews* indeed obtained it not, becaufe they fought, with you, to efta- blifh their *own* righteoufnefs). Now, how
this

this could be theirs *otherwise* than by imputation I cannot conceive: for though they
had it, it was *not* brought till several hun-
dred years *after* their death; so that was
there no *other* texts in Scripture to prove it,
it would be plain enough from hence, that
the *righteousness* for which we are accepted
is *the righteousness of God, now* brought in,
but *before* and *since* apprehended, by faith,
and *with* which we are cloathed, as our bodies with the light. (See this proved at large
in *sect* 91. II)

(70) And now, Sir, must not a man tremble to find he has insisted upon his having a
personal, inherent righteousness, and that, in
order to support the pretensions of his *flesh*,
he has set aside the merits of his *God?* for
Jesus is *God*. Must he not tremble to find
he has contended against the notion of
Christ's *bearing,* and *dying for*, our sins,
when the *unerring Spirit* of the Almighty
here plainly proposes him as such to our acceptance? Yet, you have done it. But not
to rest the proof upon this text, I will leave
this matter to be determined by a true state
of the *effects* ascribed to Christ's death, of
the *mean* by which those effects are produced, and what you have omitted of the
persons on whom they are wrought; for
then we may not only see the connection
there is between the *mean* and the *effects,*
that

that is, the efficacy of Chrift's death, as it ftands, in relation to the *effects* affigned it, but we may fee alfo the connection there is between the *means*, and the *perfons* on whom the effects are to be wrought : for, as a *mean* is a *middle* term, the connection of it with the *two* extremes will be better difcovered by fhewing the *two* extremes, namely, the *extreme* mifery of man on the one hand, and his *extreme* happinefs on the other.

(71) And this I chufe to give you at one view, in the following manner :

The perfons to be benefited by the act of Grace	The mean by which it is obtained	The effects of his mediation on us
(1) All — intentionally.	(1) 2 *Cor* v. 14 One [*Chrift*] *died for all* 1 Tim i 5 *Chrift Jefus came into the world to fave finners* Matt. xviii 14 *It is not the will of your Father that one of thefe little ones* [*meaning* children] *fhould perifh*	(1) *John* iii 16, 36 That we *fhould not perifh, but have everlafting life* 1 Theff i 10. Salvation *from the wrath to come* 1 Pet v 10 and redemption *unto glory.*
(2) Many — *eventually* and *actually* John x 15 *The fheep* Acts x 43 they that *believe* 1 Cor i 21 Gal iii 22	(2) John x 15 *Chrift laying down his life for the fheep* [and their protection from invading enemies]	(2) That we might be fecure from the fpiritual wolf, and enjoy *life,* a debt to him that *faved us,* John x 14.

(3) Sinners

(3) Sinners that had forfeited the *covenant of life and peace,* Mal ii 5 —— and had *come short of the glory of God* every way, not only by not obtaining, but by not seeking, it, in word, thought, and deed, and by assigning glory to *ourselves,* Rom iii 2 Matt ii 2 Rev. xvi 9

(3) Christ, as our *Surety,* Hebr vii 22 Psal lxv 5 *By terrible things in righteousness answered for us* He was then *jointly* bound with us to keep the conditions, and to satisfy for the breach of them, otherwise you must deny him to be a *Surety* and hence He is described to us as a *public* person, like unto the first *Adam,* who is called *a figure of him that was to come,* Rom. v 14 —*the second man,* 1 Cor xv 47 —*the last* Adam, *ver* 45 —— in whom we all lay by imputation, as we lay *in the loins* of our first parents. So that He was the *body* of mankind in their *representative,* and what was done to or by *Him,* and promised and given to *Him,* was done to or by, and promised and given *to us* in *His* person, we being *joined* parties in the *same* obligation, and *lawfully,* though mercifully, acquitted by His discharge of it. hence Christ, and what is His, is called *ours* 1 Col 1 2, 3, 22. 2 Cor xii 14. will shew what this means, *I seek not yours but you* Now as He, in *this* character, *bore,* for in *any*

(3) Our *sins* are *forgiven,* Eph i 7. Col. i 14 Dan ix 24, &c.

Our trespasses or failures are satisfied for. See (14) (15) and *sect.* 93, 94, 95, and 96 1 Cor vi 30 *we are bought with a price,* — vii 23 and therefore paid for.

other I am bold to affirm He could not bear *our fins*, 1 Pet ii 24. Heb ix 28 Isa liii 11, 12, and as He, *the Lord God*, in the flesh, was *fold*, Zech xi 2 and *delivered*, and *crucified*, and *died for us* and *our fins*, Rom iv. 25 for the *ungod'y punishable convicts* [Στ-ραιοι] *finners* and *enemies*, 5, 6, 7, 8 fo we fuffered and died in, and were *crucified together with*, Him, and are entitled to plead this as *our* fatisfaction. Hence the Scriptures fo frequently fpeak of us *as in Him, and crucified together*

(4) *Heavy laden* with fin, *Mat* xi 28 *Ifa* xxiv. 20. *Pfal* xxxviii 4

(¼) John xv 29 *Behold the Lamb of God which taketh away the fins of the world*, Pfal lv 22 *Caft thy burthen on the Lord*, Ifaiah xxx 27 *The burthen thereof* [*of the Name of the Lord*] *is heavy Taking* them away I have fhewed implies *bearing* them [from us] *upon* Him, as the *Levitical* facrifices bore them by impofition *upon* them There remaineth then for us,

(4) *Matt* xi 29, 30 *Reft unto our fouls*, an *eafy yoke*, and a *light burthen*, only to *put on Chrift*, Gal iii 17 now *without fin unto falvation*, Heb ix 28.

(5) In ruins *Ifa* xxxi 13 *This iniquity fhall be to you as a breach*

(5) Chrift, *Ifa* lviii 12 as the *repairer of breaches*, rebuilds, what we call in *Englifh reftores* us. For we find

(5) *In Him you alfo are builded together* [being raifed *together with* Him, fee *Eph* ii 6] *for an habitation of God*
ready

S 2

ready to fall. Pſal xiv 1 They are cor-rupt—there is none that do-eth good,—3 no not one — Eph iv 22 The old man is corrupt.— They that break ſtatutes, Pſal lxxxix 31 muſt be broken breach for breach, is God's law Hence we are called, Pſal cxlvii 3 bro-ken in heart Ezek xxxiv 4 broken — Hoſea xiv 1. fallen by our iniquity, and under the bur-then of it, &c

God looking, in E-zek xxii. 30 if there was any one that would make up the hedge, and ſtand in the gap before me for the land, that I ſhould not deſtroy it —— I found none [no Chriſt among them] therefore I conſumed them with the fire of my wrath Ezek. xiii 5 The Pro-phets are reproved for not going up into the gaps, and hedging the hedge for the houſe of Iſrael, to ſtand in the battle in the day of the Lord For Chriſt was to ſuffer the breach, Jer x 19 Lam ii 7 Jer vii 12 14 for the puniſhment of the iniquity 1 Cor xi 24 This is my body which is broken for you Pſ xxxi 12 I am like a broken veſſel Prov xi 15 Sure-ty for a ſtranger ſhall be ſore broken [ſee ſect 88] Then he was to be re-built, Zech vi 12, 13 —xii 8 Amos ix 11 and to be a quiet habi-tation, a tabernacle that ſhall not be taken down —the ſtakes not removed, neither the cords broken, for there [in this Jeru-ſalem] [Chriſt, but no where elſe out of him] will the Lord ſave us Iſa xxxiv 20 The Lord lifteth up all thoſe that are down——as we that believe have a covenant

through the Spirit, Eph ii 22 —have our breach bound up, Iſa xxx 26 and 1 Pet ii 5 as live-ly ſtones are built up a ſpiritual houſe, coming to the living ſtone, the ſure foundation, Iſa xxviii 16 Jeſus Chriſt, the tried ſtone, in Him we are renewed [as decayed houſes are by rebuild-ing, ſee 2 Chronicles xxiv 4 Pſal li. 10] by the renewing of the Holy Ghoſt, Tit iii 5 Pſal ciii 5 as the eagles —Pſal civ. 31. as the face of the earth by the wind, &c Pſal cxlvii 3 Gal iii 2 being all one in Chriſt Jeſus.

right to his reparation and resurrection, and to the *Spirit of him which raised up* Jesus *from the dead,* Rom viii 11 see (15)

(6) All *sore* and *wounded,* Isa i 6 Psal xiv 3

(6) Ezek xlvii 12. *The leaf thereof* [meaning of the *tree for meat,* Christ] *shall be for medicine or sore* But He, Isa. liii. 3 *Carried our sorrows,* was *feeble* and *sore broken,* Psal xxxviii 8 —xliv 19 [as every tree raised from a seed, which *dies* and is *broken*] before He *ascended* and went up thus qualified, full of *fruit for meat,* and *leaves for the healing of the nations,* Rev. xxii 2 Exod xv 26 *I am Jehovah that healeth thee.* Psal. ciii. 3. *Bless the Lord, who healeth all thy diseases.* Far hence then *human* prescriptions, when we have the recipe of the *Most High* neither let us absurdly seek to heal ourselves by aught *in ourselves,* when we should go to the Physician, and take his oil into our wounds ; that *Name* which is *as ointment poured forth,* and with which the Man *Jesus,* and we *in* Him, are anointed and made Christians, or anointed ones, *Cant* i.3 *He hath*

Sick, Isa i 5

Faint, xiii 7. —xl. 29.

Incurable, if they refuse to be healed, *Jer* xv.18.

(6) *By his stripes ye were healed*—*of all diseases* 1 Pet ii 24 Psal. ciii 3 — cxlvii 3 Isa. xxx. 26 and *have the stroke of* your *wound bound up,* and have our *health spring forth,* Isa. lviii 8 and have a *cure,* Jer xxxiii 6 For in this *holy city,* where *God dwelleth, the inhabitant shall not say I am sick, the people that dwell therein shall be forgiven their iniquity,* Isa xxxiii. 24 and the *faint* have *power,* xl. 29.

sent me to heal the broken hearted, Luke iv 18.

(7) *Stink, and are filthy,* Pfal xiv 3 Job xv. 16. *All our righteoufnefs are as filthy rags.* Ifa lxiv. 6. Zeph iii 1 *Wo to her,* &c.

(7) Zech iii 3. *Jofhua,* or Jefus, was clothed with *filthy garments,* ver 4 *iniquity* Ezek xxxvi 20 *They profaned my holy Name,* [by the connection they ftood in to Him, as *bound* to bear them like a *root* the branches] *I had pity for my holy Name, which the houfe* of Ifrael *had profaned——and I will fanctify my great Name —— fprinkle clean water upon you,* according to *Ifa* iii. 1 *The Lord will wafh away the filth of the daughter of Zion* So that though He was *made fin,* yet as He fuffered *for fin, He by Himfelf purged our fins,* Heb 1 3 *wafhed us from our fins in his own blood* [confequently we were deemed to be *in* Him and it] *Rev* 1 5 and thus we became, and are, *made,* as He with his fruit of righteoufnefs is *ours,* 1 Cor. i 2 ——iii 22 Cant. ii 3

(7) *Sweet,* 2 Cor ii 15 *for we are to God a fweet favour of Chrift* [confequently are looked upon as parts or *members* of Chrift] *Rom* xii 1 *acceptable to God,* 1 Pet ii 5 *by Jefus Chrift*

(8) *Blind,* Ifa xxix 18 Pfal cxlvi. 8. Ifa xlii 7,18. ——xliii 8 —— lix 10 becaufe they are *in the dark.*

(8) Chrift *suffered for fin,* the fiery wrath of God, and fo became, as He is called, a *light,* which muft undergo the fire to be light [See *John* 1 5 ——viii 12 —— ix 5] For us he lay in

(8) We are *called* and *tranflated* from *darknefs into his marvellous light,* 1 Pet ii 9 Ifa xxix 18 we *fee out of darknefs.* 1 John ii 8 the *darknefs is paft* Col i 13 we are *delivered from* For

For Chrift is *light*, and men not having Him *by nature*, or of themfelves, then men *by nature are in the dark*, 1 John 11 11 *Darknefs hath blinded his eyes* [They] *fit in darknefs, and in the fhadow of death*, Job x. 21 Prov. iv 19 Ifa. lx 2 ——— lxxxii 5 ——— xlii 7 —— lix. 9 John viii. 12 ——— 1 5 1 Pet 11 9

(9) *Naked*, Rev. iii. 17 Gen iii. 7 2 Chr xxviii 19. Hof ii 3.

in darknefs, and the fhadow of death, and rofe a *Sun of Righteoufnefs*, Mal iv 2 *a light* that whofoever *believeth on him* fhould *not abide in darknefs*, John xii 46 but *have the light of life*, viii 12 Pf xxvii 1 *The Lord is my light*. Ifa ix 2 *on them* [in darknefs] *hath the light fhined* Pfal xiv 9 *The Lord openeth the eyes of the blind*

(9) Chrift *cleanfed from fin, of God is made unto us righteoufnefs*, 1 Cor 1 30 which is *upon all that believe*, Rom. iii 22 Pfal cxxxii 9 let *thy Priefts* [and we are all *made Priefts*, Rev. i 6 1 Pet. ii 5] *be clothed with righteoufnefs In the Lord have I righteoufnefs*, Ifa xlv 24 —liv 17.—lxi 10 *He hath covered me with the robe of righteoufnefs,*—lxii 1 *till the righteoufnefs thereof go forth as brightnefs*, Pfal xxxvii 5. And that he might cover us,

the power of darknefs. Ifa xlii 16 *Darknefs is made light before us*. Rom xiii 12 we *put on light* John xi 9 *He ftumbleth not becaufe he feeth the light*—*it fhineth unto us* [not for itfelf, but for us] *as all light warms us with the love of God*, 1 John i 5, 7 ——ii. 10 and we have the *eyes of our underftanding enlightened*, Eph. 1 18.

(9) We have *cloathing*, 2 Cor v 21 *being made the righteoufnefs of God in* [but not out of] *him* Job xxix 14 *I put on righteoufnefs* [being therefore in myfelf without it, faith the Chriftian *Job*] *and it clothed me* — we have fhelter *under the fhadow of his wings, in his pavilion*, Pfal xxxi. 5 and *tabernacle*, Ifa iv 6 We have *righteoufnefs rained* upon us, *Hof* x 17. and *by the righteoufnefs of One the free gift came on all*, Rom v 18 We are clothed with *gar-*

(10) *De*

as the light doth, He became *a light*, which glorious covering is no more obtained by *our* working, than the day which surrounds our bodies is made by *us* Hence we are bid, *Gal* iii. 17 to *put on Chrift*, Rom xiii 12. to *put on the light*, Ifa li 9 to *put on ftrength*, Eph vi 11 *the whole armor of God,*—iv 24 *the new man* Hence Chrift is called a *temple*, a *tabernacle*, a *fanctuary*, at firft indeed, *deftroyed* for the fin of *others*, like the figures, *Jer* vii 12, 14 but afterwards *rebuilt*, and we admitted into Him, *to dwell under his cover* Hence we read of Him as a *refuge*, Deut xxxiii 7 Ifa iv. 6 —xxv 4 —— xxxii 2. *A man fhall be an hid ng place,*—*a covert,*—*a fhield* Pfal lxxxiv 11 *A fun and fhield*, a *tower*, a *fortrefs*, a *caftle*, a *city*, of which the cities of refuge were figures, *Ifa* lx 14 *Ezek* xlviii 3 *I counfel thee to buy of me white raiment, that thou mayft be clothed,* Rev iii 17

ments of falvation, *Ifa.* lxi 10 and like the mother-church, the *woman* in *Revelat* xii 1 *clothed with the fun* [of righteoufnefs] We have clothes that, like *Ifrael's*, will *not wax old*, Deut xxix 5 for *Pfal* cxi 3 *his righteoufnefs endureth for ever* For inafmuch as Jefus, who had the *filthy* garments, *iniquity*, put on Him, had them *taken away*, and received *a change of raiment*, and *a fair mitre*, *Zach* iii throughout, fo we *in Him put off the old man*, Eph. iv 22 and *put on the new*, being in Him by imputation, as we lay in the loins of *Adam*, Rom v 14 wherefore we receive *with* Him, and *in* Him, *raiment*, and a *fair mitre* of glory, *Rev* iii 17 that *the fhame of our nakednefs do not appear*, for this raiment of Chrift, like his *bodily* garment, *perfect* and entire, becometh man's *by lot*, and this *robe is parted among them as each needeth*, that they, like *Jacob*, may obtain *the bleffing from the Lord*.

(10) *Defencelefs* and expofed for the naked are fo *Job*

(10) Chrift *put on* is our fecurity · He like *a fhield*, as He is called, received the *pointed* wrath, often compared

(10) The wrath is averted from our perfons, fo that we may *ftand, having done all*, Eph vi 13 *in the day*
(11) *Poor*,

to *arrows*, and as a *houfe* or *tabernacle*, or clothing, fuftained the weather, as thefe things do For it is not a *cobweb* clothing of our own, which fhall *not become garments*, that we truft to, *Ifa* lix 6. but a raiment of the *fineft needle work, clothing of wrought gold*, wherein we hope *Chrift* will bring us to his Father, *Pfal* xlv 14, &c

of battle, under the protection of Jefus, who has *delivered us from the wrath to come*, and the impetuous ftorms in the day of trouble reach us not, through his intercepting them, and being, *Ifa* xxxii 2 *our hiding-place and covert*

(11) *Poor*,
Pfal x 14 —
xl 17. ——
lxviii 10 —
lxxiv 21
Prov xiii 8
Ifa xiv 30,
32 —xli 17
Zeph iii 12
Matth v 3
Rev iii 17
Ifa lxvi 2

(11) Pfal cxxxii 15. *I will fatisfy her poor with bread* Ifa xli 17 *When the poor and needy feek water, and there is none, and their tongue faileth for thirft, I the Lord will hear them, I the God of* Ifrael *will not forfake them I will open rivers in high places, and fountains in the midft of the vallies I will make the wildernefs a pool of water, and the dry lands fprings of water* A *fountain opened for fin* and uncleannefs Zech xiii.1 *My blood is drink indeed, it applied to* refresh our hearts, as other drink is 2 Cor viii 9 *Tho' He* [Chrift] *was rich, yet for your fakes he became poor* —— fuffered the hardfhips to which fuch poverty muft have reduced us, even *death* in mifery, that *we might not die,*

(11) We are fatisfied *with good things*, which are not in ourfelves, but are a free gift to us, as victuals and money are to the poor, *Pfal* cxxxii. 15 *Luk* i 15 We have *bread from Heaven*, Joh vi 50 ——*the true, the living bread*, vi 32, 51 prepared of God, if we will not ftand *looking* at it, and ftarve, but receive that *into* our hearts, which is as *transferrable* as bread is to *our* ufe, in order that whofoever *eateth me*, faith Chrift, *fhall live by me*, live *the life of God* by faith here, and of glory hereafter, *Gal*. ii 20 We have *living waters*, John iv 10, 11 *grace* and *peace*, and fatisfaction, from Chrift, flowing to us *like a river*, Ifa lxvi 12 that we may *drink* of them in Chrift, and rev...
H...

Thirfty, Ifa
li 17.

T

Hungry

John vi 50 Though *white* as the *manna*, Exod xvi 31 and spotless as the pureſt *flour*, he ſuffered the fire of wrath [ſee *Pſ* lxvi 12 —cii 3 —lxxx 16 *Iſa* ix 5 — xxxiii 14] to become *bread* to our ſouls, what ſhould ſatisfy all our wants, and conſequently all that God required of us, that we *might live*, John iv. 9 —vi 49 *I am the bread of life*, Rev iii. 17 *buy of me the gold tried in the fire, and ſeparated from the droſs of ſin*, for, *2 Cor* viii. 9 *Though he was rich, yet he became poor, that ye through his poverty might be rich.*

thirſt, Iſa xlix 10 Joh iv 14 — vi 35 that we may *waſh* our ſpotted ſouls, and be *clean*, Heb x. 22 We are *rich*, if ſo be we take this *gold*, and offer it in payment, as the *price of our redemption*, Rev iii 17. For, *Rom*. x 12 *the ſame Lord is rich to all that call upon him;* he giveth them the *true* riches, *Luke* xvi 11 which *riches* are, as they are called, the *riches of God's goodneſs*, Rom ii 4.—*of his glory*, ix 23.—*of his wiſdom*, xi. 33 —*of his grace*, Eph 1. 7. *the unſearchable riches of Chriſt*, iii 8. more expreſsly *the riches in glory by Chriſt*, Phil iv 19

(12) *In want*, Deut xxviii. 48. Amos iv 6 2 Cor. ix 12. Pſ xxxiv 10

(12) Pſal. xxxiii. 1 *The Lord is my ſhepherd, I ſhall not want.* 2 Cor iii 5 *Our ſufficiency is of God*, Rom v 15.

(12)We abound,*Phil* iv. 19. *My God ſhall ſupply all your need.*

(13) *Dead in ſin*, becauſe without*light*, *without Chriſt, without God in the world*,Col ii 13 Eph ii. 12 and without the Spirit, which is promiſed *only* to believers in Chriſt, *Eph.*

(13) *I am the reſurrection and the life: he that believeth in me, though he were dead, yet ſhall he live*, John xi 25. *I am the light*, viii 12. which brings every thing to light. *The Father dwelleth in me*, John xiv 10. *He will give you another comforter*, ver 16. and *if the Spirit of him that raiſed up Jeſus from the*

(13) By him we are quickened, and becauſe he liveth we live alſo, John xiv. 19 God, *when we were dead in ſins, hath quickened us together with Chriſt*, Eph ii. 5 —ver 10 *We are his workmanſhip* Col. ii. 13 *You being dead in your ſins hath he quickened together with him.* Gal. ii 19 cited ſect 120. *Our life is hid*

L 13.

i 13 and if we be dead, we cannot, with any reafon, be fuppofed to move or act, in order to our *refurrection* to any new ftate.

dead *dwell in you; he—fhall alfo quicken your mortal bodies, by his Spirit that dwelleth in you,* Romans viii 11 For Chrift died *for all,* then, as St. *Paul* fays, 2 *Cor* v. 14 were *all dead* fo we paid the debt of death in Chrift our *Surety,* and are entitled, through his purchafe, to all the benefits that were promifed to man had he ftood, to the fame *holy* influences and operations by which we had *life,* thus, as *we are buried with him,* Rom vi. 4

with *Chrift in God* [as that of the branches is in the root, *John* xv 4] therefore what we have is from Chrift, as the great *treafure houfe of God,* Col ii 3 *For the law of the Spirit of life in Chrift Jefus hath made me free from the law of fin and death,* Rom viii 2.

(14) *Enemies,* Pfal. lxxiv 10 —— vii 4 Rom v 10 Col 1. 21. *Children of wrath,* Eph ii 3.—— *of difobedience,* v 6 —— *Alienated,* Col 1. 21. Eph ii. 13.

(14) *Yea, I delivered him that is mine enemy,* Pfal vii 4 Coloff. xii 1 *Ye were enemies, yet now hath he reconciled you* [and not we ourfelves] *as a mediator,* 1 Tim. ii 5 He *intercedeth for us,* Heb vii 21 ——*pleadeth our caufe,* Ifa li 22 He *fatisfies for our offences* ——becaufe *He,* being *God, gave himfelf for the Church,* Eph. v 25 [fee fect 2, 13] [*Ye*] *are made nigh by the blood of Chrift,* for He is *our peace, who hath made both* [God and Man] *one, and hath broken down the middle wall of partition between us* [Ifa lix 2 *Your iniquities have feparated*
T 2

(14) We thus *have peace with God through Chrift,* Rom v 1 —— *in Him,* John xvi 33 *Peace and joy in the Holy Ghoft,* Rom. xiv 17 ——*in believing,* xv 13. Gal v 22 *Love, joy, peace* Phil iv 7 *Peace, which paffeth all underftanding* Ifa xxvi. 12 *a peace of his ordaining*——lxvi 12 *like a river extended* to us —— 1 Pet v 14 to all that are *in Chrift,* becaufe Chrift is our *peace,* Eph ii 13 and is *in believers,* Rom. viii 10 and therefore they have *peace,* what fatisfies God, becaufe it is a *divine* and *infinite price,* and fills us with *fullnefs,* John i. 16 Reconcilia-
Aliens

between you and your God] having abolished in His [and not leaving it to be abolished in our] flesh the enmity the law of commandments in ordinances, for to make in Himself of twain [God and Man] one new man, [so] making peace, and that he might reconcile both unto God [not in many bodies, but] in one body by the cross, having slain the enmity in Himself——— Col. i. 22 in the body of His flesh through death, to present us holy, &c. if ye continue in the faith: peace is from God the Father through Christ, through his death, Col 1. and Eph i. through his blood, and so is our reconciliation through blood as a satisfying medium : for we read, that so was the holy place reconciled, having the sin of others by imputation, even with the blood of the figurative Lamb or Goat, that bore sin upon Him [see sect 25] for, Lev viii 15 reconciliation was made upon the altar, Dan. ix 24 for iniquity——— 2 Chron xxix. 24 with their blood 2 Cor v 19 God was in Christ [the Lamb] reconciling the world to himself

Aliens.

Strangers

tion also is ours, and access unto God by the same Spirit, but through Christ, the true tabernacle, we have access, Eph i. and 11 hence the Gospel is called the ministry of reconciliation, 2 Cor v 18 Again, Ye who sometimes were far off, are made nigh by the blood of Christ. Eph 11. 13.

(15) *Cap-tives*, Ifa li 14 —— lii. 2. 2 Tim. ii. 6 Jer. xiii 17 Pf lxviii 18. Ifa xlv 13 lxi 1 Pfal xiv. 1 *Pri-foners*, Rom vii. 23 Ifa. xlii 7. Pfal. lxxix. 11. —— lxix. 33 —— cxlvi 7 Ifa. xlix.9 Zach. ix 11 To what we were *pri foners* and *captives* is plain from the above account from Scripture, of our eftate by nature.

(15) *The Lord loofeth the prifoners*, Pfal cxlvi. 7 Ifa. lxi 1 *The Lord hath fent me to proclaim liberty to the captives—— the opening of the prifon to the bound——* xlix 9. [*I o*] *fay to the prifoners, go forth——*Rev v 9 *He redeemed us by his blood* ——Acts xx. 28 *Pur-chafed us with his blood*, therefore called, 1 *Pet* i 19 *precious*, [*a price and value*] *Eph* 1 7 *Col* 1. 4 and we are faid, 1 *Cor*. vi. 20 *To be bought with a price*. Pfal cxi. 9. *He fent re-demption urto his people* [See *Lev* xxv 31 —li 52 *Jer*. xxxii 7. *The right of redemption is thine to buy it*, also *Rom* viii 23. will tell you what *redemption* is, when it is fpoken *of the body* from the *bondage of corruption*] Hence, in *Eph* 1 7 we are faid to have *redemption* [this price] *in Chrift*, and read *ver* 14. *of the re-demption of the purchafed profeffion*, which was for-feited, *Ifa* xliv 22 *Re-turn unto me, for I have redeemed thee* [as from *Egypt*, and the houfe of fervants, by the blood of the Paffover, *Micah* vi 4 2 *Sam*. vii. 23] But *he went into capti-vity*, Pf lxxviii 6 *His glory was* [for us] *deli-*

(15) We have our *chains knocked off*, the *old man put off*, and are *loofed* and *fet free from the law of fin*, Pf.cxlvi. 7 Eph iv 22 Col iii. 8 Rom viii 2 We have a happy, an eter-nal *jubilee*, Lev xxv 10 *Liberty through all the land*, not only the land of the *Jews*, but *all the land* of the whole world ; *liberty, glorious liberty, the liberty of the children of God*, Rom viii. 21 Jer xxxiv. 18. *Liberty wherewith Chrift hath fet you free*, Gal v 1 *from the law of fin*, Rom viii 2 —— *from death*, viii 2 —— *Having liberty to enter into the holieft by the blood of Jefus, by a new and living way which he hath confecrated for us, that is to fay, his flefh*, Heb x 19 We are *upheld with* his *free Spirit*, Pfal li 12 —*free from fin*, Rom. vi 7, 18. ——*free from the law*, vii. 3 becaufe Chrift is the *end of the law* to us *He that is called in the Lord is made free*, 1 Cor. vii 22. 2 Cor.i 10 we have deliverance *from death* —— 2 Tim iv. 18. *from every evil work—* Pf. xci. 3. *from the fnare of the* [fpiritual] *fowler* —Gal. 1. 4. *from this evil world*—Pfal xxxiv. (16) *Chil-*

vered into the enemies hands, yet he triumphed, and *led captivity captive* Rom viii. 2 *The spirit of life made me free from death.* John viii 32. *The truth* [Chriſt, xiv 6] *ſhall make you free*—ver 36. *if the Son make you free, ye ſhall be free indeed*— *in his righteouſneſs,* Pſal. lxxi. 2. *He came to give his life a ranſom for man,* Mat xx. 28, *&c.* [See *ſect* 90] and inaſmuch as he was ſet free from ſin and death, we, *joint* parties in the *ſame* covenant, and, in the eye of the law, *one* with him, are alſo *free,* being *raiſed together with him*; becauſe, whatever the *root* enjoys, the *branches of,* or in, the tree enjoy, *Joh.* xv 4 *Rom* xi. 16 and it is the *law of God,* Exod xxi 4 that *if a ſervant be married, the wife ſhall go out* [free] *with him*

4 *from all my fears*— liv. 7 *out of all my trouble*—Col 1 13 *from the power of darkneſs*— 1 Theſ. 1 10. *from the wrath to come.* We are *the ranſomed of the Lord,* Iſa xxxv. 10.—li. 10. Jer xxxi 11 and *live with ſongs and everlaſting joy upon* our *heads,* we obtain *joy, and gladneſs, and ſorrow, and ſighing, are done away.*

(16) *Children of the devil,* John viii. 44.—*of the world,* Luke xvi 8. 1 John iii.10 ——*unregenerate, an incompoſed maſs,* Iſa lvii.

(16) The *light of life,* in Chriſt becoming *our Father*; the Lord *our Redeemer* becoming *our Father,* Gal. iv. 6 Iſa. ix. 6.—lxiii 16. Hence we are called *children of the light,* and the church the ſpouſe or *wife of Chriſt, the Lord of Hoſts,* Iſa. liv 1 to 7.

(16) We are *paſſive,* and *begotten of God's own will by the word of truth,* Jam 1 18. We have *God for our father,* John xx 17 —viii 14. —We are *the children of God,* Rom viii 16.— *of the light,* 1 Theſ v 5. —*of the day* — We are *heirs of God,* Rom. viii.

4 *a*

4. *a feed of falsehood*

one that had committed *adultery*, and *forsaken her first love*, Hos i and ii and had been a *widow*, and *desolate* and *barren*, but was now to become a *joyful mother of children*, Psal. cxiii 9. but not without *travail* to the begetter : for *Christ*, the head of the body of the church, *gave himself for it, that he might cleanse it with the washing of water by the word*, Eph v 26 And, when he was *begotten from the dead*, Acts xiii. 33. we, *by covenant* joined with him, were *raised together with him*, Eph. ii 6 as St *Peter*, i epist c 1 [*He*] *hath begotten us again to a lively hope by the resurrection of Jesus Christ, to an inheritance that fadeth not away* We then do not beget ourselves, unless it is rational to say, *children* beget themselves ; nor is God in Christ a *mere example*, unless you will suppose children to be begotten by the mere *look* of their father. No ; as a *Father* he puts in our hearts an *incorruptible feed*, and, by his *operative* light and spirit, forms us in, and begets us into, Chrift, as into

17. *If children, then heirs ; heirs of God, and joint heirs with Christ*, who is *heir of all things*, Heb 1 2. by the death of the testator Hence we have in the *mother-church, breasts* [of life] *as clusters of grapes*, Cant vii 7, 8. conveying, if we will receive it, *the blood of the true vine*, John, to her sons *Isa* lxvi. 10 we may *suck, and be satisfied with the breasts of her consolations* —— we may *milk out, and be delighted with the abundance of her glory* —— we have *peace extended to us like a river* —— we are *borne upon her sides as one his mother comforteth* —— i Pet iii 2. *as new born babes*, we may take *the sincere milk of the word, that ye may grow thereby* —— Eph. iv 13. *unto a perfect man*. But all this is a provision as *extraneous* to our nature, as the sustenance or inheritance children are born to , like them we are begotten against our will by God's *own will* , because the grace that makes us *free* to move is, if I may so say forced upon us but then we may *chuse* whether or no we will continue in this grace

(17) *Cr-*

a new earth, that shall *not perish*, 2 Pet iii. 13. John iii 15 ——x 28. It is true then, that,

take Gods food, and live.

(17) *Un-fruitful, bar-ren, bearing briars and thorns, defert, fallow,* a *wil-derness,* with-out a *fun* to fhine upon it, *unwatered, dry, rocky* and *ftony,* Ifa xli. 18. 2Pet i 8. Fphef v 11. Ezek ii 6 Hebr vi 8 Mic vii. 4 Ifa. lv. 13 Jer xvii 6 —— iv 3 Ifa li 3 Jer xv 9 Ifa. xxxv 7 Pfal cvii 10 Luke i 79 Ifa lviii 10 Jer. v 3 Ezek xi 19 ——xxxvi 26. Matt xiii 5

(17) Becaufe Chrift *bore fin* and its punifh-ment, and was amend-ed, *renewed,* and re-formed, by fuffering *the manure* of the fire under the wife providence of his Father, the *Huf-bandman,* John xv 1 who promifed we fhould be *tilled,* Ezek xxxv 9 we being born into him, inftead of that *rocky* foil, and *heathy* confti-tution we have by na-ture, *Jer* xvii 6. are made partakers of his *plowing,* Pfal cxxix 3. Jer xxvi 18 and *fuf-ferings,* 2 Cor i 7 as of the *glory to be re vealed,* i Pet. v 1 fo that *God purgeth every branch that abideth in* Chrift, *that it may bring forth more fruit* —— *whofoever abideth in* me, *the fame bringeth forth much fruit,* John xv 2——5. *The branch cannot bear fruit of itfelf, except it abide in the vine, no more can ye, except ye abide in me* We have his *light* and his *fpirit,* without which who can have *fruits,* if fo be we are planted *in* him? For, though this *fun* fhines never fo powerfully, and this *wind* blows

(17) We have *a new heart,* Ezek xviii 31. and *new fpirit*——have our *fallow ground broken up,* Jer iv 3 Ezek xxxvi 21 *a heart of flefh* ——i Kings iii. 9 *an underftanding heart.*—— Luke viii. 15 *a good heart* —Pfal cxii 7 *are fixed,*—ver 8 *eftablifh-ed* ——Mat xiii 9 *fown with feed.*——Ifa li. 3. *like the garden of God*— lviii 11. *have a foul like a watered garden*— lv. 11 having his *ope-rative* word like *rain* or *fnow,* which *caufeth things to bring forth,* upon us—enjoying his grace, which is fre-quently reprefented as *drops of rain,* as *dew upon the grafs,* as a *clear heat after rain,* for ef-ficacy, *Deut.* xxxii 2 *Pfal.* lxv 11 —lxxii 6 *Ifa* xviii 8 —xviii 14 ——xxvi 19 ——lv 10 Heb vi. 3, 7 Hof x 11 —xiv. 5 —Poffeffed of the good influence of his *fpirit,* compared to the *wind,* John iii 8 Cant iv 16. And under this light of God's countenance, *Rom* vi 22 we are faid to have *fruit unto holinefs*—— Gal i 22 *fruits of the*

(18) *A*

never so kindly——tho' the *rains* of the *word* are moderate, and the *dews* of the *spirit* befriend Christ and his members, yet if man is not *in* Christ, he loses whatelse would raise him like the quickened seed unto *life* let us then seek an *union* with Christ, for thus *in* him

spirit, Col i 10 *tobefruitful in every good work, as God worketh in us the branches of the true vine,* Phil ii 13 Joh xv 2 —— *to flourish like a palmtree,* Psal xcvi 7 —— *a branch,* Isa lxvi 14. *like an herb —— to be upright as the fir,* and acceptable *as the myrtle,* Isa lv 13

(18) *A widow,* Isa liv. 4. Lam i. 1 Psal cxlvi 9. Rev xviii 7 *without a husband* —— Hos ii 2 *she is not my wife* [meaning the people of the *Jews,* much less then are the *Gentiles* so by *nature*] *nor am I her husband* —— *in the evening,* when darkness come on, she ceased to be his wife, *died,* to him, *Ezek* xxiv 18 *forsaken,* Amos v. 2 Isa lxii 4

(18) Isa liv 6 *The Lord hath called thee as a woman forsaken and grieved in spirit, and a wife of youth, when thou wast refused, saith thy God—*ver 4 *Thou shalt not remember the reproach of thy widowhood any more—*ver 5 *For thy Maker is thine husband (the Lord of Hosts is his Name) and thy* [אל see sect 90] *Redeemer the Holy One of* Israel, *the God of the whole earth shall he be called* Hos ii. 16 *Thou shalt call me my husband,* —ver 19 *I will betroth thee unto me for ever* Isa lxii 5 Matth ix 15 Cant. iv, 8, 9, 10 Eph v 24, 25, 29 Revel. xxi 2.

(18) We are *betrothed,* Hos ii 16 and have God for our *husband,* have from him, *Isa* lxi 10 the *garments of salvation,* the *robe of righteousness,* Gen *washed in blood from our sins,* Rev as a *bridegroom* decks with ornament, &c and what we have or plead, we have *in,* and plead *under,* his right, as all wives must, being both *one* flesh—*one* by this spiritual *relation* we have by covenant, Gen ii 24 Eph. v 30, 31

(19) *Weak,* Matth xxvi 41 Rom viii 3 —— v. 6.

(19) Matth i 21. [*Jesus*] *He shall save his people from their sins.* Psal iii 8 *Salvation belongeth unto the Lord.* Rom vi. 6. *We are cru-*

(19) We are saved, 1 Pet i 5 *kept by the power of God through faith unto salvation* —— Jude i *preserved in Jesus Christ*—— we have
(20) *Death,*

cify'd together [being deemed in him] that the body of sin might be destroyed, that henceforth we should not serve sin Isa xliii 11. I am the Lord, besides me there is no Saviour Rom vi 14. Sin shall not have dominion over you 1 John iii 9 He cannot sin, because he is born of God

(20) Death, temporal and eternal, Gen iii 17 Job xxxvi 12 Ezek xviii 4 Isa lxvi. 24 John vi. 50 for in Adam all die, 1 Cor xv 22 Rom. viii 13 Rev xx 14. being sown in corruption, dishonour, weakness, 1 Cor xv 42, 43.——— never to see light, Psf xlix 19 — but to have the wrath of God abiding on them, Joh iii. 36.

(20) I am, says Christ, the resurrection and the life, John xi 25 he that liveth and believeth in me shall never die, viii 51 shall never see death, shall live by me, vi 57 Col iv 3 for Christ is our life, 1 John v 12. He that hath the Son hath life, he that hath not the Son hath not life For being our Surety, Heb vii 22 and tasting death once for every man, ii 9. he discharged us, and being raised, he raised us in himself, if so be we plead our relation to him for it is the voice of the law, that whatever estate the husband enjoys, the wife shall partake of, as he then reigns, 1 Cor xv 26, 27, 30. we also reign in life by one Jesus, Rom v 17 therefore as in Adam all die, even so in Christ [but not out of him, not

comfort, 2 Cor 1 4 —— sufficient grace, xii 19 ——— victory over the world, 1 John v 4 and we have all necessary provision in this world. 1 Tim iv 8 Godliness is profitable unto all things, having the promise of the life that now is, and of that which is to come Heb xiii 5. I will never leave thee, nor forsake thee

(20) We have a happy repose in the Lord, Rev xiv 13 Blessed are the dead that die in the Lord, and whatever we are sown, a prince or a beggar, we shall be raised in incorruption, in glory, in power, and with a spiritual body, 1 Cor xv 42, 43 Death cannot separate us from the love of God, which is in Christ Jesus our Lord, Rom viii 38 we shall pass from death unto life, John v 24 we shall not be hurt of the second death, Rev ii 11 there shall be no death, Rev. xxi 4 for this mortal shall put on immortality, 1 Cor xv 53 Isa xxiv 23 thy God shall be thy glory, Col iii 4 we shall appear with him in glory, we shall have no need of the Sun, for the glory of God will enlighten us, and the Lamb

(21) This

without our relation to him as a *Surety* for us, as a *Root*, as a *Father*, as a *Light*, &c] *shall all be made alive*, 1 Cor xv 22 *For the trumpet shall sound, and the dead shall be raised*, ver 52 Thus,

will be our light——we that are saved shall walk in the light of him——there shall be no night there, Rev xxi 23, 25.

(21) This then is our estate by nature, in sin, as red as scarlet, Isa 1.18

(21) This then is the glorious, interposing, and regenerating Mean or Mediator, *by whom we receive the change* [καταλλαγην] change, Rom. v 11 who, like *David*, slew the *Goliah* that was against us, and *wrought salvation for* his Israel, who, by *his* own arm, overcome for us, that *we* might enjoy the fruits of his victory.

(21) This then is the invaluable *change* which Jesus hath wrought in us, making us *as white as snow*, Isa 1 18.

(22) So that old things are past away, 2 Cor v.17

(22) By him, who is *Alpha* and *Omega*; and says, *Behold I make all things new*, Rev xxi 5

(22) 2 Cor v 17 *If any man is in Christ, he is a new creature* [but not of his own creating, surely] *Behold, all things are become new*

(23) But from their *extreme* of misery there is *no* passing, but

(23) Through the *One Mediator, Jesus Christ*, 1 Tim ii 5. *The way No man cometh to the Father but by me, John* xiv 6

(23) To this *extreme* of happiness, any more than a man can pass from *one* end of a line to the *other*, but through the *middle*

(24) The evil of sin ends
Sinners put off their sins
The iniquity of sinners

(24) Here — Here

In *Him* —— In *Him*

In *Him* —— centered —— In *Him*

(24) Begins our happiness

Put on God's righteousness
The righteousness of God.

If

If men then are heavy laden, let them go, and caft their burden on	*Him* — for — In *Him*	The promife is, that we fhall be refreſh-ed.
If they are *without,*	Let them enter by *Him* the door,	And they fhall be faved,

77. And this atonement of Chriſt, which is effectual to all thefe happy ends, and works fo agreeable a change for us, extends to fins committed by them who had been dead *long before*, and fhall die *long after* He was actually crucified; for the juſtifica-tion of mankind was *now* fully perfected, though *before* and *fince* accepted and plead-ed. It redeemed *all* therefore that would come in from *the curfe of the law.*

But your notion, *feðt.* 4. is very abfurd, namely, that " abolifhing the law, as it " fubjects a man to death for every tranf-" greffion, and introducing the grace of " the gofpel, which pardons the penitent, " hath put a ſtop to tranfgreffion." Be-caufe, 1. The law did not fubject a man, in his *own* perfon, to death for *every* tranf-greffion: 2. The law is not *abolifhed* but *fulfilled,* and therefore it was not the *abo-lifhing,* but the *fulfilling,* of the law in Chriſt, *Rom.* x. 4. who *is the end of the law for righteoufnefs to every one that be-lieveth,* that puts a ſtop to tranfgreffion.

The

The blood of Jesus Christ cleanseth *us from all sin*, 1 John iii. 9. *He* cannot sin, *because he is born of God. His fulfilling* of the law for man cleared him that believed: 3. Because the law is not *destroyed*, but, on the contrary, *established*, by the preaching of the Gospel, so says the inspired *Paul*, Rom. iii. 33. its *penalties* are also *established*. But I am sorry you see not *how*, nor the *great wisdom of God* by which, the *law* has its *effect*, and yet *men* have their *discharge*. Christ *fulfilled* the law, Christ suffered the *curses* or penalties of the law *for* us : the law then had its *course*, but it was upon *Christ* ; and we have our *clearance*, but it is through *Christ*. When transgression then is said to be *sealed*, Dan. ix. 24. it is implied, that it is *covered* ; for what is *sealed*, is *hidden* and *covered* : nor can it mean, that sin is sealed up " against " the rigour of the law," as you would have it ; because then I conceive, that this is saying no more, than that sin is unpunished, uncondemned, but not that the sin itself is stopped. And how you can reconcile this, without *giving up* the Scriptures, I know not, as we are said to be *freed* from sin, *dead* unto sin, *incapable* of sin, because we are born of God, and sin, to be *condemned* and *suffered for*, so frequently, and so expresly, in these Scriptures. Nor doth

the

the ufage of the word *feal* help you out at all : for, *Cant.* viii. 6. the Church wifhes to have the *imprefs* of the renewed *image of God*, an intereft in his *heart* and *arm*, that, under his *protection* or *covering*, fhe might be fafe. The thing fealed is fhut up, *Rev.* xx. 3. *Ifa.* xxix. 11. the vifion fealed is the fame, *Dan.* xii. 9. *Ezek.* xxviii. 12. *Job* xxxvii. 7.—xli. 15, *&c.* From which the inference is the fame with that before made, that they, and they *only*, who believe Chrift to be the great *coverer*, have their iniquities *covered* from the wrath of God, and *victory* over fin, fin being condemned, fin fubdued in him. Why you conftrue *tranfgreffions under*, as if it were *againft*, the law, I know not. All I can fay is, you feem to fuppofe the law *abolifhed*, and of courfe the fins againft that law not *cognizable*; though the Scripture declares it to be *fulfilled* in Chrift, who bore its curfes for fin, and that thereby we have *redemption*, or are bought off of the *tranfgreffions* (as it is in the text) *under the firft* covenant or teftament.

Your next paragraph, 136, fpeaking of the means, I refer you thither; fee *fect.* 71. and I muft do the fame with 137.

78. And " all thefe effects relate," you fay, " immediately:" I ask your pardon; it is but *mediately*, and at *fecond* hand, to

our-

ourſelves, as you will ſee preſently. But
" our Lord's death," you ſay, " redound-
" ed to his own account, though not by
" way of atonement ;" then I muſt ſay,
you had better frankly own you receive not
the *Scriptures* for a rule of faith, than thus
all along to *inſinuate* things to be otherwiſe
than the Scriptures have declared them to
be. For we read, *Phil.* ii. 8. *He became
obedient unto death, even the death of the
croſs ; wherefore* (for this death or obedience
to death) *God alſo hath* highly exalted *him*
(whom ? Him that d˙ ˙ ˙ *that at the Name
of Jeſus every knee ſhould bow.* We read
alſo in *Iſa.* liii. 12. *Therefore will I divide
him a portion with the great, and he ſhall
divide the ſpoil with the ſtrong,* becauſe he
hath poured out his ſoul unto death. So
that whilſt theſe texts ſtand, your poſition
will be falſe, even upon your own principles, becauſe you acknowledge his death
was the atonement, *ſect.* 126, though you
would quibble upon it, *ſect.* 160. Indeed
here you ſay, " his exaltation, and univer-
" ſal dominion, are the effect of his ſuffer-
" ings," (death, I ſuppoſe, you mean) for
Rom. xiv. 9. *Phil.* ii. 8. prove no more than
this.

79. The more, Sir, I read your book,
the more contradictions I ſee in it to Scripture, to common ſenſe, and to yourſelf ; and

of a truth **I** pity you, if this be an *error* of your *judgment* : but, to make it an *error of an upright intention*, a man, in my opinion, muſt firſt have a right to plead *great ignorance* of the Scriptures. But to enquire into this is your buſineſs ; it is enough for me, in a friendly manner, to try to confute it, and to prevent its ſpreading. And, as to your concluſions from the above texts,

80. (1) You infer (77) " that Chriſt's " blood was ſhed, &c. for us, and on our " account, to free us from ſome evil, and to " procure us ſome benefit :" and, on this inference, I may ſafely be bound to over-turn your *whole* ſcheme ; for if Chriſt's blood was ſhed *for us*, and *on our account*, then *our* obligations to pay the debt of ſuf-ferings muſt have become *his*, which could only be by covenant and imputation. Se-condly, His blood is charged to *our* account as ſo much payment (becauſe it is called *pre-cious*, a *price*) made in *our* favour, or in *the ſtead of us*, for it is the ſame (ſee *ſect*. 92.) ſo that we are, in conſideration of *this*, ac-quitted of *our* obligation, and God's *de-mands* on us *ceaſe*, in proportion to the *value paid in* by him.

81. (2) You infer, " that it was an of-" fering and ſacrifice preſented to God, and " really had its effects with him." " To " us," you ſay, it had reſpect, ſo as to " give

" give us hope towards God, and to be an
" example of duty and goodneſs for our
" imitation; but it was offered to God, as
" the object of his regard and approbation,
" on our account." Now, from this latter
conceſſion I might argue, as I did juſt now,
to the confutation of your whole ſcheme,
and in vindication of a *vicarious* payment
made by Chriſt. And, as to the effects it
had with us, I have already ſhewed from
Scripture, that they are ſomewhat more
than an *example* to us, and nothing leſs
than *juſtification*, and, in conſequence of
this, *ſanctification*, through *the renewing of
the Holy Ghoſt*, that we might be *worked
upon* to walk after his example, and to be
conform to his image. See *ſect.* 101.

82. 3. " It was offered unto God," you
ſay, " for our ſins, in order to their being
" forgiven by him." But, give me leave
to add, upon the *demonſtrable* nature of all
ſacrifices *for ſin*, in order to *ſatisfy* for ſuch
ſins, as ſatisfaction muſt, in the nature of
the thing (ſee *ſect.* 86.) be previous to forgiveneſs; and this is the neceſſary conſequence of your *own* reaſoning · for you here
ſay, " it is certain, that the ſhedding of his
" [meaning *Chriſt's*] blood had its effects
" with God, as it ſupplied ſuch a reaſon for
" the forgiveneſs of ſins, as the wiſdom and
" goodneſs of God our Saviour thought moſt

X " proper

" proper and expedient, and without which
" he did not think it proper or expedient to
" forgive them." Now, upon your own
principles, Chrift's facrifice was a *reafon*
with God for our forgivenefs, and therefore
it muft, as a *reafon* with the infinite wifdom of God, in *every* refpect, be fatisfactory; but that which fatisfies *not* his juftice,
as well as his other attributes, cannot be
thus *fatisfactory*; and, unlefs fin be condemned and punifhed, juftice *cannot* be fatisfied. Chrift's facrifice then being a *reafon* for the remiffion of our fins, muft needs
have been a *fatisfying* facrifice, fuffering the
condemnation of fin, as we read *Rom.* viii. 3.
*God fending his own Son in the likenefs of
finful flefh, and for fin* condemned fin *in the
flefh*: In *what flefh?* In *the flefh* of his Son,
who, to be thus *condemned for fin*, muft in
juftice have been, as we read, 1 *Cor.* v. 21.
(*He was*) *made fin for us.* You find, Sir, I
adopt your own conceffions, as being pre-
mifes enough for me to argue upon againft
you. You grant Chrift's offering to be a
reafon of remiffion in God, a *ratio*, a certain *proportion* of what God *required*, and
what man *wanted*, previoufly to our forgivenefs. What man *wanted* was original
innocence or righteoufnefs, *now brought in*,
what God *required* was fatisfaction for fin,
condemnation of fin in the flefh, which was
executed

executed on the *body of Chrift*, who was *made a curfe for us*, Gal. iii. 13. But how agrees this with your faying, *fect*. 167. " God wants no facrifice to excite or affift " his mercy:" For, if reafons excite, in- duce, or promote actions, as, in my opinion, and, I believe, in the opinion of every man of fenfe, they moft affuredly do, then Chrift's facrifice being, as you allow it to be, a *rea- fon* with God for the forgivenefs of fins, it is of courfe the *motive* which *excites* God to mercy, and that inducement which *not only* affifts but *raifes* his compaffion towards us. Had he not wanted it, you muft con- ceive ftrangely of all his attributes, to fup- pofe him to have required it *at all*. But he has required it of *another* to fulfil his will, *Pfal.* xl. and therefore he *needed* it for the *confiftent* difplay of his mercy: fo that you again contradict yourfelf.

83. 4. " He offered, you fay, *fect*. 148. " one facrifice for fins." Tiue ; all good Chriftians believe it : but do you believe it ? No ; you fay " he was not made fin for us " —he bore no fins"—He could not then in juftice be offered for fins : nor can I conceive, as you affert he did *fuffer*, how, on your *ftrange* fuppofition, the juftice of God can be vindicated. As far as I fee, you have framed a fcheme repugnant to his *juftice*, which infidels may make a handle

X 2 of,

" proper and expedient, and without which
" he did not think it proper or expedient to
" forgive them." Now, upon your own
principles, Chrift's facrifice was a *reafon*
with God for our forgivenefs, and therefore
it muft, as a *reafon* with the infinite wifdom of God, in *every* refpect, be fatisfactory; but that which fatisfies *not* his juftice,
as well as his other attributes, cannot be
thus *fatisfactory*; and, unlefs fin be condemned and punifhed, juftice *cannot* be fatisfied. Chrift's facrifice then being a *reafon* for the remiffion of our fins, muft needs
have been a *fatisfying* facrifice, fuffering the
condemnation of fin, as we read *Rom.* viii. 3.
*God fending his own Son in the likenefs of
finful flefh, and for fin* condemned fin *in the
flefh*: In *what flefh?* In *the flefh* of his Son,
who, to be thus *condemned for fin*, muft in
juftice have been, as we read, 1 *Cor.* v. 21.
(*He was*) *made fin for us.* You find, Sir, I
adopt your own conceffions, as being pre-
mifes enough for me to argue upon againft
you. You grant Chrift's offering to be a
reafon of remiffion in God, a *ratio*, a certain *proportion* of what God *required*, and
what man *wanted*, previoufly to our forgivenefs. What man *wanted* was original
innocence or righteoufnefs, *now brought in*,
what God *required* was fatisfaction for fin,
condemnation of fin in the flefh, which was
                                    executed

executed on the *body of Christ*, who was
made a curse for us, Gal. iii. 13. But how
agrees this with your saying, *sect.* 167.
" God wants no sacrifice to excite or assist
" his mercy:" For, if reasons excite, induce, or promote actions, as, in my opinion,
and, I believe, in the opinion of every man
of sense, they most assuredly do, then Christ's
sacrifice being, as you allow it to be, a *reason* with God for the forgiveness of sins, it
is of course the *motive* which *excites* God
to mercy, and that inducement which *not
only* assists but *raises* his compassion towards
us. Had he not wanted it, you must conceive strangely of all his attributes, to suppose him to have required it *at all*. But
he has required it of *another* to fulfil his
will, *Psal.* xl. and therefore he *needed* it
for the *consistent* display of his mercy: so
that you again contradict yourself.

83. 4. " He offered, you say, *sect.* 148.
" one sacrifice for sins." True, all good
Christians believe it: but do you believe it?
No; you say " he was not made sin for us
" —he bore no sins"—He could not then
in justice be offered for sins: nor can I
conceive, as you assert he did *suffer*, how,
on your *strange* supposition, the justice of
God can be vindicated. As far as I see,
you have framed a scheme repugnant to his
justice, which infidels may make a handle
of,

of, but no man of fenfe can come into confiftently with his *belief* in the Bible, or
with his own *reafoning*.

84. Yet you fay, *fect.* 148. " It is with
" refpect to his facrifice that our fins are
" forgiven, whenever they are forgiven." But
how, with refpect to his facrifice? You will
not allow it to be *propitiatory for*, or *in the
ftead of*, fin, tho' St. *John*, and *all* the Apoftles and Prophets, affert it to be fuch : how
therefore we can be forgiven " with refpect
" to his facrifice," I know not. This I am
taught to know, if we are not looked upon
as *members of his body*, as *crucified together*, as *fuffering together*, as *dead together
with him*, as *circumcifed in him*, as *rifen
with him* by the power of the operation
of God, as *renewed in him*, the *fentence
of death* is *ftill* in us; we are *ftill* liable to
the condemnation of fin, and have our debt
to pay : for, *fhall not the Judge of the whole
earth do right?* He who hath faid, *Whofoever hath finned againft me, him will I blot
out of my book*, Exod. xxxii. 33. *He that
will* by no means clear *the guilty*, xxxiv. 7.
vifiting the iniquity *of the fathers* upon *the
children.* And we *ftill* are guilty, if, as
you fay, *none* hath juftified us, though
the Scripture offers Chrift to us as our
Juftifier, as none *can* juftify us but he
who fuffers what the *guilty* deferve ; and
if

if *none* will cover us, like the ark, and *intercept* the ftorm, we muft evidently *die* in our *fins :* fo that the queftion is now, Whether it is, or is not, agreeable to reafon, and the Scriptures, for God to *clear the guilty ?* Scripture is evidently againft it, *Exod.* xxxiv. 7, and I would not be guilty of arguing with you upon the footing of a *Deift,* as if you thought there was *any* truth revealed which is not *equally* true in the reafon of the thing. However, pleafe to recollect, that to fuppofe God to pardon the *guilty,* is to fuppofe what is *contrary* to nature, and to common fenfe ; that light and darknefs, corruption and incorruption, holinefs and unholinefs, can agree, when it is a known truth in nature, as well as in Scripture, *Amos* iii. 3. that no two perfons or things *can walk together,* or fort together, *except they be agreed :* and, before God and Man can agree, Man's *guilt* muft be removed ; which cannot be done by a *pardon* of your defining : for *pardon,* in your fenfe of it, makes *no* change in the fubject. He is ftill *in himfelf* the *finner* he was, *corrupt* as he was, and *guilty* as he was. Nay, if there are certain *immutable* relations in things, that relation between the *juftice* of a righteous God and a *guilty* man muft *ever* remain, and juftice recompenfe to the finner, according to his fins.

the

the equal, the righteous *retribution*, which
our fubtleft reafoners *all* own to be difcover-
able by *every* man of fenfe.

Again, *Heb.* x. 17, 18. *Their fins and iniquities will I remember no more: now
where remiffion of thefe is, there is no more
offering for fin*; becaufe, by a previous offering *for fin*, fin is remitted: fo that this
text is built upon this fundamental truth,
that *Chrift died for us*, and *in our ftead* fuffered the punifhment due to finners, as we
read 1 *Tim.* i. 15. *Chrift Jefus came into the
world to* fave finners.

85. Indeed you fee, that " if God [*to ufe
" your own words*] of his own mere grace
" had pardoned fin, *&c.* there would have
" been no occafion at all that Chrift fhould
" have offered himfelf a facrifice for the re-
" miffion of fins :" Whereby, fetting afide
how much you contradict what you fay, *fect.*
167. it appears how neceffarily you are concerned to allow Chrift to have offered himfelf *for fin*, though you deny what I muft
aver can *only* make his offering *confiftent*
with divine juftice, namely, " that it was
a *vicarious offering*, and *inftead* of finners,
or that he *bore our fins* by imputation *in
his own body on the tree*, 1 Pet. ii. 24. (compare *Ifa.* xliii. 35. with *Col.* ii. 14.) *blotting
out the hand-writing of mene, mene, tekel,
upharfin, numbered, weighed, found wanting,*

ing, and *divided*, Dan. v. 25. *which was against us.* Obferve, how much a man muft wreft the Scriptures to put your fenfe of forbearing or forgiving fins (*fect.* 51.) upon the word we conftrue *bare*, 1 Pet. ii. 24; for it would run thus, *He* forbare *our fins—He* forgave *our fins, in his own body, on the tree*; which interpretation manifefts neither the wifdom nor propriety of the infpired author.

86. Hence you fay, *fect.* 149. " the of- " fering of Chrift was needful not only for " us," whereto you feem very narrowly to confine its ufefulnefs, 167. not without further inconfiftency in your argument, " but " alfo for God, to be merciful, becaufe of " his own mere grace, without any refpect " to the offering of Chrift, he has not par- " doned fin." Which is a plain proof to me, with *all* due reverence do I mean to fpeak it in vindication of the *confiftent* difplay of his Divine Attributes, that he *could* not *confiftently* do it; becaufe God would not ufe means that were *unneceffary.* The mediation of Chrift, as a *vicarious* facrifice, is therefore fo *neceffary*, that without it we *could not* be faved, nor God in his *wrath* remember *mercy*; and that man, who will *not* plead this gracious payment of his debt *in* and *by* Chrift, muft be thrown into prifon till he pays the *uttermoft farthing*, that
is,

is, *for ever*; becaufe *there remaineth* no *more facrifice for fins*, no *other* means of paying his debt. Such a *poor* but *proud* man, who is of the number of thofe *poor* that think themfelves *rich*, muft live in *everlaft-ing* chains of darknefs, brought on him by a *bankruptcy* wilfully incurred.

87. You make further conceffions, *fect.* 150, 151. that the blood of Chrift was a *reafon* with God for the remiffion of fins, and therefore fatisfactory; fee *fect.* 82. There-fore I conclude, that the facrifice of Chrift was *truly* and *properly*, not only in the *higheft* degree, and *infinitely* far beyond *any other*, but alfo the *only real, piacular, ex-piatory, propitiatory, meritorious, fatisfac-tory*, and *reconciliatory facrifice*, not only to give us an *example*—not only to *affure* us of remiffion of fins, or to procure our Lord, in your fenfe of it, a commiffion and right to *publifh* and *grant* forgivenefs, to which you would confine it;—but *moreover* to *bear* our fins by imputation in his body —to *fuffer* for, and *in the ftead of*, us, what we ought to have fuffered—to *perform* the obedience *we* ought to have performed, in order to *deferve* eternal life — thus to *clear* us, and to convey *merit* to us: in fhort, *to do* what God, in his infinite wifdom and goodnefs, judged *fit* and *expedient* to be done, in order to the *maintenance* of his juftice,

justice, to the *consistent* display of his mercy, to the *forgiveness of our sins*, and to
the making us *worthy* of the inheritance reserved for us.

85. We come then in the next place to
shew, wherein the *virtue* and *efficacy* of
Christ's death consists, as it stands in relation to the *effects* assigned it above. And,

I. We see the whole design of it was to
make or qualify *God*, as *God*, to be merciful, and to dispose him to spare and pardon
us. For what you deny is, to the increase
of the glory of the *Lord*, true to all intents and purposes, That had not Christ in-
terposed, we must have been destroyed:
how else doth he *save us* from *the wrath to
come*, as the Scriptures expressly assert,
if it is not true that, without *his* salvation,
we had suffered *the wrath to come*. You
say indeed (144), " That this is directly
" contrary to the most plain and certain no-
" tions of the Divine Goodness, and to the
" whole current of revelation." But, in
answer to this most hasty, I hope, because
it is a most deadly, assertion, I must say,
that *God*, who cannot, and will not, look
upon sin in an approving light, nor *clear
the guilty*, Nahum i. 3. but in *his soul
hateth the wicked*, Psal. xi. 5. cannot, according to the whole tenor of the above
Scriptures, and according to our most cer-

Y   tain

tain notions of *Divine* Juſtice or Wiſdom,
be diſpoſed to pardon ſinners, till the difference there is between him and them is
changed. Nay, how he could otherwiſe
love man, or bear him in his boſom, I know
not, unleſs you will take not only juſtice
but purity from the idea of God. What
you urge in ſupport of your aſſertion, that
the pure love of God to a ſinful world was
the *firſt* mover, and original ſpring, of the
whole of our redemption by Chriſt, *John*
iii. 17, though it proves from whence our
redemption aroſe, is very improperly urged
to prove, that *Chriſt* was not offered to
make *God* merciful; becauſe it remains un-
proved, that, without *any* reſpect to a ſatisfaction, *God* would be merciful to man.
" But all that Chriſt did and ſuffered was
" by the will and appointment of God (154)."
True; what he did was the will of God,
becauſe he firſt himſelf willed not to do his
own will, but the will of him that ſent
him, *John* vi. 38. But this, inſtead of
proving *God* could be merciful without his
ſatisfying offering, proves the very contrary: for either it was *not* neceſſary, that is,
not ſomewhat without which the end could
not be wrought, or it *was:* if it was *not,*
pray tell me how it is conſiſtent with our
notions of *God,* to ſuppoſe him to *will* or
appoint it. Where, on ſuch a ſuppoſition,
would

would *his* Wifdom, *his* Juftice, and *his*
Goodnefs, be manifeft, in ordaining the *fufferings* of an *innocent* perfon for an end
which could have been accomplifhed *without* them. This, then, is not a true ftate
of the matter; and it remains that *Chrift's*
offering muft be *neceffary*, and if fo, it was
fo needful to difpofe *God* to mercy, that
without it he could not have been merciful
to a finful world: for love towards man
came to him through the fatisfaction *in
view*, as it now does through this mediation *actually* eftablifhed, why then do you
fay (I cannot acquit your expreffion, though
I would your *intention* of blafphemy) "that
" Chrift's offering was conducive to our re-
" demption, only in virtue of his will and
" appointment." As to the Scriptures you
cite for a proof of it, they are all againft
you, as they only prove Chrift fulfilled
God's *will for us*, Heb. x. 7. John v. 30.
—xxvii. 3; and no wonder they fhould be
fo. for is Chrift's offering a mere piece of
ceremony required on the part of God, or is
it not effectual, in its *own* nature, to obtain *eternal redemption for us?* I remember
St. *Paul* afferts this its efficacy, becaufe it
was the offering of *God*, and of courfe muft
be of infinite efficacy, *Heb*. ix. 12. And,
if it is not *thus* effectual to anfwer the end,
but a mere piece of *ceremony*, then, in the
Y 2

reafon

reafon of the thing, it is an appointment of means *without* an effect ; and Chrift is no *price.* He is not a Mediator that hath *of himfelf,* or by any *merits,* or *valuable confideration paid down* by him, *obtained eternal redemption,* and *purchafed* and *bought* it for us. But, firft, this is indeed contrary to the *whole* current of the Scriptures, which affert (*fect.* 55, 56.) Chrift *to be* God, and a *price* wherewith we are *bought* ; that *thro'* him, and *by* him, and *in* him, we are *reconciled,* and *made nigh* ; that *without fhedding of blood there is no remiffion* ; and, that God fent him, that *whofoever believeth on him fhould not perifh, but have everlafting life,* Heb. ix. 22. John iii. 15. Secondly, it is contrary to our notions of infinite *Wifdom,* that he would appoint a means not *in itfelf* adapted to work the end. Thirdly, God, becaufe he is *wife* and *juft,* with reverence do I fpeak it, cannot make that a *means* by his will, which, after *his* appointment of it, is *not* adapted, by its *nature,* to anfwer the *ends* of fuch appointment. Fourthly, It is highly derogatory to Chrift, who is God, to think his infinitely valuable offering to have *in itfelf* no effect, but only that which arifes from the will of *another,* when in truth God appointed Jefus, by his *own* confent, to be the *means* of mercy ; becaufe his offering *himfelf,* by virtue of the

infinite

infinite worth of his nature, was conducive
to accomplifh that *redemption* which God,
in his *council*, determined to bring about.
I really am concerned to fee fuch things
drop unexamined from your pen. Deifts or
Infidels fay not things worfe than thefe.
For you fee, Sir, that the value of Chrift's
offering arofe from the *effectual* nature of
it, and was therefore willed and *chofen* of
God, becaufe of this its *forefeen* and *fore-
known* efficacy.

86. II. The defign of it was by fufferings to fatisfy juftice, or the law of God.
But, plain as it is to every reader of the
above ftate of the means, you very boldly
fay, " Nor can it be true ;" yet it might be
true, though it did not appear fo to you.
However, to juftify your affertion, you, in
your note, diftinguifh between *juftice* and
righteoufnefs (which is the fame thing, take
them in what light you will) and make
juftice and *law* one *thing*, when, by your
own account, " law is the rule, and juftice
" is acting according to fuch rule." Nor
would God be *righteous*, in your fenfe of
righteoufnefs, as a branch of his *moral rectitude*, if he did not act *juftly* and *lawfully*.
After this unavailing diftinction, you proceed in your argument, and fay, " It is
" very certain and evident, that juftice and
" law can no otherwife be fatisfied, than by
" the

" the *juſt* and *legal* puniſhment of the of-
" fender." Now I beg leave to ſay, this
is neither *certain* nor *evident*. But, to ad-
journ the proof of it to

III. Let us ſuppoſe this to be the caſe,
that " law, in its *own* nature, muſt always
" *condemn* the criminal; and juſtice, acting
" according to law, muſt *always preciſely*
" inflict the penalty:" You own, the tranſ-
greſſion of the law is worthy of *eternal*
death, *ſect.* 150. what then muſt become
of you and me? As to myſelf, I am a
ſinner, and obnoxious to *all* the penalties;
and, was the above account true, I muſt
expect to be *executed* every minute; nay,
you muſt allow me to wonder, as I cannot
reconcile it to my reaſon, that I am *re-
prieved* ſo long. Is it to be guilty of *more*
provoking iniquity? to incur *more* wrath,
and to make our puniſhment the greater?
Surely, you do not think thus of God: and
it cannot be, on your ſuppoſition, for me
to *repent*, becauſe juſtice, acting according
to law, muſt *always preciſely* inflict the
penalty: what then is the reaſon of this
reſpite? You ſay indeed, " the pardoning
" grace of the Law-giver is not obſtructed
" by any demands of law and juſtice." In
reply to this I muſt obſerve, that the voice
of the law of God is poſitive: *In the day
that thou eateſt thereof thou ſhalt ſurely die.*
Curſed

Curfed is every one that continueth not in all things that are written in the book of the law; *to do them* is the *eternal* and *immutable* language of law; and the *Law-giver* is one who is *immutable*, and in whom there is as little *variableneſs, or ſhadow of turning*, as ever you can ſuppoſe to be in his *law*. If *he* hath ſpoken, then *ſhall he not do it ?* When he *purpoſeth*, who can *let it ?* " *Juſt* conſiderations," you ſay, " may poſſibly occur to *ſatisfy* the Law-" giver." True; *juſt* conſiderations may occur to *ſatisfy* the Law-giver; this is what I am contending for: but you, throughout your book, *deny* that Chriſt is this *juſt conſideration*, which God *in juſtice* can accept, becauſe it *ſatisfies* him; and yet, here you *own* there may be one. Perhaps you mean, that an earthly *Law-giver* may pardon an offender *without* inflicting the penalty on him, or receiving *any* ſatisfaction from him: and this again is true; becauſe earthly Law-givers have *received* mercy, they may *ſhew* mercy; but Chriſt is the *conſideration*—he ſuffered *once for all*; and forgiveneſs or pardon from man may, on *this* account, be granted to an offender: but then it is not granted *without* an adequate *ſatisfaction* for him, becauſe *Chriſt ſatisfied* for all, *ſect* 32; otherwiſe pardon of offences or offenders cannot be juſtified, that is, made to be

agreeable

agreeable to juftice. But the cafe is *other-wife* with God: *Who hath given to him that it fhould be recompenfed to him again?* Rom. xi. 35. Doth he need expedients which he doth *not forefee before* he publifhes his law? No; therefore when God, notwithftanding his *forefight* of times and occafions, fhall fay *it fhall be fo and fo*, I conceive, as he is *unchangeable* and *juft*, it *will*, it *muft*, be fo. What then, I fay ftill, muft become of you and me? Nothing, upon your *own* principles, can *in juftice* hinder the law from being put in execution upon *offenders*; and if God cannot *in juftice*, he cannot *at all*, difcharge us. But you fay, " he can " fet law and juftice afide;" and with this your account I cannot be fatisfied: for it is *impious* to imagine this to be the cafe; becaufe I am perfuaded, without wrefting your expreffion, this is none other than faying, " God can act *without* law and juftice, " nay, *contrary* to law and juftice, which " demands the *condemnation* and *execution* " of the criminal." This is none other than faying, " Chriftianity is, though a *Di-* " *vine* fcheme, a fcheme founded *neceffarily* " upon the *overthrow* of law and juftice." But this account of Divine Grace is repugnant, 1. To our notions of the *juft* Judge of the *whole earth*: 2. To the exprefs Scriptures of God, *Ifa.* xlv. 21. *I the Lord, a*

juft

juft God and Saviour.—Zech ix. 9 *He is juft, and having falvation*; fo that we have it *not* in ourfelves, it is he that *has* it, and *gives* it us, and yet is *juft* in giving it; therefore, *John* 1. 19. he is faid to be even *juft to forgive us our fins* — he gives us it as an *act of juftice in* him, and we claim it in the *right* of our *Saviour* as an *act of juftice to* us, Rev. xv. 3. *Juft and true are thy ways, thou King of Saints*, Pfal. lxxxix. 14. — cxix. 21. — vii. 8.—lxxvi. 1.— ix 8.— xxxvii. 61.—lxxvi. 9.— xcix. 4.— ciii. 6.— cxi. 7.—cxix. 149. Ifa. i. 27. *Zion* is promifed to be *redeemed with* or *in judgment*, iv. 4. — ix. 7. — xxx. 18. — it is faid to be the·motive of pardon, xlii. 1. Mat. xii. 20. John ix. 39.—for *judgment came I into the world*, Rom. v. 16. James ii. 13. Hof. ii. 19. Pfal. ix. 9. — cxix. 39. the *Pfalmift* places his *hope* in God's *judgment* , and when Chrift was fuffering he fays, *John* xii. 31 *Now is the judgment of this world.* From *Matt.* v. 17. *John* vii. 23. *Rom.* iii. 21.— viii. 4.—x. 4 —xiii. 8. *Pfal.* cxix. 42,44. it is plain our falvation is according to *law* , that Chrift *fulfilled the law*, and that as he fulfilled it, we, his *fpoufe*, have a right *by law* to his freedom and clearance, according to *Exod.* xxi. 3. *fect.* 71 (15). So that *Chriftianity* is founded, as all God's ways are, *in juftice* and *judgment, truth* and *equity* · fo

7.   fai

far are they from being *set aside*, that they
are the *basis of God's mercy*, and our releafe It is true, God's *righteousness* is like
the great mountains, and his *judgments* like
the great deep, Pfal. xxxvi. 6. It is not in
the power of the natural man to *climb up*
to the one, or to *dive* to the *bottom* of the
other; though they will always be found,
as *Ifa.* xl. 12. to be *weighed in scales* by one
that reafons upon thofe right principles,
which he cannot have but from the *revela-*
tion of the *Moft High*. Befides, allow God
to be *righteous* in faving us, and he does
what is *right*; and if he does what is *right*,
he acts according to his own *immutable law*
and *justice*; for this only is what we mean
by *right*. You fee, then, the reafon of the
thing, upon your *own* principles, tells us,
for *our* acquitment from the penalty of the
immutable law of an *immutable God*, human nature (in Chrift) muft *satisfy*, and muft
fulfil the law, that is, its demands of curfes
or punifhment on us: for I have equally a
right to infift, 1. That Chrift performed the
commands, and fatisfied the *demands*, of the
immutable law, or elfe he *never* fulfilled it,
which yet he is faid to have done or, fe-
condly, That if he did *not* fulfil it, the law
is ftill in force *against* all mankind, as there
occurs not that *just confideration* to *satisfy*
the Law-giver, which you are here forced

to

to *plead* as the reason of our pardon. You talk of a prerogative in God to take the matter into his *own* hands, as if it was not in his hands *before:* but God has a right to support his character as a *just*, as well as a *merciful* God, and no right can belong to him which would supersede this his *essential* right; because he cannot, he will not, *cease* to be God, so a dependance upon this is in vain; and a dependance upon his wisdom, presupposing *no* satisfaction in view, is *equally* weak. It is God's wisdom to maintain his character, amongst the rank of beings, as a *just* dispenser of his providence, however we prostitute ours. *Law*, and *justice*, and *wisdom*, and *goodness*, beautifully and most consistently tempered, are therefore the *rules* of pardoning mercy, even according to yourself, who, whilst you deny this in *one* line, introduce a *just consideration to satisfy the Law-giver* in the next line or two, as the *rule* or reason of forgiveness, in order to the vindicating his wisdom by such legal satisfaction. So that I cannot but oppose, with boldness perhaps, your gainsaying misrepresentation of Holy Writ, *p.* 95. where you affirm, ". the Scripture never speaks, nor in any " consistency can speak, of Christ's satisfy- " ing the Divine Law and Justice," that

" there

" there is no neceffity for it, and all the
" ends of redemption may be obtained with-
" out it:" For I anfwer, and will venture
my reputation to fhame, if, from the texts
I have produced, it is clear, that the Scriptures throughout do, as, to fupport a *due*
confiftency in the fcheme of our redemption,
they muft, fpeak of Chrift's *fatisfying* the
Divine Law and Juftice, and of his *buying*
off (fee 55, 56.) and efpecially 1 *Cor.* vi. 20.
and throughout, declare *none other Name,*
Way, or *Means,* by which the ends of redemption could be obtained, or we *come to*
the Father (fee *fect.* 19, 21. *John* xiv. 6.
Acts iv. 12) 1. Becaufe *without* it I take a
pleafure to affirm, on fo *fair* and *firm* a
ground as the Scripture affords me, that the
wifdom of the Law-giver cannot be *fatif-*
fied without a *previous* fatisfaction to his
juftice It is hence *Chrift* is called *the wif-*
dom as well as *power of God,* which *did,*
and always *will,* though deemed foolifhnefs
by the world, *make foolifh the wifdom of*
the world. for by the fufferings of Chrift,
in order to our falvation, was manifeft *the*
wifdom of God in the fatisfaction of his
juftice, confiftently with *our* acquitment, and
with *our* being made of *criminals* righteous
and *juftified* (fee *fect.* 71. (3).

And here, Sir, you have opened a door
to infidelity for if Chrift was offered without

out *any* respect to his satisfying justice, then his offering was *not a matter of justice*; and if it was *not*, then to say he suffered *at all* is *not* to be held consistently with reason, or that he was *in the world* at all; because at his *coming* he suffered an eclipse of his glory, being veiled in *flesh*: so that the questions, *Why did Christ come? Why was Christ crucified?* on your principles, remain, and must ever remain, to be answered. Hence,

88. (III) It is evident, the design of Christ's offering was to *pay an equivalent*, by dying in our stead, and by suffering a *vicarious* and *adequate* punishment for sin: because if the language of the law of God is, that *thou shalt surely die*, if it is plain, from the *unchangeableness of God*, that he will execute his law; if Christ came to save man, or what is the same, if man is to be exempted *from* this execution; then it is evident, from your own principles (155), there must be one of, and in, the human nature, that must *suffer*, in this nature, what the *law of God*, and his *justice*, required to be *executed* on this nature. But, plain as this is, I am shocked to hear you boldly assert, that " this notion will not bear the test of " Scripture or reason;" when I may boldly, in the cause of truth, aver, that it is agreeable to both. 1. It is so agreeable to Scripture, that it speaks of no atonement
without

without it (fee *fect.* 42 to 50, 71, *&c.*)
2. It is agreeable to all *right* reafon : for the
firft thing we hear in this court is, that
when we are *numbered* and *weighed,* we are
light in the *ballances,* and *found wanting.*
The evidences are, the *nature* of God, and
the *nature* of our offences againft him and
his image. The nature of God is *infinite,*
and all his attributes are *infinite,* and therefore a contempt, or an offence done in the
face of, or in oppofition to, thefe, though
arifing from a *finite* creature, is neceffarily
infinite, by reafon of his *infinite* nature, to
which they reach, and becaufe they are fo
many forfeitures of *infinite* life in happinefs.
To this we muft plead guilty. As God,
then, can fee *nothing* in his *infinite* felf
which his creature hath not defpifed, and
againft which he hath not offended, by de-
fpifing or offending *againft* him ; fo it is but
highly juft, fitting, and reafonable, that
there be no part of *infinity* wherein this
creature ought not to *fuffer.* The judgment,
then, is paft upon us, and what can ftop
the execution? God is *good,* it is true, but
he will not be *good* at the expence of his
juftice. You may fay, man can repent ; but
he cannot without God's grace, which he
hath forfeited : for both Scripture and reafon
tell us, *to whom ye yield yourfelves fervants to obey, his fervants ye are to whom*

ye

ye obey; whether of fin unto death, &c.
Rom. vi. 16 ; therefore man can do *no* good
of himfelf, as he is by nature (fee his fitua-
tion, *fect.* 71.) and *without* a reconciliation,
much lefs can he *work* it to procure *one*.
Who then fhall make his peace for him ?
None but an *infinite* perfon can pay an *infinite* debt. But where can we find fuch a
one ? or, if we could, how could *we* know
he would be accepted *for* us ? So that if
there is not more than *one* perfon in the
Godhead, befides which *Divine* Nature nothing is *infinite*, if he fhall not pay the debt
for us, and if the *Father* fhall not fignify
that with him he is *well pleafed*, man muft,
from God's immutability, undergo the wrath.
And is this our cafe ? No ; our continuance
in being is a proof God has mercy left for
us ; otherwife our punifhment would be *lefs*
than juftice is concerned to make it, by the
time of our life *out* of it. But I fhewed
(1) God cannot be merciful *without* refpect
to a fatisfaction ; and I have, I think,
proved, that this fatisfaction *cannot* be given
by us, unlefs we live *for ever* in mifery, and
therefore muft be given by *another* for us,
as it was by Chrift, when he faid, *Now is
the judgment of this world*, John xii. 16.
Mercy, then, by a *vicarious* fatisfaction to
the Divine *law* and *juftice*, is the voice of
right reafon.

(89) But

89. But " law and juſtice," you ſay,
" can never admit of one man's dying in
" the ſtead of another, or of his ſuffering
" the puniſhment which, in law and juſtice,
" is due to the offender only." Now, in
anſwer to this, *no* man, it is true, can, in
law and *juſtice*, ſuffer the puniſhment which,
in *law* and *juſtice*, is due to the offender
only. No Chriſtian *ever* aſſerted it. But
this is not proving, that law and juſtice can
never admit of *one* man's dying in the ſtead
of *another*; becauſe they do admit, in certain caſes, of a *vicarious* ſatisfaction for,
in pecuniary caſes, the *obligation* is tranſ-
ferrable to a *joint* bondſman, and his payment of the money ariſes from the *previous*
transfer of the *obligation* to his perſon:
therefore your conſidering the money, and
not the obligation, as *transferrable*, is
miſtaking the matter *alluded to*, and from
whence I argue in defence of a *vicarious*
ſatisfaction. Beſides, you own *money*, in
its nature, is a *transferrable* property; I
ſuppoſe you mean, by its being a paſſible
or *paſſive* matter: Now, if Chriſt was *paſſive* (and to denote his being ſo he is called
bread, price) if he, the *original* Proprietor of
his own precious endowments, condeſcended
to be *paſſive, not to do his own will, but the
will of him that ſent him*, John v. 30 —
xxvi. 38. then he might be *transferred* to
what

what ufe he and the *Father* fhould think
fit; and this upon your *own* principles.
But you fay, " guilt is *my* doing wrong,
" whereby *I* become obnoxious to punifh-
" ment, and therefore guilt, in its own na-
" ture, cannot be transferred; for *punifh-*
" *ment* is neceffarily connected with the
" *wrong* done, and the wrong is done, and
" therefore can be done by none but my-
" felf; therefore *punifhment* can be due to
" none, and confequently can poffibly be in-
" flicted upon none, but myfelf." Let us
fee how this will hold in matters of trefpafs. Failure is *my* doing wrong, whereby
I become obnoxious to the *penalty* or *punifh-*
ment, and therefore failure, in its *own* nature, cannot be transferred; for the *penalty*
is neceffarily connected with the *failure*
done, and the *failure* is done, and therefore
can be done by *none* but *myfelf*; therefore
penalty can be due to *none*, and confequently can poffibly be inflicted upon *none* but
myfelf. And is this a true ftate of the
thing? Have you not omitted *any* material
confideration? Is there *no* cafe wherein fuch
reafoning will not, and cannot, in *law* and
juftice, be admitted, but which would be
laughed at were it urged in a *court of judi-
cature?* Ask any perfons skilled in the law,
whether there is *no* fuch thing as bonds of
indemnification, or making *two* parties *one*

A a   in

in the eye of all *law* and *juſtice?* They
will inform you how trifling your argument
is, becauſe ſuppoſing a *previous* covenant,
engagement, or bond, whereby *one* party
enters into an obligation, tho, in the end,
to his own hurt or impriſonment, to *ſatisfy*
for the treſpaſs and failure of *another*; the
whole is equitable, juſt, and reaſonable. It
was juſt then for *one perſon* in the *Godhead*
to demand ſatisfaction for the offence of man
againſt the whole. it was equitable to inflict the *puniſhment* due by the *law* on him
who, by his *previous* engagement, was *bound*
for to make good all men's treſpaſſes againſt
the law; becauſe, though it was *in law* due
to men, the offenders, yet it was *in law*
due to the ſurety alſo, and he was, *in law
and juſtice*, liable to it, by virtue of his
own obligation *freely* entered into, to be re-
ſponſible for man's proper uſe of his *talents*.
And pray, Sir, if this *other* jointly-obliged
perſon could, in the end, *ſtand* the demand,
and *pay* the *debt*, though by ſuffering impriſonment in the grave, and *with pain and
ſorrow*, for a *time*, and man could not do
it but by *ſuffering* in the priſon of miſery
throughout *eternity*—Say, when the ſatiſ-
faction may *in juſtice* be taken on *either*
party, whether it is not *more* agreeable to
all goodneſs and benevolence, to take the
payment of him who *can* make it, and,
after

after a fhort time, overcome it, rather than of us who *cannot* pay *it* ? Is it a wonder, then, that *God*, that *Divine* Goodnefs, and *Divine* Benevolence, fhould do this ? No; it is more to be wondered, that, when he in kindnefs does it, a man fhould arraign the *juſtice* of his proceedings. However, then, you may determine this to have been well argued againft in *fecond thoughts, concerning the fufferings of Chriſt*, it is plain fuch men have miftaken the matter. They confider the *transfer* of the obligation to fatisfy to man's *Surety*, without *any* reference to the *cove-nant* whereby Chriſt became a Surety to fa-tisfy for man, *previouſly* to man's failure, which clears all, and *neceſſarily* connects man with his Surety, and confequently his *obnoxiouſneſs* to the penalty. They never think, that, as *death is the wages of fin, Chriſt* could not die for *himſelf*, becaufe he had *no* fin of his own, and therefore, as he did *die*, he died for *others*. They never think, that thus he became *transferrable* to our ufe, becaufe he wanted *nothing* for him-felf, and that for this reafon he is called *bread, price, gold tried in the fire* (fee the ftate of the means, 77) which are, in their nature, *transferrable* things. And, now I am talking of likenefs of cafes, give me leave to add *one* more obfervation of a pa-rallel in them. *Juſtice* and *law* requires,

that

that a debtor satisfies *somehow* or *other*, or else, that the prisoner be *confined* in prison, till he *pays* the *uttermost farthing*, nor does *justice* on earth, in matters of *trespass*, for misapplying of talents committed to a man by another, so *much* respect the person's *bodily* hurt, as a *satisfaction* to the offended: therefore in the administration of *Divine* Justice (for, by your example, you justify my reasoning from things on earth) it must and does (see the parable in *Matth.* v. 24, 25, 26.) demand *satisfaction* of the offender, *somehow* or other; and if he *cannot* give it, confines him till he pays the *uttermost farthing*: and, though the *medium* or *means* of satisfaction is not *originally* ours but *another's*, as *Christ's* is mercifully consigned to *our* use, it is enough, but it is the *least* that is expected of us by our heavenly, as by an earthly Judge, that *we* plead it as *our* satisfaction for *our* misapplication of the *talents* he has committed to us, for *our* trespasses, and for *our* breach of trust: if we do not, the gaol of death, and eternal confinement, must be *our* portion: *He that hath not the Son hath not life*, because he hath not the price of his redemption. *Note,* That the sufferings, or labour, or pains, with which such price, or gold tried in the fire, is obtained, *all* go to make up its value.

(90) Besides, hear the voice of the *eternal* law of God, *Levit.* xxv. 24. *Ye shall grant a* redemption (גְּאֻלָּה) *for the land.*
—ver. 25. *If thy brother be waxen poor, and hath* sold *away some of his possession, and if any of his kin come to* redeem *it, then shall he* redeem *that which his* brother *sold.*——
ver. 47. *And if a sojourner or stranger wax rich by thee, and thy* brother (*that dwelleth*) *by him wax poor, and* fell himself *unto the* stranger *or sojourner by thee, or to the* stock *of the strangers family:* 48. *After that he is* fold, *he may be* redeemed *again (there shall be* redemption *for him,* תְּהִיֶּה לוֹ
גְּאֻלָּה) *one of his* brethren *may* redeem *him:* 49. *Either his* uncle, *or his* uncle's son, *may* redeem *him, or (any) that is* nigh *unto him, of his* family, *may* redeem *him; or if he be* able, *he may* redeem *himself.* Deut. xxv. 5, 6. *If* brethren *dwell together, and* one *of them die, and have no* child— *her husband's* brother *shall go in unto her, and take her to him to wife, and perform the duty of an* husband's brother *unto her. And it shall be, that the* first-born *which she beareth shall* succeed *in the* name *of his* brother *which is dead, that his name be not* put out *in* Israel. Hence *Ruth* says to *Boaz,* ch. iii. 9. *I* Ruth *am thine handmaid:* spread therefore thy skirt *over thine*
hand-

handmaid, for thou art a near kinfman. Hence *Boaz,* ver. 13. promifes to *do the part of a* kinfman *to her* ; and when, in *chap.* iv. 6. *Boaz's* kinfman fays, *Redeem thou* my right *to thyfelf, for I cannot* redeem *it, Boaz,* ver. 9. faid unto the *elders,* &c. *Ye are witneffes this day, that I have* bought all *that was* Elimelech's (God the King) *&c. Moreover,* Ruth (the refrefhed one) *have I* purchafed *to be my* wife, *to raife up the name of the dead upon his* inheritance. Such was the allowance of *redemption* of land and a man, and the allowance of children to *inherit,* though begotten by *another,* if he was of the *fame* family ; and this granted by a *law* which yet enjoined a *perfect* and *juft weight,* a *perfect* and *juft meafure,* Deut. xxv. 15. Forafmuch then as *Chrift was made of a woman under the law,* and became our kinfman and brother to redeem them (fays St. *Paul,* carrying on the fame allufion, *Gal.* iv. 4, 5.) *that were under the law, that we might receive the adoption of fons,* he, by his *voluntary* condefcenfion, bound himfelf to *do the part of a kinfman,* according *to law,* to *redeem* the inheritance *we* had *fold* for the ill-conceived pleafures of fenfe, and being *poor* could *not* redeem ; to *redeem* us his *brethren,* who were in *bondage,* and to *take* the *poor* church to *wife,* who now had *no* husband ;

for

for *God* was now, by her *fins, feparated* from her (fee *Ifa.* lix. 2. and *Hof.* ii.) and to raife up a *feed* to *God* the *Father* by her, that he and his brethren, in his right, as *joint heirs,* might take the inheritance of the Father: and, therefore, 1. When God required this of Chrift, he required no more than what was *in law* due *from* him as *our* kinfman, by *his* covenant. 2. When Chrift did *this,* he did *no more* than what he came to do, namely, fulfilled *the law.* 3. When he *had* done it, God, by his *own law, freely* made, was *engaged* to let us *go free,* to *reftore* our poffeffion, and to *admit* us to the *inheritance* of children; and it is in allufion to this that we read of *the redemption of the purchafed poffeffion,* Eph. i. 14. and of being bought with a price, 1 *Cor.* vi. 20. Surely then, Sir, you will not fay, *law* and *juftice* cannot allow, when *Divine* law and *Divine* juftice has thought fit to allow, a *vicarious* fatisfaction and redemption; nay, when it required a גאל a kinfman, *fhould,* if he *could,* redeem, when Chrift did *not* fulfil the law, except he *did* thus redeem our forfeit natures and inheritance; and when the *Levitical* priefthood, the figure of Chrift's, was vicarious (fee *fect.* 6 and 11). No, let us fay with *Naomi, Bleffed be he of the Lord, who hath not left off his kindnefs to the living and to the dead.* Notwithftanding

ing this, you fay, " If the Law-giver
" fhould infift upon a vicarious punifhment,
" or require the innocent to die, or accept
" the voluntary death of the innocent by
" way of commutation for the death of the
" nocent: this feems more inconfiftent with
" righteoufnefs and juftice, and more re-
" mote from all the ends of moral govern-
" ment, than fimply to pardon the nocent,
" without any confideration at all." Now
reafoning upon the cafe as it *really* is, we
find, 1. There was no *infifting*, though there
was a *requiring in juftice*, what Chrift was
in juftice, by his free contracted obligation,
bound to do for man. 2. That here was no
perfon required to fuffer as *innocent*, but as
furety for man, and as thus obliged to fatisfy. 3. That it is agreeable to *all law
and juftice*, not only for Chrift to fuffer, and
pay the debt, but for God to accept him as
a *furety*; otherwife you muft arraign *all*
laws in *all* realms. 4. That it is inconfiftent with all the ends of a reafonable,
moral, and methodical government, to pardon the guilty *without* a reafonable confideration, and, that God fays he will not *do*
it. 5. That this facrifice, as being that of
one who could not be *holden* of the pains of
death, *Acts* ii. 24. and by the efficacious
merits of which men, numerous as the *fand
on the fea-fhore*, fhould be faved, was, in
truth

truth, *a sacrifice of a sweet-smelling favour,*
Ephef. v. 2. pleafing and acceptable unto
God as delicious, as fragrant odours are to *our*
fenfes, preventing the abominable fmell of
fin : Yet you call it, with *uncommon* oppofition to Scripture, and the common fenfe of
mankind, " an unequitable punifhment ; "
and fay, what I aver can only make it fo,
" that it is not a vicarious one :" for, if
death is only the *wages of fin,* and Chrift
bore not our fin, why did he *die ?* I chal-
lenge the whole creation, and the moft malicious fpirit, to fhew me, that it *otherwife*
was due to this fpotlefs Lamb. But why
muft it not be a *vicarious* offering ? Becaufe
" it gives us too low ideas of the fufferings
" of the Son of God, as it finks them to
" the pain and fufferings of a malefactor."
But why, Sir, let me freely afk you, have
you at all reafoned from Scripture, when
here you are directly oppofing it ? The Scriptures fay, *He was numbered with the tranf-*
greffors — He was made fin for us ; for the
voice of the enemy and blafphemer ; for the
enemy and avenger — He bore our griefs —
He carried our forrows — the chaftifement of
our peace was upon Him — He died for us —
He was taken by force, &c. You will fay,
perhaps, *He was numbered with the* tranf-
greffors in the fight of men ; which was the
cafe ; though this would be enough to prove

B b   he

he suffered as a transgressor, but I must add, in the sight of God too, who could not otherwise, *in justice*, see him with such on the *cross*. Thus to *low*, indeed, and to *insipid* and *tasteless*, circumstances he was reduced for *you* and *me*, and *all*: He had not whereon to *lay his Head*—He was a *stranger to his brethren—black for our hurt*. But consider how low a sinner stands in God's eye: sink yourself as low as you *can*, lower than this we *all* stood, and as the satisfaction a *surety* must make is in proportion to the *breach* of trust, so, before we could be exalted, it was necessary some *one* should stand thus *low* for us: and, when Christ has done it, shall I, as you have done, call *his sufferings low and insipid*, and that *idea* so which the Scriptures give me? No; though the scenes he appeared in for us were *low* and *insipid*, i. e. what would not be agreeable to our tastes, and were such as only suited one who *bore sin*, and the *evil* of sin, yet think, if you can, on the *noble* ends in view—think how wonderfully *mercy and truth* have *met*, and *kissed* each other, in this wisely disposed mediation—how consistently every attribute is displayed in Christ, and all to justify God's ways before his creatures, that he *might be justified when he speaketh, and clear when he is judged*, Psal. li. 4. Rom. iii. 4. and that all the race of of men might *in juſtice* be ſaved from *the wrath to come*—then think what God has choſen, 1 *Cor.* i. 27, 28. *the fooliſh things of the world, to confound the wiſe, and the weak things of the world, to confound the things which are mighty; and baſe things of the world, and things that are deſpiſed, and things which are not, to bring to nought things that are;* and you will call Chriſt *the power of God,* and *the wiſdom of God;* and own this mediation of his to be as full of *juſtice,* as it is of *condeſcenſion;* as *neceſſary* for our juſtification, as they are *worthy* to be accepted of God : it is a humiliation Chriſt glories in ; it is a ſcheme *every* way manifeſting the *unfathomable* depth of the riches both of the *wiſdom* and *knowledge* of God, of his unſearchable judgments, and his inſcrutable ways, *Rom.* xi. 33 ; it is a ſtage becoming the only-begotten Son of God, and alſo the Divine Majeſty of that Moſt High God who dwelt *in* him, to appear in.

(91) But, ſecondly, you object againſt the vicariouſneſs of Chriſt's offering ; becauſe " this notion, as it includes the im-
" putation of our ſins to Chriſt, and of his
" righteouſneſs, or fulfilling of the law to
" us, ſupplies conſequences very hurtful to
" piety and virtue, and ſome Chriſtians have
" actually drawn ſuch conſequences from

" it."

" it." *Christian* charity, and your *own* declaration, induces me to believe this is not
an error of your will: I wish your want of
examining the evidence for these truths may
never make it so For, should it ever be
an error of *will*, no error could be entertained in the face of so *high* an authority, and
under so *many* great and terrible aggrava-
tions. For,

I The imputation of sin to Christ is, 1. Clearly
set forth in *these*, among *many* other Scriptures
He was made sin *for us, who* knew *no* sin—*Who
bore* our *sins* in *his own body on the tree—Cast thy*
burden *on the Lord—He shall appear the second time*
without sin. 2 It is plain, from the *Levitical*
priests and sacrifices which *bore*, and *suffered for*,
sin : see this fully proved in *sect* 10, 11, 31, 32
3 It is necessarily implied in Christ's death for,
as death is the *wages of sin*, and Christ had the
wages, he had, like *Issachar*, the *burthen* of sin
and served *under* it by imputation *upon* him, *Gen*
xliv. 15 Like *Benjamin*, he bore the blame for
his brethren, *Gen* xliv 11. See also the state of
the means, *sect.* 16, 25, 27, 34, 41, 71, 88, 89,
92.
II The imputation of *his* righteousness, or fulfilling the law, *to* us, is, 1. Most evidently declared in the law , for the *trespass offering* is *most
holy*, so is the *sin offering* and *meat offering*, Exod.
xxx 10 Lev. vi. 17. so is *every thing* in the *tabernacle*, Exod xxxix. 26, &c. and *every one that
toucheth them shall be holy* Lev vii. 18, it is said,
*If any of the flesh of the sacrifice of his peace offer-
ings*

ings be eaten at all on the third day (on which day the true peace offering was to be no more broken, but to rise entire) *it shall not be accepted, neither shall it be* imputed unto him *that offereth it*; so they knew their sacrifices and offerings, as figures of Christ, were *imputed* to him that offered them *in faith*; and the Lord took particular care to let them know, whatever they had they had not for *their* righteousness but for his word, which he had promised to their fathers, *Deut.* ix. 5. They were to be *clean*, because of the atonement, *Lev* xvi 30. 2dly, The Prophets declare it. *Daniel* ix 24 remarkably speaks of it as to be brought in by the Messiah, though *Abraham* is said to have it. See *sect* 69 (4). *Isa* liii. 11 *My righteous servant shall* justify *many*. Psal xxiv. 5 we are said to *receive* it *from the God of our salvation*, xlviii. 10. therefore his *right hand* is said to be *full of righteousness*, which he deals out to believers, cxviii 19. There are *gates of righteousness*, lxix 27. to *be come into*, and therefore it exists *previously* to, and *out* of, us, xlv 8 The *skies* are said to *pour down righteousness*, xlv 24. *In the Lord have I* righteousness, lxi 10 *He hath covered me with the robe of righteousness* Jer li 10 Mal. iv 2 *The Sun of righteousness* is said to arise *on* us, hence, *Isa* lxii 1 *Psal* xxxvii 6 it is compared to the light *Psal* cxliii 7 *David* says, for *thy righteousness sake bring us out of trouble* His righteousness was to be *openly shewed* in the sight of the heathen, xcviii 2. *Isa.* xlii 2 the Lord is well pleased for *his righteousness sake Psal* xxxi 1 *David* begs God to deliver him *in his righteousness*——lxxi. 16. *I will make mention of thy righteousness, of thine only*—lxxxix. 16. *In thy righteousness shall they be exalted*

tinued—cxliii. 2 *In thy sight shall no man living be justified.* Isa. xlv. 25. *In the Lord shall all* Israel *be justified* 3dly, The Apostles speak of it, hence Rom. iii. 10 *There is none righteous, no not one—* v 19. *By the obedience of* one *shall many be made righteous.* Matth. iii. 15 *Thus it becometh* us *to fulfil all righteousness——x* 4 *Christ is the end of the law* for righteousness *to every one that believeth ——*iii. 21. 22. *Now* (but not before) *the righteousness of God* without the law *is manifested, being witnessed* (as just now proved) *by the Law and the Prophets, even the righteousness of God by the faith of Jesus Christ unto all,* and upon *all them that believe ——*ver 24, 25, 26, 27 *Being justified freely by his grace, through the redemption that is in Jesus Christ, whom God hath set forth to be a propitiation, through faith in his blood, to declare his righteousness* (and not to admit *ours,* or any *works of righteousness which we have done,* see *Tit* iii 5 *) for the remission of sins that are past, through the forbearance of God, to declare,* I say, *at this time his righteousness. that he might be* just, *and the* justifier *of him which believeth in Jesus Where is boasting then? It is excluded,* for all *the world is guilty before God, and by the deeds of the law shall no flesh be justified in his sight,* ver. 19, 20 The righteousness then whereby we are accepted is *the righteousness of God,* apprehended *by faith of Jesus Christ,* which is *imputed* to us, ch. iv 24. which St *Paul* desired, *Phil.* iii. 9. to *have,* though as *touching the righteousness which is in the law* he was *blameless.* 4thly, It is plain from Christ's being a *light,* a *refuge,* a *shield,* a *cover* (see *sect* 9, 71, *&c.*) *One* under whose wings we dwell, as *Boaz* and *Ruth,* that he and his righteousness is *imputed, imposed,*

imposed, or *put on*, us, who are naked by nature. 5thly, It is plain from his being called *bread*, and what is his *an inheritance*, &c that what he has is *ours* if we will but apply it, *all things are for your sakes*, 2 Cor. iv 15 See the state of the means, *sect* 71. 6thly, It is plain from Christ's being God, for he could not want *any* thing for himself, *all* he did then was for *us*, and his *obedience*, being the obedience of God in the flesh, was of *infinite* value, therefore it was *sufficient* for *all*, and it was therefore *intended for all*, unless you will say, God provided a *means* without having an *end* to answer by it. From all this, though I could multiply my proofs, I conclude, that the *merits* and *righteousness* of God in Christ are *imputed* to us, and that we are justified only on account of our *being found*, with St *Paul*, Phil. iii 9. *in Christ*, and consequently *in*, and *cloathed with*, the bright *righteousness* of God in Christ, *who*, 1 Cor. 1 30 *of God is made unto us righteousness*, and who *was made sin for us, that we might be* made *the righteousness of God in him*, 2 Cor v 21. wherefore the law runs thus, *Num* xix. 15 *Every open vessel which hath no covering bound upon it, is unclean*

III. It is false, to all intents and purposes, that the consequences which this notion, a vicarious satisfaction, supplies, are very hurtful to piety and virtue, when it is evident, that they must of necessity owe their *being* to it, are *promoted* by it, and cannot *stand* without it First, it is evident, all piety and virtue must of necessity owe their *being* to it for, let me beg of you to take a view of your circumstances by nature, in *sect* 71, you see, both you and I, and all, are prisoners and captives by nature.

natuie ; *that there is none that doeth good, no, not one* But you fee *Chrift*, the *Son*, fets us *free*, by a *ranfom* for our lives, that in confequence of *his righteoufnefs* we have *remiffion of fins*, Rom. iii 21. and that, ch vi 13. being *free from fin*, we aie made feivants of iighteoufnefs, and are *created in Chrift Jefus unto good works*—being *his workman-fhip* ; fo that the *righteoufnefs of God* is the *merito-rious* caufe of our regeneration, according to the *Pfalmift, Thou haft quickened me in thy righteoufnefs* , and, if we cannot be quickened *without* the righ-teoufnefs of God, much lefs can we *live* without it the life of God, which makes St. *Paul* fay, *I live not of myfelf, but by the faith of the Son of God*, and that it is *Chrift* that liveth *in* him Se-condly, All piety and viitue is *promoted* by it ; be-caufe, as we thus ieceive *life* through oui having Chrift, and confequently *his* righteoufnefs · in *us*, except we be ieprobates, 2 *Cor* xiii 5. it is veiy plain, our movement in life muft be piomoted by it, as it is written, we aie the *Sons of God* , have the *Spirit of adoption* ; are *led by the Spirit* ; have *fanctification unto obedience* , are *kept by the power of God through faith unto the falvation* , *God giveth the increafe* to us *his hufbandry in Chrift Jefus, fanctified, elect*, and *preferved*, that we may bring forth fruit as the *branches* of the *vine :* He, like *David*, deals among the multitude of his *Ifrael bread*, &c. to fuppoit them, 2 *Sam.* vi. 19 Thiidly, Piety and virtue cannot *ftand* without it, becaufe without it we *cannot* have remiffion of fins, and muft remain *captives* of fin : if Chrift is our *life*, or if the Spirit is *life, becaufe of righteoufnefs*, then he who has not *Chrift* has not *life*, becaufe he has not *righ-teoufnefs*, and cannot do good any more than a

branch

branch that abideth *not* in the vine. You may say you can; but I will not admit any proofs drawn from your prefent ability, becaufe I am contending, that you owe this to your being fet *free* in *Chrift*, who fet us all free, to admit or reject the influence of his grace; fo true is this of St *John*, xv. 5 *without me you can do* nothing, but are dead, and cannot move in fpiritual life. Yet, true as it is, you boldly deny it, and would tempt us to return into our natural *Egypt*, to ferve in the worft of fervices, to make bricks without ftraw, to leave the *grace of God*, which *bringeth forth fruit* in them that *know it in truth*, and to feek, without feafons, a fine harveft of piety and virtue But, whilft I have the example of the poor difeafed woman, who had fpent her fubftance in order to remove her diforder, I fhall feek, with her, to ftop what other means *cannot* ftop, by touching the hem of *Jefus*'s garment; believing, with her, that if I only touch the garment of *his* righteoufnefs, I fhall be whole, fee *fect.* 71; for the promifes are *in Chrift*, confequently in his righteoufnefs, but not out of him. They *may be afhamed* therefore, *that falfly accufe our good converfation in Chrift.* For hence you may obferve, how unwarrantably you have rejected, in one period, what you are in vain labouring, throughout your treatife, to difprove, and what I have produced the plaineft teftimonies of *Scripture* and reafon to ratify and confirm, throughout thefe fheets. See *fect.* 101.

92. But ftill you fay υπερ, when applied to Chrift's dying for us, means not *in the place*, or *ftead, of*; when, both in *facred*

and

and claffical ufage it is ufed to denote *fub-
ftitution*, like our *Englifh* prepofition *for*:
Why, then, muft it not be conftrued fo
here, when *other* Scriptures lead us to give
it this fenfe? efpecially *Ifa.* xliii. 3. where
תחת is ufed, which fignifies *for*, and *in
the ftead of.* Nor doth αντι, you fay, denote this ; when it does, in fome places, by
your *own* conceffion : and, though it is con-
ftrued *for, on account of,* &c. yet this
amounts to the fame thing. For, if a man
pays aught *for* me, he does it in *my ftead,*
and is *my legal* reprefentative, and takes *my*
concerns into *his* own hands : and if he does
any thing to another *in my behalf,* or *on my
account,* he kindly makes *my* cafe *his own,*
and fatisfies this *other's* demands, or procures
his favour, and I am difcharged and accepted by what *he* does. So that your diftinction between *for,* and *in the ftead of,* is
without ground ; and, by granting the *one*
to be the fenfe, you make good room for
the *other,* as in כפר *fett.* 61. The texts
then, *Matt.* xx. 28, &c. muft ftand as they
are, and ever remain proofs, that *Chrift
gave himfelf a ranfom for, and in the ftead
of, others.* Nay, Chrift calling his *life* a
ranfom, leads us to conceive the true fenfe
of υπερ and αντι, for a *ranfom* is always a
valuable confideration and equivalent, given
and

and fubftituted *in the ftead* of the party for whom it is paid.

93. You are indeed aware, that *Ifa.* liii. 6. may be brought againft you; and, to evade it, you fay, " who knows not that " our redemption is imaged by various figu- " rative expreffions." But remember, Sir, that *figures* neceffarily fuppofe fomewhat *figured,* fomewhat in the *originals* which an- fwers to the things *alluded to* · but *healed by his ftripes, wafhed in his blood,* are no figures, in your fenfe of them; and the ex- preffion, *He was made fin for us,* is literal: for Chrift was *made fin for us,* otherwife he could not *in juftice* have fuffered *for fin.* Ask you, How? I anfwer, by the *imputa- tion* of it , it was *for* us in *our ftead,* other- wife *for us* is, both here and in all the other texts, an improper addition. Nay, that it was fo, is plain from the expreffion, *He was* made *fin,* which implies he was not fo *in himfelf,* but *made fo,* by the imputation *of fin for us.* Taking thefe texts then as they ftand, we ought in reafon to interpret *Ifa.* liii. 6. agreeably to the tenor of the reft of the Scriptures, which, as exprefsly as words can do it, relate to the *fame* thing, and which, without underftanding them of the *fame* thing, cannot be made fenfe of: ver. 5. *He was wounded for* our *tranfgreffions, he was bruifed for* our *fins; the chaftifement*

of

C c 2

of

of our *peace was upon* him, *and with* his *stripes* we *are healed—And the Lord has laid on* him (it is in the margin, *hath made to meet on* him) *the iniquities of* us all: you fay, " that is, the fufferings." I wonder you cannot fee (for in charity I dare not fay you will not fee) the notorious difference there is between *iniquities* and *fufferings*; though as he fuffered he had *our* fin : and I fee not how you can render it, *the Lord hath made to meet* by *him the iniquities of us all.* But waving the common phrafe of meeting *in* a place, meeting *by* him is fuppofing him the *medium,* the *way,* the *place, by* or *through* which the iniquities of us all *meet*; there can be *no* meeting without a place; but Chrift is here faid to be the *place* of their meeting : fo that whilft you allow a *meeting* of them *by* or *through* Chrift, or in any *other* manner, you muft make Chrift the centre where they meet. *Exod.* xxiii. 4. will tell you what it is to meet: *If thou meet thine enemy's ox or afs going aftray, thou fhalt furely bring him back to him again.* For, if the ground was the place *whereon* they met, Chrift is the place *where* our iniquities met, and who, like the ark, his figure, for *our* fins was carried captive.

94. However, you fay, " you are per-
" fuaded, that neither upon this, nor any
" other

" other part of Scripture, can this doctrine
" be grounded :" which, I confeſs, gives
me little hopes of my ſucceſs with you, and
ſome room to doubt the *uprightneſs* of your
intention : for, how you can reconcile this
previous prejudice and perſuaſion with it I
cannot tell. But it is enough for me to
have propoſed to you the uniform evidence
of the plaineſt Scriptures againſt your perſuaſion, which muſt have weight with every
impartial reaſoner.

95. You proceed, *ch.* 10. to ſay, " the
" word of God gives us much more juſt and
" ſublime ſentiments ; and ſhews, that our
" Lord's death took its value not from pain
" or ſuffering, imputation or puniſhment,
" but from obedience and goodneſs, *&c.*"
But, till you diſprove or confront the evidence I have brought from Scripture, it is
plain our Lord's death muſt be held to take
its value from pain or ſuffering : ſee *ſect.* 71,
91 ; and, indeed, your own reaſoning proves
it, *p.* 101 : for you are to ſhew, that Chriſt's
death took not its value from pain, *&c.* but
from obedience : and how do you do it ?
Why, by including his ſufferings in it ; for
his death was a *ſuffering*—his death was a
pain—his death was a *puniſhment* (ſee *ſect.*
89, 71.) ſo that you give up the point you
are contending for. Beſides, his obedience
was *active* and *paſſive* for us, and was valuable

luable becaufe it was fo : how you then can exclude the *paffive* part of it, contrary to *Heb*. ii. 10.—v. 8, 9. I know not ; for we fee Jefus, for the fuffering of death, crowned with glory and honour, xii. 9.

96. But " the obedience of *Abraham* " was a reafon for beftowing bleffings upon " his pofterity." True ; but it was becaufe this obedience was manifeft in his acknowledging of an equivalent, in his intention to offer his fon, as one in whom *all nations fhould be bleffed*, and, confequently, have what fhould be neceffary to their juftification. And this obedience, if we apprehend *Abraham*'s ftory as a fymbol, according to *Gal*. iv. 22 *to* 28. and *Heb*. xi. will prove much againft you. 1. That it is on account, or by the *obedience*, of the true *Abraham*, or *Father of the Faithful*, that his children (Chriftians) are bleffed with juftification. 2. That this obedience was reprefented to men in the *intended* fufferings of *Ifaac*, the joy of all people, and in the pain and concern of the father.

97. And the fcriptural notion of atonement will not, as you affert, admit this way of accounting for our redemption by the blood of Chrift, as you may fee, *fect*. 48, 61. For the Sciptures fpeak of a ranfom or equivalent, confifting of active and paffive obedience, as the ground of our redemption :

demption: for the reafon is, *Chrift died for us.*

> *Note*, Repentance or renovation is a *gift* in Chrift, *Acts* v. 31. and cannot be had by him that receives not Chrift, and puts not on him the *new man*; and, therefore, fuch a one *cannot* receive pardon.

As to finlefs, fteady obedience, I know of *none* in man.

98. The Father of mercies was *good*, but to a finner contrary to what you fay: he needed in juftice a mean to make him fo (fee *fect*. 86, 87.) and do not we receive all *through* this mean, *Jefus Chrift*.

True holinefs, befides *Chrift*'s, I am a ftranger to. The pious *David* talked of *no* other all the day long; and, upon full conviction, after a long fearch, that there is *no* other, I am refolved to follow his example. He was *accepted* who faid, *There is none that doeth good*, and I truft *I fhall*; though he could fay, *The Lord is on my right hand, therefore I fhall not fall.*

99. You fay, 107, " God wants not our " information, our affiftance, for the relief " of the indigent, nor facrifice to excite or " affift his mercy." Why, then, are we bid to pray, or to believe, or to love? God would not require what he wants *not*, in
order

order to *our* happiness : but he has required it, and therefore he wants it *from us* as free men feverally entrusted with talents, and qualified to acknowledge him, in order to *our* being entitled to the reward of a proper ufe of them : for we are not enquiring what God could do *without* us, but what he wants of *us*, now that we have being, that he may, *in juftice* to himfelf and us, make us happy. As to his needing a facrifice, I think I have fully proved it, *fect*. 87, 88, 89. *Rom*. iii. 26. *That he might be* juft, *and the* juftifier *of him that believeth in Jefus*.

100. I am forry, *p.* 168. to fee the drift of your book laid open : As " Chrift's death " difcountenances fin, and engages men to du- " ty and obedience," you approve it ; but not as a fatisfying, vicarious mean, " as the " example of him who was, in the higheft " degree of felicity with the fupreme father, " of the brighteft mind by far that ever ap- " peared on earth ; and gives us a fenfe of " our higheft perfection, leads us to account " true holinefs the glory of our nature, " and convinces us of the immenfe value of " goodnefs and obedience;" you approve it: but you fay, 110, " Beyond this he could " not carry his obedience to God, or his " good-will towards men :" fo that we are *without* a Redeemer, on your fuppofition.

But

But why did not you shew the texts in the state of the means, *sect.* 71. to be spurious? Whilst these stand so conspicuously in the holy page, it will be true God carried his love and obedience in Christ *far* beyond your *narrow* conceptions of it. 1 *John* iii. 16. *Hereby perceive we the love of God, that he laid down his life for us*——iv. 19. *that we might live through him*—*Christ died for the ungodly*—*for the sheep*—*and greater love indeed hath no man than this, that a man lay down his life for his friend's,* as Christ reasons, *John* xv. 13. And, 2. he did *God's will by law,* redeemed his *brethren* and their *inheritance,* paid the *price* of their redemption, as *in law* he was *bound to do* by being our *kinsman* ; see *sect.* 90. Thus he not only deters us from sin by being an *example,* but also by being a *propitiation :* He *bought* us to what we have, to *all* that grace *wherein we stand,* and *by* which only we can walk in *his* steps, as we can plead our sureties payment for us, and *by law* claim the inheritance *in right of his redemption* ; see *sect.* 71, 90. 3. It is not, and cannot be, that *any* personal obedience of us should justify us. *Abraham* had nothing whereof to *boast,* St. *Paul* positively says, and therefore I conceive it to be *now,* as it *always* was determined, that *by the obedience of One many shall be made*

D d   *righteous.*

righteous. So that the offering of Chrift in active and paffive obedience, for *our* fakes, is the reafon and ground of our redemption: nor is *any* fcheme which is different from this able to ftand the teft of the *leaft* found reafoning, neither to bear up the *finner* under that weight which confcience muft, fooner or later, put upon his mind. It is this *Divine* fcheme he muft embrace to be happy, and to avoid that *bitter* remorfe *all* the devices of human wifdom will infallibly betray him into.

101. But ftill, *ch.* 11. you claim Scripture evidence in proof of Chrift's being held forth to us as an *example* only, and of its redeeming us as it *fanctifies* our minds by the *virtue* and *efficacy* of it. You urge, *Heb.* ii. 10, 11. I fhall add, *ver.* 9. *We fee Jefus, for the fuffering of death, crowned with glory and honour, that he, by the grace of God, fhould tafte death* for *every man · for,* fays St. *Paul, it became him* for *whom are all things, and* by *whom are all things, in bringing many* fons *unto glory, to make the Captain of their Salvation perfect* through *fufferings; for both he that* fanctifieth, *and they that are* fanctified, *are all of one.* Whence what can we infer, but that Chrift, intending to bring *many fons into glory,* qualified himfelf for this purpofe by *fufferings,* and *tafting death for every man,* and, being

crowned

crowned with glory himself, had a right to bring them to the fame glory, by *fect.* 71, 90.; for both he that *fanctifieth*, and they that are *fanctified*, are of *one flesh* ; fee *Eph.* v. 30, 31, 32. and confequently *coheirs* with *Chrift*, and entitled to the benefit of his fatisfaction and difcharge as their *furety.* As to *Heb.* x. 11. you read (if you make a fair citation) we are *fanctified* through *the offering of the body of Jefus once* (for all, ver. 12.) fo Jefus, being offered for us, and redeeming us, is the *meritorious* caufe of our fanctification; and the ground of our redemption is the death or offering of Chrift as a *valuable* confideration and *equivalent* for every thing offered in *exchange*, as this for every man is fo, and our fanctification is the effect of it. And I cannot but obferve to you, that you have miftaken the procedure in our redemption: for a *captive* muft be *redeemed*, firft, by the payment of his *ranfom*, for and in the ftead of him, before the party who pays the ranfom can affign him *any* work, or direct him, or the captive can be in a *capacity* to hear, obey, or to fubmit to be led by him. We, therefore, the *captives* of fin, are, in the nature of the thing, firft *redeemed* with the blood or death of Chrift, the equivalent *ranfom* for our lives, before Chrift, who pays the ranfom, can affign us *any* work, or direct

us,

us, and before we the *captives* can be in a *capacity* to hear, obey, or submit, to be *led by* his spirit, as we read, *Gal.* iii. 13. *Christ hath redeemed us, that we might receive the promise of the Spirit* through *faith.* Wherefore I am bold to say, it is the *death* of Christ, his *laying down his life a ransom for* us, which is, as *all* ransoms are, the *ground* of our redemption, and the ground of our sanctification : witness *Rom.* vi. 18. *being made free from sins, ye became the servants of righteousness.* Heb. xiii. 12, 13. *Jesus, that he* might sanctify *the people with his own blood, suffered without the gate,* as the heifer, *Numb.* xix. 3. His *sufferings,* then, are the means of *every* blessing we enjoy, even of *sanctification,* for he *suffered* that he *might sanctify* us, consequently *without* it, as we were, he could not : wherefore sanctification is so far from being the *ground* of our redemption, that the Scriptures speak of it as a building upon the ground-work, the *ransoming death of Christ* ; which makes the Apostle conclude, *Let us therefore go forth unto him without the camp* (as bearing *our* uncleanness, for none but the unclean were to go out of the camp, see *Numb.* xix. throughout). Let us go thus bearing his reproach, looking upon ourselves as members of him the head, suffering *in* him, crucified *in* him, and dying

in

in him, being *in law one* with him wherein
was no blemiſh, and upon whom never came
yoke.   You ſay, in imitation of him, en-
during any ſufferings rather than ſin againſt
God : but I muſt anſwer, here is not a
word of this.   For, why doth St. *Paul* ſay,
let us go to him ? Is he not to be imitated
without *going* to him ? It is our *going* to
him, and to him as having our uncleanneſs,
and ſuffering *without* the camp, before we
can, by virtue of his cleanſing, be ſanctified, and re-enter *into* the camp of God. So
we read, *Heb.* ix. 14. of the *blood of Chriſt
purging our conſcience.*   How ? 1 *Pet.* 1. 2.
*by the ſprinkling of the blood of Jeſus upon
us,* unclean as we are by nature, *by the
waſhing of our bodies with pure water,*
Heb. x. 22. as of thoſe of the unclean *Iſ-
raelites without the camp,* Num. xix. Nor
can you evade the proof from *Heb.* i. 3. by
your very unjuſtifiable addition to the word
of God, *by* (the ſacrifice of) *himſelf he
purged our ſins,* for it is *by himſelf* in the
text : whence it is evident, 1. That Chriſt
is the *ſole* and *ſeparate* cauſe of the purging
of our ſins ; ſo man has *nothing to* do, but
to be a *patient* of this great *Phyſician* of
our ſouls.   2. That they, as *all* filth, are
purged by the application of a cleanſer,
namely, *his blood,* Heb. ix. 14. 3. That
therefore we muſt have been deemed *in*
Chriſt

in Christ by imputation, as we are *by law one with* our surety, because otherwise we never could have the *blood of Christ* applied to *our* sins by Christ; for *flesh and blood cannot inherit the kingdom of God,* 1 Cor. xv. 50. We cannot have it *now*; it must have been applied to us, when he was on earth, *once* for all, for it is said, *He washed us from our sins in his own blood,* Rev. i. 5. then we must have been *in* him, otherwise he did not *wash us*: nor were the Apostles, I suppose, any more than we, bodily *bathed* in it, therefore we were there by *actual* and necessary relation to *him*, who, by *covenant*, was *our* surety, and *one in law* with us: and it is thus we are *purged, cleansed,* and *sprinkled, in* and *with* the blood of this great Name, which was *profaned* and *sanctified.* I conclude then, that the *death of Christ*, as a ransom for us, is the *ground* of our redemption, and that because we are *redeemed* we are *sanctified*; that when *he*, like *David*, 2 Sam. vi. 18. in the *tabernacle of his* body, had made an *end of offering his burnt offering and peace-offering, he blessed the people in the Name of the Lord of Hosts.*

102. As to the *robes washed white in the blood of the Lamb*; consider, the *covering* Christians wear is not their *own*, but of *God's Spirit and Righteousness*—wore *over*

their

their natural nakednefs as *Chrift's garment,*
without feam. It is *his* blood that makes
them *white,* for we are come to the *blood of*
fprinkling, precious, becaufe it is an *equi-*
valent, which will neceffarily fall *upon* the
patient receiver, and *whiten* his nature, as
it manifefts his acquitment, and *clears* him.

103. But, *p.* 118. you fay, " more par-
" ticularly the fufferings, death, and blood
" of Chrift, fanctify as an example to us."
That the fufferings, *&c.* of Chrift have an
influence, as an example to us, is true, if
you prefuppofe us *juftified* by them as a *ran-*
fom for our redemption and reftitution to the
grace of God, and raifed *together with* and
in our furety, 1 *John* i. 3. to a communion
with the *Divine* nature, and, *Eph.* i. 13.
fealed with the Holy Spirit of promife. On
this footing the Apoftles urge the example
of Chrift as that after which we fhould
walk ; becaufe, on fuch it has an influence :
but then it does not fanctify them, the
Holy Spirit is that with which we are fanctified, *Eph* i. 13. *Rom.* xv. 16. and Chrift,
and not his example, is the fanctifier, 1 *Cor.*
i. 2. *Heb.* xiii. 12. Sanctification is not in
words, but in *fpirit* and in *power,* Eph. v.
26. 1 Theff. v. 23. Exod. xxxi. 13. John
xvii. 17. Acts xx. 32. 1 Cor. vi. 11. 2 Tim.
ii. 21. 1 Cor. i. 30.

But

But example only operates upon us *outwardly*, and needs a mind *free* to follow it, and *inclined* to pursue it; and that which *frees* the mind, and thus *inclines* it, is the sanctifier: but Christ's sufferings as an example only, and if it be not a ransom, cannot *free* us; and therefore doth not sanctify us; see *sect.* 88. Besides, his example cannot have any effect upon men not *previously* redeemed by Christ, not *previously* sanctified by his spirit · *without me* (my communicated strength and support, conveyed as nourishment from the vine to the branches) *ye can do nothing*, John xv. 5. What then can your scheme avail us, which supposes Christ's death the ground of our redemption, as it is a mean of sanctification, and this *sanctification* to arise to us from it as an example, when, without this, *justice* cannot bear with us, God cannot dwell with us? and, unless Christ not only died for us, but is risen again, ye are *yet in your sins?* when we are *without the spirit* of Christ, *without life*, because *without Christ*, and *dead* in our sins, and, consequently, can neither *see* what is good, nor be *moved* nor *excited* by it; see *sect.* 71. But, God be thanked, we are not left in this helpless estate. As God hath given us a *Mediator*, so he hath qualified him to answer the *ends* of his mediations. He hath not left us in the

the evil propenſity of our nature, but hath *given us the victory through our Lord Jeſus Chriſt*, holding him forth to us as a ſuffering *ſurety*; *one* in whom, as in a ſurety, we are *cleared*, and *raiſed* unto the *grace of God*, and exalted to a dominion *over* ſin. I muſt ſhew then, that the example of Chriſt is not urged to men as merely acted upon by it, in thoſe texts which you have cited in proof of it, as a ſanctifying mean.

104. I. *Rom.* vi. 10. *In that he died he died unto ſin once*; obſerve, *unto ſin once:* what, only *once?* in your ſenſe it ought to have been *always*, but in the Scripture ſenſe, as a *propitiation for*, and *in the ſtead of*, ſin. It is true, he died but *unto ſin once*, ver. 11. *likewiſe reckon ye alſo yourſelves to be dead indeed unto ſin, through Jeſus Chriſt. Jeſus Chriſt*, then, is he in whom we are *dead unto ſin*, iii. 24. being *buried with him*, vi. 4. *having our old man crucified together,* —7. being *many are one body in Chriſt, in whom ye are circumciſed.* So that God exhorts them to conceive themſelves (as they are in his eye, being *one in law* with their ſurety) *to be dead indeed unto ſin.* 1 *Pet.* ii. 21, 24. urges them to ſuffer patiently, as Chriſt did, though it is for the *imputation* of crimes of which they were not *actually* guilty; for ſo did Chriſt, who bare *our ſins in his own body on the tree.* But to what

E e   perſons

But example only operates upon us *outwardly*, and needs a mind *free* to follow it, and *inclined* to pursue it; and that which *frees* the mind, and thus *inclines* it, is the sanctifier: but Christ's sufferings as an example only, and if it be not a ransom, cannot *free* us; and therefore doth not sanctify us, see *sect.* 88. Besides, his example cannot have any effect upon men not *previously* redeemed by Christ, not *previously* sanctified by his spirit: *without me* (my communicated strength and support, conveyed as nourishment from the vine to the branches) *ye can do nothing*, John xv 5. What then can your scheme avail us, which supposes Christ's death the ground of our redemption, as it is a mean of sanctification, and this *sanctification* to arise to us from it as an example, when, without this, *justice* cannot bear with us, God cannot dwell with us? and, unless Christ not only died for us, but is risen again, ye are *yet* in *your sins?* when we are *without the spirit* of Christ, *without life*, because *without Christ*, and *dead* in our sins, and, consequently, can neither *see* what is good, nor be *moved* nor *excited* by it; see *sect.* 71. But, God be thanked, we are not left in this helpless estate. As God hath given us a *Mediator*, so he hath qualified him to answer the *ends* of his mediations. He hath not left us in

the

the evil propensity of our nature, but hath *given us the victory through our Lord Jesus Christ*, holding him forth to us as a suffering *surety*, *one* in whom, as in a surety, we are *cleared*, and *raised* unto the *grace of God*, and exalted to a dominion *over* sin. I must shew then, that the example of Christ is not urged to men as merely acted upon by it, in those texts which you have cited in proof of it, as a sanctifying mean.

104. I. *Rom.* vi. 10. *In that he died he died unto sin once*; observe, *unto sin once*: what, only *once?* in your sense it ought to have been *always*, but in the Scripture sense, as a *propitiation for*, and *in the stead of*, sin. It is true, he died but *unto sin once*, ver. 11. *likewise reckon ye also yourselves to be dead indeed unto sin, through Jesus Christ. Jesus Christ*, then, is he in whom we are *dead unto sin*, iii. 24. being *buried with him*, vi. 4. *having our old man crucified together*, —7. being *many are one body in Christ, in whom ye are circumcised*. So that God exhorts them to conceive themselves (as they are in his eye, being *one in law* with their surety) *to be dead indeed unto sin*. 1 *Pet.* ii. 21, 24. urges them to suffer patiently, as Christ did, though it is for the *imputation* of crimes of which they were not *actually* guilty ; for so did Christ, who bare *our sins in his own body on the tree*. But to what

persons

persons doth he address himself? *ver.* 1, 2. to the *elect through sanctification of the spirit unto obedience, and the sprinkling of the blood of Jesus,* v. 8. to them who *cast* their *care upon God,*—10. who are *perfected, established, strengthened* and *settled* by the *God of all grace*—i. 21. who *obey the truth through the Spirit*—ii. 5. are *built up* (and do not build themselves) *a spiritual house upon Jesus Christ*—9. and *called out of darkness into light.* These might *arm* themselves with the *like* mind, by putting on Christ, the *new Man,* the *whole armor of God;* for the *spirit of glory,* and *of God, rested u*pon them, iv. 14. by the *laver of regeneration,* and *the renewing of the Holy Ghost,* Tit. iii. 5. Phil. iii. 10. St. *Paul,* who, as I have shewn, most expressly asserts the doctrine of the *imputation* of our sins to Christ, and of *his* righteousness to *us,* was desirous to know the *power of* his *resurrection, through faith of the operation of God,* Col. ii. 12. *and what is the exceeding greatness of his power to us-ward who believe, according to the working of his mighty power; which he wrought in Christ, when he raised him from the dead,* Eph. i. 19, 20; not the force of his *example,* but the actual *efficacy* of his omnipotent *power,* which raised Christ. He sought that *fellowship* of Christ's sufferings, and *conformity* to his death,

death, which he, under the covenant, had a right to by faith: in short, suffering and dying in his surety, he sought that sonship, and *the riches of that inheritance*, unto which God, of *his own will*, begets us, *John* i. 12; or, in other words, *effectually* to be risen with Christ, by *experiment* of his power, as God had *intentionally* raised us together with him, and blessed us, if we will not quench it, with the same spirit that raised up Jesus. The example of Christ is not therefore, in these texts, urged as a sanctifier to the *regenerate*, much less to un-regenerated nature; though it was set before the *regenerate* as the *way* by which they should come to God, because they were *in Christ* the way, and not mere *spectators* of him; because they, receiving in him the *seal* of the same *spirit*, must of necessity receive the *same impression*, namely, the *new Man*. Still, you say, Christ's blood sanctifieth as an *example* to us in particular instances.

105. I. Usefulness. *Matth.* xx. 26, 27, 28. *Whosoever will be great among you, let him be your minister——Even as the Son of Man came not to be* ministered *unto, but to* minister, and *to give his life a* ransom *for many*, 1 John iii. 16. and we ought to lay down our lives for *the brethren:* now these doctrines, which oppose your strange errors,

 p. 96,

p. 96, &c. are built upon Chrift's miniſter-
ing as a *ſervant* (which is contrary to what
you ſay, *p.* 97) unto others, and upon his
giving his life a *ranſom for* many, for their
redemption, and of courſe, upon their being
thus *ſet free*, to follow his example.

II. Love, *Epheſ.* v. 2. urged upon the
ſame grounds, and to men who are *quickened* by Chriſt to move in the life of God, and
reconciled and *ſanctified by the ſpirit.* See
ch. 1 and 2. throughout, and *ſect.* 71.

III. Humility, *Phil.* ii. 2 *to* 8. The
perſons ſpoke to are, the *ſaints in Chriſt,*
i. 1. to whom the Apoſtle wiſhes *grace and
peace from our Lord Jeſus Chriſt*—they *in
whom God had begun a good work,* and
would *perfect* it—perſons *filled with the
fruits of righteouſneſs, which are by Jeſus
Chriſt.* To theſe he recommends *likeneſs of
mind* with Chriſt Jeſus, in conſequence of
the *conſolation, and fellowſhip of ſpirit,*
which there is *in Chriſt Jeſus,* ii. 1. who
(far from vain glory, and) *being in the form
of God* conſequently as much God as he was
a ſervant) *thought it not robbery to be equal
with God, but emptied himſelf* (of his glory)
*and took upon him the form of a ſervant,
and became obedient unto death, even the
death of the croſs.* Your making his *glory*
the gift of the *Father,* and ſuppoſing the
divinity of Chriſt to be *dependent,* is to ſet
up

up an *image*, and to bring Scripture, as construed by *heathens*, to juftify *idolatry*. The text makes him *equal*, for *ισος* fignifies *equal*; and the heathens thought their *heroes*, which were *made* gods, equal to their other gods, who were alfo *heroes*.

IV. Truft in *God*, 1 *Pet.* ii. 21, 23. See *fect.* 104. what perfons urged to truft in God : not men *unredeemed* and *unfanctified*; no, by nature we are fervants of *fin*, and *dead*, and therefore if dead men cannot truft; we cannot truft in God after his example, unlefs his death is *more* than an example, and our *life*, unlefs it is a *fatisfying ranfom for*, and in the ftead of, us, we have no room to truft in him. To truft in God after his example, is, firft, to be *without fin* after his example, and therefore, unlefs we are clean *in* Chrift, and by *his* death, we cannot truft in God : though to fuch as will accept him, to fuch as chufe not to *die in their fins*, he is not only an *example*, but the *object* of truft : *Believe on the Lord Jefus Chrift and thou fhalt be faved, and thy houfe*, was St. *Paul's* advice to the gaoler, *Acts* xvi. 31.

V. Mortification of flefhly lufts, *Gal.* v. 24. *They that are Chrift's have crucified the flefh with the affections and lufts*, i. e. they only who are his, whom he hath *bought* and *paid for*, and *created unto good works.* I
know

know of but *one* crucifixion, that of *Chrift, in whom ye are circumcifed, by the putting off the fins of the flefh*, Col. ii. 11. And to fuppofe yourfelf capable of *firft* killing, and then *quickening*, your nature, is to pretend to nothing lefs than *raifing the dead*, jointly with this abfurdity, your making a *dead* fubject to act upon itfelf: for it is man's misfortune, that he is *dead in fin*; and yet, in thefe circumftances, you would advife him to *kill* what has *already* killed him. Wherefore, unlefs Chrift has overcome fin *for* us, and *raifed us* with him our furety, as St. *Paul* reafons, *ye are yet in your fins, and Chrift died in vain*, and we are unable to refift, much *lefs* to mortify after his example, what has killed us; when in him, though *dead in fin*, we fuffered *for* fin, and are thenceforward *dead* with him *unto* fin, being *freed* from it, and *alive unto God*, Rom. vi. throughout.

VI. Patience, meeknefs, and fortitude, under fufferings, *looking unto Jefus —for confider him who endured fuch contradiction of finners——left ye be weary*, Heb. xii. 1, 2, 3. Yes; *looking unto Jefus as the* AUTHOR *and* FINISHER *of the faith*, who hath *begun a good work in* us, and will perfect it; becaufe, confidering him in thefe lights, will give us a pleafant conviction, that, as what we are, we are by the endowment of *him, the* AUTHOR

of

of our faith, reconciliation, life and peace, and by *his* purchase of us; so, under the right of *his* discharge of our debt, and of *his* redemption of the inheritance of grace, we know we are entitled to God's fatherly care; and, however we suffer with his *Son* here, we know we shall be glorified with *him* in eternity. But, otherwise, what would Christ, as an example only, avail us? He had the *fullness of the Godhead dwelling in him:* but does he dwell in *sinners* out of Christ? if he does, you must have more *gods* than one to suit your scheme; and you must say, they dwell in *unholy* temples of flesh; unless then you own *our union* with Christ; that he dwelleth *in* us, and we *in* him; and that our bodies, by virtue of this *union* (*for being many we are one body in Christ*) are also *the temple of God,* 1 Cor. iii. 16, 17, 19. 2 Cor. vi. 16. Christ's example will not be any motive to our practice: you would have done as well to have proposed a single man's fighting the *French* army after the example of the Duke of *Marlborough,* when he had his thousands to assist him in his enterprize. But, blessed be God, we are *one* with Christ; we have fellowship with God, and, *by his blood* that bought redemption for us, and by the *word of his testimony,* whereby we *are made partakers of the Divine nature,* we must *overcome,* if
we

we *stand in the grace we have accefs to through Jefus Chrift*, Rev. xii. 11. Rom. v. 1.

VII. Deadnefs to the world, *Gal.* vi. 14. *God forbid that I fhould glory fave in the crofs of our Lord Jefus Chrift, by which the world is crucified to me, and I to the world.* In this text the *crofs of Chrift* is not fet forth as an *example*, but as that *by* which we are crucified, the body of Chrift being by imputation (fee *fect.* 91 (I) and the places there cited) the body of *fins*, Colof. ii. 11. 1 Pet. ii. 24. is *deftroyed, crucified,* and *circumcifed,* by the *circumcifion of Chrift* ; and we, as one with him *our* furety, and, in the relation of *members* to their *head,* are, as we are faid to be, *circumcifed in him* ; which, left we fhould miftake, is repeated to have been done *by the circumcifion of Chrift* ; confequently we died *with* him unto fin, and were, as we are faid to have been, *crucified together,* and made clean, that as he, the *firft fruits,* was raifed to the life of God, we alfo the reft of the *harveft,* the *branches of him,* John xv. 5. being *holy,* Rom. xi. 16. might, by virtue of our being branches, enjoy the fame *light,* and the fame *fpirit,* and *fet* our *affections on things above,* and grow upwards *from* the world though *in* the world, for the *feed of* Abraham, according to the *faith* of *Abraham,*

die

die in Chrift, the *feed* from whence we *all*
fpring; and becaufe he died like a giain,
we, dying in him, become, and are raifed,
a *holy feed*, Ifa. vi. 13. For Chrift is our
ground and foundation; *here* we are fown;
here we die; *here* we are quickened together
with him, and enjoy life eternal under the
light of his countenance: the world being
made dead and impotent to fuch, and we
dead to it, unexcited by its Sun-fhine, and
unmoved by its fpirit. Why? Becaufe we
have the *fpirit of glory and of God refting
upon* us in Chrift, to direct our defiies elfe-
where, becaufe we have *our lufts*, that only
hold the world has of us, *circumcifed by the
circumcifion of Chrift* : in fhort, becaufe we
are tranflated into *another* fyftem, into the
*kingdom of Chrift, from darknefs into his
marvellous light*; and are under *other* influences, not under thofe *of fin* and *corruption*, or *the devil, who ruleth in the hearts
of the children of difobedience*, Acts xxvi.
18. which we all are by nature, but *under*
thofe of *Divine* love, the *renewing of the
Holy Ghoft*, and *the Lord God* in our *hearts.*
But you, Sir, have chofen a *new* means of
crucifying your affections and lufts: you
have, with the *Pelagians*, found out *another*
crofs, in your own imitation of Chrift: you
glory in the *inherent* perfection of your nature, in being accepted by a juft and holy

F f

God

God *without* law and juftice, becaufe without a *fatisfaction* (fee *fect.* 87, 88, 89. and *p.* 95, 96. of your book) by virtue of being *fufpended* on the crofs of your defires, wherein fetting afide that you cannot *crofs* your defires without God's grace, unobtainable but *through* a fatisfaction, you run counter, in my eye, to St *Paul's* requeft of his God, and rank yourfelf amongft the *enemies of the crofs,* Phil iii. 18. For, who is an enemy to a King fo much as he who makes himfelf the King? Who, therefore, is an enemy to the *crofs of Chrift* fo much as he who fets up *another,* in his own rectoral goodnefs, a certain ability in *himfelf* to kill his lufts, and to work out a *righteoufnefs,* on account of which God will give him happinefs, an ability that needs but fomewhat to *fhew* wherein true holinefs confifts (*pag.* 110, 111, 113. of your book) and as an example to excite to the practice of it. Indeed, either the fprings by which we are carried on, and the movements we make in life, are Chrift's, or elfe he is neither, to fuch, *the refurrection nor the life,* neither *the* AUTHOR *nor* FINISHER *of their faith.*

106. *We are baptized into Chrift's death,* Rom. vi. 3. as you fay, *p.* 122. But how? Neither the *Romans,* nor *we,* were ever bathed or dipped in it, nor even prefent at

his

his death; so that it remains we died, being by imputation *in him*. As to saying, it means *our* death unto sin, this will explain away, but not account for, nor be agreeable to, the expression, for the words are, *We are baptized into his* death, which can only be by *imputation* of it to *us*, who are immerged *in* it by water, the *sign* of it.

107. And, in the Lord's Supper, you say, " doubtless, eating Christ's body, and " drinking his blood, are to be understood " figuratively." Do you mean, that we eat the one, and drink the other, in figure? or, that it is not true we, by faith, apprehend and receive Christ's body and blood to our use? If you mean the *former*, it is true, if the *latter*, you have *no* warrant for it from Scripture, for they evidently assert our *communion* with Christ, 1 *Cor*. x. 16. 1 *John* 1. 3. 2 *Cor*. xiii. 14. And, when we thus have Christ in us, pray on account of what righteousness are we accepted? Of Christ's, doubtless; unless you say it is overlooked, and is not the reason of our forgiveness, which yet you own it to be, *p*. 87, 91. As to the Scripture instructions being called *meat*, &c. this is far from proving we receive not Christ in the Sacrament, as we receive the earth in its fruits, because the *word, which liveth and abideth for ever,*

F f 2   *is*

is by the gospel preached unto you, 1 Pet. i. 23. as a seed under a husk. In the Sacrament, then, we receive Christ as certainly by faith, as by faith we receive him when we receive the written word: and we do not, as you say then, first *receive* him " when " we tread in his steps," but we receive him then only, when knowing and owning *our* inability to tread in his steps, and confessing and believing *him* to be *our* righteousness, *wisdom, sanctification,* and *redemption,* and pleading *our* right, by his purchase, we take him, and the quickening grace *in* him, with a view not apart *from* him, but in *union* with him, and under his rule and power to fight and strive against sin unto victory, and to reign with him. This is eating the body of Christ, as it was *broken for us:* this is drinking *his blood,* as it was shed *for the remission of sins,* both together making up the *price* of our redemption, which we here plead in payment *for* our freedom, and *for* the inheritance *reserved for us.*

108 And all this to me is a clear proof, that the *cross* and *blood* of Christ, as it is the *ground* and *reason* of the remission of sins, is considered not immediately, as you say it is, as the means of our sanctification, but as it is the vicarious, substituted offering for sin, which, by *his* suffering, like as the

the light fuffers the fire, puts a bright *robe of righteoufnefs upon* our natures, and clears them , and, being *made* known for this very purpofe, *Rom.* iii. 25 we are obliged, at our eternal peril, to ufe it as fuch; which if we do, we fhall be forgiven, and we fhall obtain eternal life, if not, our fins will not be forgiven: we fhall bear our fins, and perifh eternally. For, however Chrift's death was the *valuable* confideration, on account of which not only " antecedent," but alfo confequent bleffings, even the *end of our faith,* the *falvation of* our *fouls,* are freely beftowed upon us; yet, with refpect to our intereft in it, we are then only held to have it in the eye of God, when our hearts *receive* it. If we receive not the faith of *Chrift crucified* in our ftead, that is, for us, *fect.* 88. and making reconciliation for us by his infinite merits, we cannot, *in juftice,* and therefore not at all, *receive the end of* it, *the falvation of our fouls* (from fin) or, in other words, fanctification, which is to me a ftrong confirmation of the whole fcheme.

109. As, therefore, our Lord's death is fo plainly reprefented as a fatisfying mean, in like manner as *Sheba*'s death faved the people from the fword of *Joab,* 2 Sam. xx. 21 ; as we have *no* ground, in Scripture or Reafon, to confider it as of *any* virtue in

any

any other abstracted light; and as we cannot be pardoned, or saved, or sanctified, because we cannot be set free from sin, unless
we are *justified* by it; I conclude, it is a
reason with God for the forgiveness of sins,
and the donation of blessings, as it is *made*
a proper mean of cleansing us from all fil-
thiness of the flesh and spirit, by being a
valuable consideration given for the *redemption of the purchased possession*, of all that
inheritance we have in the kingdom of
God.

In *sect.* 186 and 187. you most strangely
contradict yourself: for you make *our imitation of Christ* (confuted in your sense of
it, *sect.* 117.) and prayer, the *reason* of our
forgiveness, when, at the same time, you
make Christ's righteousness and death the
reason of our forgiveness, *p.* 147, &c.

110. Judge now, Sir, whether I can look
upon what you have said to be *silencing*, as
you call it, all infidel objections against the
doctrine of *atonement*. Suppose I had argued against some *sacred* truth, to which
unbelievers, in their *uncommon* ignorance,
object, would you say, I had silenced their
objections? No; you must in justice say,
that I had changed sides, taken the unbeliever's part, urged new objections, and,
through a good confidence in the strength of
my reasoning, boasted that I had set aside
my

this doctrine; though, for a skreen, I softened the expression, and only said, with you, that I had " silenced the objections " against it." For, if the commander of a garrison should aim at silencing the batteries of the besieger, by this *new* method of your's, by giving up the works they were battering, what could we call him but a traitor to his Prince. I wish, therefore, you would carefully consider, whether or no you have not been doing *so*; and take this for a certain truth, that though ten thousand objectors, backed by all the malicious spirits that set them on work, should assault the sacred doctrines of *atonement* by a *Vice-man suffering* and *obeying for us*, and consequently by the imputation of his righteousness *unto all*, and *upon all, them that believe*; yet these will stand their attacks, and make the enemy fly like stubble before the whirlwind.

" Thus," you say, " we are well guard-
" ed *against* the dangerous error of expect-
" ing to obtain mercy by a presumptuous,
" inactive reliance upon the blood or merits
" of Christ, or by the imputation of his
" righteousness to us." Now, that the Scripture recommends a *reliance* on him, as being *all in all* to us, is plain from both testaments; else, Why are we bid to *believe to cast our burthen upon the Lord?*
Why

Why faid to be *borne by him as on eagles wings?* Why to be *one with him*, if fo be that we are not to *rely* on the *blood* and *merits* of Chrift, which fuch an union, in *law* and *juftice*, makes *ours?* If it is prefumptuous then to *rely* upon thefe, as it is an injunction of my Bible, may I never prefume, by any other means, to obtain pardon, fanctity, and happinefs (fee this proved, *fect.* 71, 86, 101.) and this *faith* and reliance, as it entitles us to the promifes, connects us with Chrift, and is faid to have the *falvation of* our *fouls* for *the end of it*, cannot be inactive in the *members*, unlefs you make God the *Head* fo, whofe *gift* it is: and, furely, *his* gifts are not ineffectual and inoperative, but *good* and *perfect!* Happy, then, is the man who receives this *gift* as propofed to him in the Scriptures: *After* he *believes*, he is *fealed with the Holy Spirit of Promife*, as *Chrift's workmanfhip*, Eph. i. 13.—ii. 10. As to your calling our *faith*, in the imputation of *Chrift's righteoufnefs*, a *dangerous error*, I have faid enough, *fect.* 71 and 91. II. to prove it to be the doctrine of the Scriptures, and abfolutely neceffary to our juftification, that God *might be juft:* therefore let me beg of you well to confider, *Exod.* xxx. 31. where you will find there was an *holy ointment* appointed for the anointment of the Prieft, *ver.* 37. *for the*

the Lord; but, that it was *death* for man to *imitate* it, or to *put it upon* his flesh. In *sect.* 71 and 91. II. you may also see this righteousness is not wrought by this spiritual *Bezaleel*, Exod. xxxi. 2. nor imputed to us that we may *not* obey, but that we might thus have in Christ, thus made of God *righteousness to us*, a reason *for the remission of* our *sins*, that God may be *just*, and yet the *justifier of* us, and that we, being accepted of him, *Heb.* xiii. 12. *might* be sanctified and supported *under* the shelter of his wings in all spiritual life, without which sanctification and support we cannot *move* in obedience unto God : For, as *Noah* was covered in the ark that he *might* be saved, so are we clad with *the righteousness of God*, that we *might* be *preserved in Jesus Christ*, wherefore you have wholly mistaken man's circumstances. Man is not admitted to mercy *without* any respect to law and justice; for, since Christ, our Surety, hath fulfilled the law, we, one with him, have fulfilled it in him, and because we are, by his *one* offering, perfected, and set free, from the condemnation and penalty of the law; God is even *just*, as well as he is *faithful, to forgive us our sins*; he sees upon us what shall justify us, and can, *by law*, acquit and protect whom, *by law*, he was *before* bound to punish. And if, notwithstanding

G g

this,

this, a man will feek to be juftified *by the law*, and by his perfonal obedience, it is plain he becomes *a debtor to do the whole law*, and, as St. *Paul* reafons, *Gal.* v. 4. is *fallen from grace*, becaufe he is fallen from that gracious connection which he had with Chrift and *his* righteoufnefs, and wherein he once ftood, and only can *rejoice in the houfe of the glory of God*, Rom v. 2. *Chrift is become of no effect to you*, Gal. v. 4. So that if the Scriptures, or common fenfe, are a guard, we are *well* guarded againft the dangerous error of expecting mercy by a prefumptuous reliance on *any* rock but Chrift, on *any* blood, merits, or confideration, but *his* : for thus, and on *no* other footing, the Scripture exhorts me fay, the *atonement* by Chrift's blood ftands in perfect *confiftency* not only with all the principles and declarations of the Gofpel, I muft add, with our current notions of God's juftice and wifdom, and infinite dignity, but ftrongly enforces every command of duty, and every threatening to difobedience, as it makes us, and what, *without* it, we could not be, free to be awed by the one, and to be deterred by the other; and precludes all hopes of ever feeing God without an inveftiture of the New Man *Chrift Jefus*, and of his righteoufnefs, and of that love of God and our brother unto which we are fanctified, in confequence of fuch a

powerful

powerful inveſtiture ; which, ſo far as I can
ſee (to uſe your own words) is clearly and
univerſally true of no other ſcheme of redemption but this.   For, 1. *If ye be led by
the Spirit ye are not under the law*, Gal. v.
18. *Whoſoever of you are juſtified by the
law, ye are fallen from grace*, ver. 4. 2. On
your ſcheme, or *any other* ſcheme , you ſuppoſe man unredeemed, unranſomed, and in
the ſervice of ſin, *free* to work out his ſal-
vation, to do good, and to *deſtroy the works
of the devil*, which is contrary to Scripture, that ſays, *beſides God there is no Saviour — without Jeſus ye can do nothing —*
and, that our bleſſed Lord was *manifeſt to
deſtroy* theſe *works* ; and then it is contrary
to the reaſon of the thing, becauſe it is
making the Devil very weak, and blind too,
to let man, of himſelf, eſcape him ; and
making God's aſſignments for the confinement of his rebel ſubject very ineffectual to
anſwer the end intended by them. I ſay,
you ſuppoſe man *unredeemed*; becauſe, if
redemption beſpeaks ſome one a *captive*,
ſome other paying an *equivalent* for his *ranſom*, and the *liberty* of this captive obtained
by the *payment* of this ranſom ; then, ſince
theſe things have *no* place in your ſcheme,
I muſt inſiſt upon it, that your ſcheme is
no ſcheme of *redemption*, ſince if it was, it
muſt be the Scripture ſcheme ſtated in *ſect.*

G g 2   71.

71. But, that it is a scheme, whose very *name* carries its confutation with it; a scheme, which, I hope, for your soul's sake, you have framed in the *dark*; and a scheme, whose parts *correspond* not with each other, as you are well apprized, in *such* circumstances, must *always* be the case.

In 19o. you contradict your account in the first chapter, as you may see, *sect.* 5 to 26.

111. Because, then, our blessed *Redeemer*, having made trial of our infirmities, and bought liberty, and power, and glory, for the patient receivers of him, is exalted to universal rule in his human nature, that he might dispense them, because he appears in the real *Holy of Holies*, in Heaven, as our *High-Priest* and *Advocate*, making a *legal* intercession for us with the *incense* of his merits, and the *blood* of his sacrifice, because he is perpetually, " not receiving, but" conveying to us the blessed consequences of his satisfaction, a *legal* acquitment, and the effectual power of the *Holy Ghost*, and *peace* and *joy* to all who, as the stars, *borrow* their lustre, are content to receive their glory from *him*. By this means, the *mercy of the Lord* is set far above the sheltering light which these Heavens affords us, his *justice* is maintained with due consistency, as its demands *are attended to*, and, in the midst

of

of them, fhine forth his *wifdom* and *omni-potence* in their full fplendor, by a recon-ciliation of his *juftice* and *mercy* in the paf-fion of *Jefus Chrift once for all*   Thus the love of God, manifeft in the grateful prac-tice of every virtue by all intelligent men, is put upon a proper ground, and is raifed, and brought forward, by means that cannot fail of having effect on the patient receiver of thefe *precious things of Heaven* above ; which fhews, that the everlafting dominion and priefthood of Chrift is a conftitution moft rationally, moft deeply, becaufe moft juftly, and yet moft beneficently, contrived : and this not only as it is " the public re-" ward and exhibition of the moft confum-" mate holinefs," I add, condefcenfion and good-will, but alfo as it is that *availing* interceffion, by whofe *fatisfying* efficacy God is difpofed to mercy, and we are enti-tled to it ; as it is the reward of *us* in the perfon of our *Surety*, as it is the exhibition of *our* holinefs in the holinefs of *him*, on account of which the reward is given to him, and intentionally to us *in* him ; and, laftly, as it tends of neceffity to raife, as well as " to fpread and propagate," the love of our brethren after Chrift's example, and, in proportion, to diffufe happinefs throughout the whole creation of God, by tranfplanting us into *that* foil, and under the

the prolific influence of *those* feafons of grace which can only produce in us the *fruits of the Spirit.* For, whilft we are redeemed unto God in *juftice* and *judgment*, in *mercy* and *truth*, that he may *work in us to will and to do*; and whilft we are praifing him for the happy effects we feel under his faving grace, the created fpirits, wondering at the wifely complicated fcheme of redemption, fall down and worfhip JESUS, the AUTHOR and FINISHER of fo much mercy to mankind, and devils, confounded to fee with what due fupport of the Divine Attributes God hath retaken his creature, and ftruck with fhame and remorfe to fee their deadly purpofes baffled, by the fuperior ftrength and counfel of the *Almighty*, are forced to confefs the manifefted *Godhead*, and that he is *juft to forgive us our fins.* Shall man then, *more* fenfelefs than they, boldly affert, that, in the bufinefs of our redemption, in God's difpenfation of his pardoning grace (I tremble almoft to fay it) he hath *fet law and juftice afide.* See *p. 95* of your book.

112. How you, then, have difcharged the part of a faithful *fteward of the myfteries of God*, I muft leave to the reader's judgment, and to your *own* confcience, to determine. For, how you have preached and explained, as you fay it is a minifter's
duty

duty to preach and explain, the *crofs of Chrift*, after the example of St. *Paul*, muft appear to you, if you will but ferioufly confider, that you take away *all the myfteries of Godlinefs* ; for what *myftery* is left to us, in faying God pardons us without a confideration, I fee not. Add to this, that St *Paul* preached *nothing* but *Chrift crucified, God juftified in the Spirit*, for us, becaufe otherwife he needed *no* juftification : but you, I muft fay, have, I hope in an error of your *judgment*, preached yourfelf, and not *Chrift Jefus the Lord*.

113. What faith, then, that precludes the pleafing and neceffary relations which God gives us to Chrift, and detaches from it our interefts in him and his merits (fee *fect.* 71.) can afford the poor finner any fort of complacency and comfort, when it leaves the unchangeable law of an unchangeable God in full force *againft* us? This cannot be the *Gofpel of peace* ; with this faith *Jerufalem* could never be *comforted*, for, on your fuppofition, fhe is far from having *received, at the Lord's hands* (aught much lefs) *double for all her fins*. However, let us examine your account of it. " Faith," then, you fay, " is not merely believing " what is related in the Scriptures concern- " ing Chrift's incarnation or fufferings, but " it is fuch a right knowledge, fentiment, " and

" and perſuaſion, concerning his blood, as
" purify our hearts, confirm our hope in
" God, and diſpoſe us to univerſal obe-
" dience." Now, in this account, ſetting
aſide that, *without Chriſt*, you unſcriptu-
rally ſuppoſe a man to have *hope towards
God* now only " confirmed," you mighty
odly deny the exiſtence of what you would
prove to be. You ſay, " faith is not mere-
" ly believing;" when, if there is ſuch a
thing as faith or belief, it can be nothing
elſe but faith, or merely believing. Poſſibly you would mean, it is not a mere aſ-
ſent of the mind, unſupported by any inward conviction. If ſo, you are right: for
St. *Paul, Heb.* xi. 1. ſays, *It is the evidence
or demonſtration* (that is, in part, 1 *Cor.*
xiii 9.) *of things not ſeen, the* ſubſtratum or
ground of things hoped for : therefore, it
preſuppoſes inſtruction, or a revelation of
the things of Heaven by ideas, or evidence,
from God, on the one hand, and an ability
in man to receive theſe ideas, or this evidence of them, on the other; and is the
middle term which confides in, depends on,
and accepts, the things thus revealed, on
the one hand, and thus underſtood on the
other. So that faith in Chriſt is the hand
of the ſoul, which receives him as the Scripture or Revelation gives him, as our ſurety
for ſin, who offered up himſelf once for, or

in

in the ſtead of, all; ſee *ſect.* 71. It is the hand which applies *his* blood that we may be waſhed, and *his* righteouſneſs to our hearts, that we may be forgiven, that God may ſee it, and, in the final judgment, as at the rehearſal of it in *Egypt* upon them who *know not the Lord,* may paſs over us. It is the hand that takes and *puts on* the *armor of God,* that he may fight againſt ſin unto victory; and, though he fall down under the arrow of death, may riſe again by *the operation of God,* thus received, and ſit down conqueror with Chriſt, at the right hand of God. Its influence may be conſidered,

114 1. In reference to our temper and conduct; you ſay, " as it leads us to a con-" formity to Chriſt," but I muſt more explicitly ſay, as it ſets us free from ſin, apprehends, and lays hold of, the operative grace of God, inſomuch, that it is Chriſt, our life, which lives in us, and, as a quickening principle of ſpiritual life, animates us to this or that thought or action; which makes the Apoſtle ſay, *Gal.* ii. 20. *that the life he lived, he lived by the faith of the Son of God, which gave him his intereſt in Chriſt;* for he here poſitively ſays, *he lived it not of himſelf,* as he ſays 2 *Cor.* iii. 5. *Not that we are ſufficient of ourſelves to think* (much leſs to do) *any thing as of ourſelves, but*

H h   *our*

our sufficiency is of God; for he was not *under*, but *dead to, the law*: he was *mar-ried to another*, to Chrift, and his mainte-nance was from him, as a wife is from her husband (fee 71) *Gal* v. 18. *Rom.* vii. 4. *It is of faith, that it might be by grace*, Rom. iv. 16 —v. 5. *The love of God is fhed abroad in our hearts, by the Holy Ghoft that is given to us* —vii. 4. *that we fhould bring forth fruit unto God*—Gal. iii. 14. *we receive the promife of the fpirit through faith*, fo that *we are kept by the power of God through faith unto falvation*, 1 Pet. i. 5. We model not ourfelves, but are mo-delled, fince we are *created in Chrift Jefus unto good works* by the grace of God, who gives us to partake of the anointing of Chrift, and anoints us in him, 1 *John* ii. 20, 27, for the Chriftian covenant runs thus, *Jer.* xxx. 11, 22. *I will be to you a God, and they fhall be to me a people.*

115. II. In refpect to our approaches to God · you fay, not without contradiction to yourfelf, *fect.* 167. " Chrift is a mercy-feat,
" the ground or bafis upon which God has
" fixed the throne of his grace, and, there-
" fore, the ground or bafis of all the inter-
" courfe we hold with him, and he with us
" and, as the antient worfhipper drew near to
" God, with fuch thoughts as the blood of
" the fin offering, fprinkled before or upon
" the

" the mercy-feat, would fuggeft, fo we
" Chriftians fhould draw near to God for par-
" don, &c. through faith in his blood, *Rom.*
" iii. 25. or with fuch thoughts" (mentioned
more exprefsly, and confuted, in *feft.* 19)
" as his blood, fhed for the remiffion of fins,
" will naturally fuggeft. ' Now give me
leave to ftate fome things, concerning the
nature and manner of our acceptance, which
you feem to have overlooked, and which I
have, to my own fatisfaction, proved, in
feft. 6, 7, 8, 9, 10, 11, 21, 26.

1. The temple and tabernacle were both figures
of the body of Chrift

2. In this temple dwelt the token of the prefence of the fulnefs of the Godhead.

3 To this token of God's prefence none could
come, fave the High-Prieft once a year.

4 In this temple, in the holy place, *Lev* xvi.
3 a figure of the Holy One of God, he, who was
cloathed in holy garments, officiated in the Name
of the Lord, and bore the iniquity of the congregation, and the judgment of the people, upon
him, offered a fatisfactory and vicarious facrifice
in figure, fpotlefs and perfect in his nature, but
bearing the fin of others, by imputation or impofition, upon him, and therefore receiving the
wages of fin, *death*, and flain and fuffering for
their offences

5. After the death of this his fatisfying facrifice,
he came into the fymbolical prefence of God,
within the veil, and fumed the fweet-fmelling in-

cenfe

our sufficiency is of God; for he was not *under*, but *dead to, the law :* he was *married to another*, to Christ, and his maintenance was from him, as a wife is from her husband (see 71) *Gal* v. 18. *Rom.* vii. 4. *It is of faith, that it might be by grace,* Rom. iv. 16 —v. 5. *The love of God is shed abroad in our hearts, by the Holy Ghost that is given to us* —vii. 4. *that we should bring forth fruit unto God*—Gal. iii. 14. *we receive the promise of the spirit through faith*, so that *we are kept by the power of God through faith unto salvation,* 1 Pet. i. 5. We model not ourselves, but are modelled, since we are *created in Christ Jesus unto good works* by the grace of God, who gives us to partake of the anointing of Christ, and anoints us in him, 1 *John* ii. 20, 27; for the Christian covenant runs thus, *Jer.* xxx. 11, 22. *I will be to you a God, and they shall be to me a people.*

115. II. In respect to our approaches to God . you say, not without contradiction to yourself, *sect.* 167. " Christ is a mercy-seat,
" the ground or basis upon which God has
" fixed the throne of his grace, and, there-
" fore, the ground or basis of all the inter-
" course we hold with him, and he with us
" and, as the antient worshipper drew near to
" God, with such thoughts as the blood of
" the sin offering, sprinkled before or upon
" the

" the mercy-feat, would fuggeft, fo we
" Chriftians fhould draw near to God for par-
" don, &c. through faith in his blood, *Rom.*
" iii. 25. or with fuch thoughts" (mentioned
more exprefsly, and confuted, in *fect.* 19.)
" as his blood, fhed for the remiffion of fins,
" will naturally fuggeft." Now give me
leave to ftate fome things, concerning the
nature and manner of our acceptance, which
you feem to have overlooked, and which I
have, to my own fatisfaction, proved, in
fect. 6, 7, 8, 9, 10, 11, 21, 26.

    1 The temple and tabernacle were both figures
of the body of Chrift

    2 In this temple dwelt the token of the pre-
fence of the fulnefs of the Godhead.

    3 To this token of God's prefence none could
come, fave the High-Prieft once a year

    4 In this temple, in the holy place, *Lev* xvi
3 a figure of the Holy One of God, he, who was
cloathed in holy garments, officiated in the Name
of the Lord, and bore the iniquity of the congregation, and the judgment of the people, upon
him, offered a fatisfactory and vicarious facrifice
in figure, fpotlefs and perfect in his nature, but
bearing the fin of others, by imputation or impofition, upon him, and therefore receiving the
wages of fin, *death*, and fhen and fuffering for
their offences

    5 After the death of this his fatisfying facrifice,
he came into the fymbolical prefence of God,
within the veil, and fumed the fweet fmelling in-

cenfe

cenfe that was raifed by being burned; and then brought of the blood of his facrifice, and of that for the people, and fprinkled it with his finger upon the mercy-feat feven times, *Lev* xvi.

6 In confequence of this he, in the ftead of *Ifrael*, made an *atonement for the holy place*, the figure of the body of Chrift, becaufe *of the un-cleannefs of the children of* Ifrael, and for the *ta-bernacle of the congregation that remaineth amongft them, in the midft of their uncleannefs*; no man be-ing admitted into the tabernacle of the congrega-tion whilft he was doing this, agreeably to what Chrift fays in *Ifa* lxiii 3. *I have trodden the wine prefs alone, and of the people there was none with me.*

7 " The worfhipper," therefore, or penitent finner, came not at all *into* the tabernacle, or holy place, but was admitted into the *temple*, in confe-quence of what was done by the *High Prieft* in the *holy* place, and the *Holy of Holies* and pleaded by him in payment

8. The temple, in which he knew and confef-fed the *typical* fatisfaction to be made, was the in-terpofing *medium* or means, and not his perfonal qualifications, by which he drew *nigh* unto God

9 This temple, therefore, was not only to be *looked* at as an *example* of building, but to be *en-tered* into

10. And, becaufe the Faithful *Ifraelite* content-ed not himfelf with taking a furvey of this tem-ple as the *ftandard* of all buildings, but *entered* into God's *gates with thankfgiving*, and *into his courts with praife*, he, by virtue of being *in* it, and under its fhelter, received *the bleffing from the* reprefentative of *the God of his Salvation*, which

this

this reprefentative, by a *typical* fatisfaction and blood, had obtained for him.

And, from thefe fhadows of *good things*, of *better* facrifices, of a *better* miniftry, and a more *perfect* tabernacle, in fhort, of the *heavenly things themfelves*, our inferences, Sir, muft of neceffity be thefe following

I That the body of Chrift is to us, what the temple was in *figure* to the *Ifraelites*

II That in him dwelleth the *fullnefs of the* GODHEAD *bodily.*

III That none could come directly to God but *Jefus*, our great High-Prieft, in the *temple of his body*

IV. That, in this *temple of his body*, he, who was cloathed in *holinefs*, and *undefiled*, the *Name of the Lord*, who *bore our fins in his own body*, and the evil of fin, offered an infinitely fatisfying, tho' *vicarious* facrifice, namely, himfelf, fpotlefs and perfect in himfelf, as the unblemifhed *Pafchal* Lamb, but as a *Surety*, bearing our fins and failures by legal imputation, and therefore receiving *the wages of fin, death*, and flain and fuffering the fiery wrath *for our offences*

V That, after the death of him, our *equivalent*, fatisfying facrifice, *he rofe again*, and, having rent the *veil* of fins *in his flefh*, went up into the real *prefence of God*, and tendered the fweet-fmelling incenfe of his all-fufficient merits, which arofe from his fuffering the fiery wrath of God, and *fprinkled the blood* of his facrifice for fin *feven times*, that is, fatisfactorily and abundantly for all.

VI. That,

VI. That, in confequence of this, he made an atonement for himfelf as our *Surety*, that, like the *tabernacle*, had remained in the *midft* of our un-cleannefs, made *his* by imputation, and reconciled us *in the body of his flefh*, *none* of the *people* being *with him*, Ifa. liii. 3

VII. That, therefore, the worfhipper, or penitent finner, comes *not* into the *tabernacle* of *his body* prefumptuoufly to offer what he *only*, by his Divine *nature*, is qualified to offer, but is admitted into a *communion with the temple of the body of Chrift*, in confequence of *what* was done by Chrift in the true holy place of *his body*.

VIII. That the *temple of the body of Chrift*, in which a man knows and confeffes the real and adequate *fatisfaction* to be made to God *for him*, and not any *perfonal* qualification of man, is, that *interpofing medium* or means through which he muft *draw nigh*, as it is that by which he is *made nigh unto God*, dwelling *bodily in Chrift*.

IX. That this *temple of the body of Chrift* is not only to be *curioufly* eyed at a *diftance*, becaufe it is not only held forth to us as an *exemplar* of what we *ought* to be, and by which we fhould *model* our conduct, but is alfo to be *entered in* by us, *John* x 9 as the *houfe not made with hands*, that we may be fheltered from the ftorm and tempeft of judgment in the day of vifitation.

X. That, becaufe the faithful *Chriftian* contents not himfelf with *looking* at Chrift as an *example only*, but *enters into* him, the *door* and *gate of righteoufnefs*, John x. 9. Ifa. lx and into *communion* with *his* body, he, by virtue of fuch *communion* or *incorporation*, for *being many we are one body in Chrift*, receives the *invefiture* of a glorious righteoufnefs,

righteoufnefs, and the blefling from this High-Prieft of his profeffion, who, by a *fatisfying* facrifice, has obtained it *for*, and *in the ftead of*, us.

116 Whence we fee, that " the anticnt wor-" fhipper drew near," not " with fuch thoughts " as the blood fuggefted," according to your account of it, confuted *fect* 19. but with *faith*, in what the *Ifraelitcs* faw in *figure*, in the blood of Chrift, fhed and fprinkled by *another* for him Nor could he draw near, under the law, to the *fymbolical* prefence of God ; there was a *veil*, emblematical of fin, to be *rent*, which none did or could *put* afide but the *High-Prieft*. and, if he owned it not put *afide* by him, it was *not* rent *for* him, and the prefence of God was *not* to be come at Wherefore, if we confefs not that Chrift rent this veil of fins, which *feparated us* from God, in *his* (and not in our) *flefh*, the *way* to God is open to *none* of us, and fuch a man is a *ftranger*, an *alien*, an *outcaft*, *without God*, becaufe *without Chrift in the world*. The *blood of Chrift*, then, muft be confidered as the *medium*, not only " through which our minds fhould look to the " throne of God," but *through* which, *in* which, and *on account of* which, as an *equivalent* fatisfaction, our perfons, prayers, &c are accepted 2 As the throne of God is *in* Chrift, as well as " fix-" ed *upon* Chrift," none can fee God but who are members *of* and *in* Chrift 3. His righteoufnefs muft not *only* be confidered as the " moft perfect" and exemplary, but as the *only perfect One*, in oppofition to any *other* righteoufnefs *falfly fo called*, and as to be *put on* by us *previoufly* to the *remiffion* of our fins, that God *may be juft*, and yet our

juftifier,

justifier, Rom iii 26. 4. It is not man " that
" sets this *medium* before his eyes when he draws
" near to God," but God that *declares* it, and
sets it *forth* as the *light*; and, it is not exhibited
before us " as a character of spotless virtue" only,
nor are we accepted because we *previously* imitate
it thus set before us no, it is exhibited as that
wherewith we must be *clothed* in God's *kingdom*, as
with *light* in this earthly kingdom, *previously* to
our *moving at all*, or *seeing how* to move in spiritual life 5 " The image of the Son of God upon
" our hearts" is not, in *your* sense of it, the reason
of our acceptance, because you declare against the
imputation of the image, p 98; and, where it is
not by imputation, it *cannot* be at all, because it is
an image existing in *another* subject for, as your
meaning must be, that God can be pleased with
nothing more than seeing the image, the copy of
his Son, as an example upon our hearts; so, because this absurdly presupposes persons (found by
Scripture, and by experience, dead in trespasses)
previously to their justification, or spiritual quickening, to be qualified to work within themselves
what shall justify them, I must deny this to be the
reason of our acceptance, for, though I read,
This is my beloved Son, in whom I am well pleased,
yet I find not this is the image of my image, in
which I am well pleased As far as I see, to support this notion, Sir, you must assume to yourself
a creative power, and imagine you can act before
you can, with any reason, be supposed to have
existence in spiritual life. But why, Sir, will you
do this in the face of so many absurdities ? when
the unalterable law of God is, that the imitator
of this holiness, when he imitates it with a view

to

to be accepted by such imitation, shall die without mercy, *Exod* xxx 31 Besides, what saith the Scriptures, *In the Lord shall all the seed of* Israel *be justified, and shall glory* (but not out of him) Isa xlv. 25. *I am the Lord----and my glory will I not give to* another, *neither my praise to graven images,* Isa xlii. 8 *Besides me there is no Saviour,* xliii. 11 Phil iii 2 *Beware of dogs------ for we are the circumcision, which worship God in the Spirit, and rejoice in Chrijt Jesus, and have no confidence in the flesh, though I might, touching the righteousness which is in the law blameless* How you, then, could be led to set up an *image graven* in the flesh, and to give the glory to *it,* I know not But I hope you have overlooked those Scriptures ; then, Sir, and then only, you have *excuse.*

117. In drawing thus near to God, with a heart *cleansed* from all sin, we gain not only a " *double* advantage," as you say, but *manifold* and innumerable benefits and blessings.

(1) " We contemplate," as you rightly observe, " the surest pledge, and strongest " confirmation, of the love and mercy of " God to us ," but then you limit them : you say, " they are for the encouragement " of our faith and hope, that our sins are " pardoned, *&c :*" when you should, I think, have said, they are for the raising of our faith and hope, as without this love and mercy they could not exist : for we read, *God* (that will not give *his glory to another*)

I i   gave

gave him glory *that our faith and hope might be in God.* And, of a truth, appeareth it not from the sense of the Scriptures cited in this letter, that it was God's greatest glory to manifest his wisdom in the reconciliation of his justice and mercy, that he might consistently display his love to man? Yes Indeed, man seems to be the object of all the regard of the Almighty, and the exaltation of our *degraded* nature into an union with the Most High, to be the concern of our *Maker* · what he has done or promised is to make man happy ; so that we cannot contemplate these manifestations of a kind but just God, without perceiving our interests in him. However low we are in ourselves, we see ourselves exalted by grace in Christ, who for our sakes *became* poor. We rejoice in Jesus Christ, and in the *communicative* nature of his infinite merits and grace, and under the rule of this *King of Kings,* and *Lord of Lords.* We boast in *nothing* but in that *mediation* by which we are accepted, and through which we are sanctified, daring not to put *any,* no not the *least,* confidence in the flesh ; for we are aware, that such a man becomes obnoxious to that *terrible* denunciation in *Jer.* xvi. 5. *Cursed is the man that trusteth in* man, *and maketh flesh his arm, and whose heart departeth from the Lord.* We know
whom

whom we have believed, and chufe not to
be as the heath in the defert, but like the
tree planted by the waters, that fhall not
ceafe from yielding fruit. Alas, Sir! I am
naked without him, and would fain have
you turn your eyes upon yourfelf to fee
whether you have a covering of your own
works, or are not my brother in this I
wifh I could, and I hope I foon may, call
you my brother in another refpect, as a fel-
low citizen of Chrift, *the city of the Lord.*

118. (2) " Thus," you fay (145) " we
" fhall lift up our fouls unto God, charged
" with ideas of the moft perfect duty and
" goodnefs, which, if our hearts are pro-
" perly feafoned with them, will difpofe us
" to a conformity to them, or change us
" into the fame image." Now, Sir, this
will fhew us what man *ought* to be. But,
when we look into our earthly tabernacle,
where can we find a confcioufnefs that we
have acted according to thofe ideas of the
moft perfect duty and goodnefs? To our
fhame be it fpoken, our accounts will foon
*fhew us the debt is great, infinitely great on
our fide.* Our hearts, therefore, being " fea-
" foned with thofe ideas," will not avail
us, as you fay it will: where is our power
to do the good we fee? Is there no law in
your members? There is mine, and, I be-

gave him glory *that our faith and hope might be in God.* And, of a truth, appeareth it not from the sense of the Scriptures cited in this letter, that it was God's greatest glory to manifest his wisdom in the reconciliation of his justice and mercy, that he might consistently display his love to man? Yes. Indeed, man seems to be the object of all the regard of the Almighty, and the exaltation of our *degraded* nature into an union with the Most High, to be the concern of our *Maker* · what he has done or promised is to make man happy; so that we cannot contemplate these manifestations of a kind but just God, without perceiving our interests in him. However low we are in ourselves, we see ourselves exalted by grace in Christ, who for our sakes *became* poor. We rejoice in Jesus Christ, and in the *communicative* nature of his infinite merits and grace, and under the rule of this *King of Kings,* and *Lord of Lords.* We boast in *nothing* but in that *mediation* by which we are accepted, and through which we are sanctified, daring not to put *any,* no not the *least,* confidence in the flesh, for we are aware, that such a man becomes obnoxious to that *terrible* denunciation in *Jer.* xvi. 5 *Cursed is the man that trusteth in* man, *and maketh flesh his arm, and whose heart departeth from the Lord.* We know
whom

whom we have believed, and chuſe not to
be as the heath in the deſert, but like the
tree planted by the waters, that ſhall not
ceaſe from yielding fruit. Alas, Sir! I am
naked without him, and would fain have
you turn your eyes upon yourſelf to ſee
whether you have a covering of your own
works, or are not my brother in this· I
wiſh I could, and I hope I ſoon may, call
you my brother in another reſpect, as a fel-
low citizen of Chriſt, *the city of the Lord.*

118. (2) " Thus," you ſay (145) " we
" ſhall lift up our ſouls unto God, charged
" with ideas of the moſt perfect duty and
" goodneſs; which, if our hearts are pro-
" perly ſeaſoned with them, will diſpoſe us
" to a conformity to them, or change us
" into the ſame image." Now, Sir, this
will ſhew us what man *ought* to be. But,
when we look into our earthly tabernacle,
where can we find a conſciouſneſs that we
have acted according to thoſe ideas of the
moſt perfect duty and goodneſs? To our
ſhame be it ſpoken, our accounts will ſoon
*ſhew us the debt is great, infinitely great on
our ſide.* Our hearts, therefore, being " ſea-
" ſoned with thoſe ideas," will not avail
us, as you ſay it will : where is our power
to do the good we ſee? Is there no law in
your members? There is mine, and, I be-

lieve,

lieve, in every natural man's: who then shall
make me dead to this law, and smite his *rod*
upon this *sea* of wickedness, *after the manner
of* Egypt, *to* break this *yoke* off *us*, Isa. x.
26, 27. Man has obeyed sin, and sold himself for nought, and is sin's captive till redeemed: take away redemption, which, I
must frankly say, *your* scheme does *to all
intents and purposes*, and these ideas will
serve a man only as so many memento's of
what he *ought* to be, of what he is *not*, and
of what he *cannot* be till he is redeemed.
" Still," you say, " every part of our duty
" is absolutely necessary to our happiness :"
then, Sir, either you and all are *righteous*,
or you and all are *lost* for ever; the pardoning grace you mention can now do man no
good: all is absolutely necessary, because
pardon, in your sense of it, cannot convey
merit or *obedience* to us: but point me out
the man that works it; if you cannot, some
man must do it *for all*, upon your *own*
principles, or all are *lost, irrecoverably lost:*
and you can shew me none; your heart
will tell you, you are not the man, as it
must tell all that enquire of it: there must
then be *imputed* obedience to make up
for *our* failure, that we *may* be saved.
How unfit, therefore, your sentiments for
your subject! for you see they necessarily
lead to the very truths you are contending
against.

against. Indeed, the advantages, you would, under this head draw from coming to God through the blood of Chrift, are but imaginary, they never can be obtained by man, unlefs Chrift's offering is, what I have proved the Scriptures fpeak it, in other words, *all* that you, I think, deny it to be, *fatisfactory* and *meritorious for us.* How much the Scripture account of thefe advantages is unlike to your's, will appear from reading St *Paul's* rehearfal of them; in the firft and fecond chapters of his epiftle to the *Ephefians*, to which I refer you. And how much more fuitable to the nature of the thing is Chrift's account? They who walk in the light *fall not* (willingly) and when they do fall, they fee *how* to rife, and will be cautious how they walk in fuch a place amongft fuch ftumbling-blocks; the more cautious, as they advance in growth—*Little children* fall often, *men* lefs frequently in this world; and this is the cafe in the kingdom of God—God's power is manifeft in *our weaknefs*; and, did not men want *evidence* of their weaknefs, I leave you to judge how they would *boaft*, when even now fome are fo blind to their own *unworthinefs*, as to think they ftand in no need of *another's* merits or abilities to fave them. To come unto God by the *blood of Chrift* is to come unto him in fuch a way

as

as naturally fuggefts to us the accepting of the *Father*, the fatisfaction of *Chrift* for us, and the fanctification of the *Spirit*, promifed to thofe who believe; for it fuggefts not, as you fay, " that purity and " holinefs" which you fuppofe to be " the " principle and rule of our whole conduct," but that difplay of love on the part of God, by which we are faved, and that promife of the Spirit which the Apoftles make, contrary to your notion of the principles of our actions, the fpring of all our movements in life, for *Chrift is our life*, we are *led by the Spirit*.

119. And, (2) yet you would fay, St. *Paul*, taking his images from the *Jewifh* worfhip, confiders this advantage of drawing near unto God by the blood of Jefus, *Heb.* x. 19—22. whether with any truth, judge you yourfelf. For, 1. The *Jewifh* fymbols figure out Chrift, in whom a fatisfactory equivalent was paid by way of ranfom for us, as the only ground of our acceptance when pleaded by us (fee *fect.* 116.) 2. St. *Paul* had before-hand fhewed, that Chrift's facrifice was a *facrifice for*, and *in the ftead of, our fins*, ver. 12. that by *one offering* (and confequently by no additional offering of man's mifcalled merits and obedience) he had *perfected* for ever *them that are fanctified*: and, xvi. 19. that we have *a hope*

*hope set before us as an anchor of the soul,
sure and stedfast, which entereth into* (and of
course is connected with) *that* (scene of action which was done in our favour) *which is
within the veil,* &c. and, after this, he con-
cludes thus, *Now where remission of these*
(sins) *is, there is no more offering for sin —
Having therefore brethren* (through this assurance of remission of sins by this offering
for sin) *boldness* (or liberty, what before we
had not) *to enter into the Holiest* (Heaven, whither the anchor of our hope reach-
eth) *by the blood of Jesus* (there pleaded as
in the Holiest) *by a new and living way,
which he hath consecrated for us* (made holy
for us, and in our stead, as being only our
forerunner, and consequently having more
to come the same way) *through the veil,
that is to say, his* (and not our) *flesh* (in
which the veil of sin was rent) *and having
an High-Priest over the House of God* (into
which we are builded upon the foundation
Jesus Christ, for an habitation of God
through the Spirit) *let us draw near with
a true heart* (not let out to self, or the
world, but given and resigned to God) *in
full assurance of faith* (in that within the
veil, whither this anchor of our hope entereth) *having our hearts sprinkled from an
evil conscience* (or guilt, by the blood of
Christ, received by faith and patience) *and*

our bodies wafhed with pure water (as the *Jews* were typically with the impofition of that righteoufnefs which is as the fea)—*Let us hold faft the profeffion of our faith* (as the Scriptures, and not mens darkened minds, propofe it to us, as an active, quickening faith, rooted in *knowledge*, and working by *love*) *without wavering* (one tittle from them, unftirred by the deftructive blafts of worldly fpirits, for he is faithful, and will reward us as we build or ftumble upon God's precious *Stone* Jefus Chrift — *and let us confider one another as members one of another* (only as being by imputation members of one body, even of Chrift) *to provoke unto love and good works*, that each member, moved by *one hope*, and led by *one fpirit*, may work, in his peculiar ftation, to *one* end, the edification of the whole under the guidance of one *Head*, even *Chrift*, Eph. iv. 16. *from whom the whole body fitly joined together, and compacted by that which every joint fupplieth, according to the effectual working in the meafure of every part, maketh increafe of the body, unto the edifying of* the whole. How forry am I to fee you, who call yourfelf a Minifter of Chrift, are defirous to cut off from our interefts in, and connection with, this *Head*, by denying our *fellowfhip* with the merits and righteoufnefs of our dear Redeemer. becaufe, muft it not argue a man's inattention to his great and chiefeft good, as well as betray his ignorance of the natural means of fupporting life, when he would propofe to maintain the life of a body or member independently of its communion with its *head*, from whence, according to the nature of things, it muft of neceffity receive them   If thefe things are fo, then I conceive it lies upon you, henceforward, to difcountenance what only ftands upon fuch untenable ground ; for, if members muft be *dead* that are cut off from a communion with their *head*, and ever difqualified from raifing themfelves, then your detaching men from an intereft in Chrift's merits, is making them dead eternally.

120. You muft alfo own, Sir, that your fuppofing " afking in his Name," means our " afking as his fincere difciples and fol- " lowers," without any refpect to its fanctifying efficacy with God, is not to be juftified . for, unlefs the *dead* can be fincere, or follow at all, or move otherwife than they are moved, you predicate of them an evident contradiction. Asking *in his Name*, then, will always mean our fupplicating the Father as members of Jefus Chrift, in and for the fake of him, as he is the *Name* above every name, being the *Lord God omnipotent*, and an infinitely fatisfying media-

K k   tion.

tion I muſt beg, on this occaſion, to refer you to the Prophets, where we find God
ſaid to be merciful to man for his great
Name's ſake, and men ſaid *to walk in the
Name of the Lord* their *God*. For this
proves, that this phraſe beſpeaks as much
our connection *with* and *in* him, and with
and in whatſoever things were done by him
for our juſtification, as *walk in the light*
beſpeaks us in the light.

121. Your laſt paragraph, therefore, will
hardly need a particular reply: for, when
you conſider ſeriouſly how you have not,
without great boldneſs, ſet aſide the *inter-
ceſſion* of Chriſt as intercepting the blow for
us, and interpoſing his merits to cover our
ſins, which, I have ſhewn, is ſo ſtrongly
inſiſted upon in Scripture, you cannot, I
think, believe, much leſs ſollicit others to
believe, that " happy is the man who forms
" his principles and temper upon the blood
" of Jeſus, as a perfect model only;" according to the Scripture account, he is the
moſt miſled and ungrateful man living, becauſe man cannot form his *own* principles
and temper: the *formation* of man belongs
not to man, but to God; this would be to
make contrary to all reaſon, the *ſubject* to
be formed, and the *former* the ſame: and
the holineſs of our *High-Prieſt* is not to
be imitated by us with a view of being accepted

cepted by it ; it is the law of God, that such
shall die. And, when a man sees his infinite demerits, the infinite justice of God,
who will not clear the guilty, and his infinite power to punish the wicked, say, whether this man is happy, whether his con-
templation of the most perfect virtue or
goodness, wherein he knows he has so no-
toriously failed, can make him happy, or
rather say, would you describe the most
miserable man alive, it should be by saying, his case was that of the *Jews*, *God
was not for him*, he was *without Christ* in
the world—without his merits about him,
keeping him as a memento of what he is
not before his eyes (which cannot see it,
unless the *dead* can see) instead of taking
him into his heart to supply his wants, and
to perfect him for Heaven. A sober and
dispassionate mind cannot conceive any circumstances so piercingly painful to his soul
and body, whilst, on the other hand, there
is such unspeakable comfort arises, from a
consciousness that *Christ* is *God*, that his
merits are, therefore, of *infinite* availance,
and that my soul has an interest *in* them, so
as to have them made over to my use, that,
with all the strength of my scanty imagina-
tion, I cannot conceive any circumstances so
agreeable, nor any happiness but this founded on a rational and everlasting ground, for

K k 2

human

human nature, without this infinite worth put upon it, is far beneath our most unworthy conceptions of it, and unentitled to the least of mercies.

122. Excuse, nay commend me, Sir, when these things are so, if I have endeavoured to vindicate, from your exceptions, the things I hold to *belong unto* my *peace*; if I cannot, without cause, part with those merits which I look upon to be my *right* and *lawful* heretage. Had you an estate upon what you thought a good title you would try it, and I cannot see, upon cross-examining your witnesses, that they either agree with reason or nature, or amongst themselves, much less with the Divine Laws and Statutes. The principles I have gone upon are mostly your own, as the texts I have used are mostly of your own citing, from which, as far as I can see, I have fairly proved that common right of Christians in the propitiation of our blessed Lord, against which, who would think it, you, under the name of a *Minister*, have argued. Sometimes, indeed, when I could substitute more rational premisses, or bring further evidence in my favour, from Scripture, I have done it. And, as the matter in hand is of such great concernment to the world in general, being nothing less than an enquiry whether Christ did, or did *not*, redeem us;

whether

whether he did, or did *not*, make our cafe *his*, and, laftly, whether, on account of *his* payment, we are, or are *not*, fet free, fo, as a Chriftian, I require you to do what, as a *Minifter*, you are bound to do, for the peace of my own, as well as others fouls, to fignify any objections you have againft my conclufions concerning thefe truths. If I have reafoned from premiffes not given me in Scripture, and not countenanced by nature, or, if the inferences I have drawn from them ftand not in proper connection with my principles, be fincere, and tell me as freely as I have told you. If your intention is, as you fay it is, " upright," you muft do it. an " upright intention" will never leave the faith of Chriftians unfettled, but will fupport its fentiments by Scripture or Reafon; or, when this is not to be done, will honeftly recant them; apprized, however, narrow minds are fufpicious of drawing fhame upon them by fuch acknowledgment, that fhame can never, with any propriety, belong to him who, in the honefty of his heart, feeks to be informed, and only errs for want of information. Befides, Sir, hundreds may read your book, and imbibe your tenets only becaufe they are in print: and, fhould thefe have fallen off from the faith through your means, and continue in their belief for want of your recantation,

I dread

I dread to think what a heavy burden you muſt one day bear *for* thoſe miſled ſouls. As, therefore, it is but charity in me to caution you againſt the danger, it is but reaſonable for you to defend yourſelf, or, if you cannot do it, it is but honeſt to own your miſtake, and that *Chriſt died in the ſtead of us*, and is *our wiſdom, righteouſneſs, ſanctification*, and *redemption*. And, as to my part, the ſame ſpirit that led me to write theſe ſheets to arm you againſt thoſe pointed arrows of doctrine, which were firſt ſhot from the quivers of *Arius*, who denied Chriſt to be the *ſupreme God*, and of *Socinus*, who denied he ſuffered in the ſtead of us ; this ſame ſpirit, I ſay, will lead me to glory in your acknowledgment no otherwiſe than as it brings you to Chriſt, the *Power*, as well as *Wiſdom, of God*, and to *know the Grace of God* in truth, and as it undeceives them who may have come too haſtily into your way of thinking. Nor let it be thought a juſtifiable reaſon of your ſilence that I conceal my name ; for I have not put on a cloak to act a baſe, unworthy part. I have endeavoured indeed to caſt down your high thoughts, but to exalt your perſon, for to be one with Chriſt, who is one with God, and thus to receive his impreſſed image on our hearts, is an exaltation ſo great, that it is beyond our ambition

bition

bition to afpire higher. My intimations,
therefore, being thofe of a friend, defirous
to acquaint you with the wifdom and power
of the Gofpel, and zealous for your happinefs, as well as for the propagation of the
knowledge of the *myftery of God, and of
the Father, and of our Lord Jefus Chrift,*
I muft, in the name of all Chriftians, expect, from your upright intentions, either
your further exceptions, to which I promife you, God willing, a candid reply, or
your fair and honeft recantation. A fincere
and upright Chriftian cannot ask *lefs,* and
you cannot, in juftice to yourfelf and the
world, but do the *one* or the *other.* One
of us muft be miftaken, one of us muft fee
thefe things in a different light . and, I proteft to you, I have ufed no other than
that which God has given me in the Scriptures, which fhews this facred doctrine of
atonement in the colourings I have propofed
it Search then the Scriptures, and compare Scripture by Scripture, you may fee
what difficulties *Socinus, Fofter,* &c. labour
under for want of it, and the advantage I
have got from it. And if you are bleft with
the fenfe of feeling your wants, and hunger
and thirft after what you therefore want,
the renewing means of God , if you feek acceptance of God, and a light to enlighten
your underftanding to fhew you how you
may

may be accepted, and a spirit to give you a new life unto God, and, lastly, if you seek these in the Scriptures, where this Divine Light and Spirit first manifest themselves to us, and, by the faith of this then wisdom, then manifest themselves, and their power, unto our hearts, that they may be glorified in us, and we in them, I doubt not but that, upon a review of the passages in the Scriptures relative to the point in hand, as well as by reasonable induction, you will come to the knowledge of the things which belong unto your peace, and be changed, by *the powers of the world to come*, into that one image wherein alone God can delight. This is my hearty desire, as it is the end proposed by the labours of one who cannot deny Christ to be the supreme God, and his offering to be meritorious and satisfactory for, and in the stead of us, and believers, to have a saving interest in Christ's imputed sufferings and obedience, renovation and victory unto life under his shelter, because, *in nothing terrified by* his *adversaries*, he is

PHILO-BIBLOS.

F I N I S.

ERRATA

PAGE 17. l. 11. after *blind* read *broken*.

P. 21. l 15. after *feafts* read *and*.

P 25 l 25. put a Colon [·] after *No*.

P 40 put from l. 22. *altar* to *mercy-feat* in a paren-thefis.

P 42. l 25 for *brought* read *made*, and l 26. add *v*. 13.

P. 44. l. 17 prefix 23.

P 45. l. 10. omit the ftop after *obtained*.

P 53 l 14 for *Chrift* at the end read *God*.

P. 56. l. 25 after *Hebr*. read ix 7.

P 67 l. 1. read *call* for *calls*—l. 5 for *connect* read con-nects.

P. 76 l 29. after *and* read *the*.

P 78. l. 5 after *as* read *a*.

P 86. l 5. for *they* read *men*.

P 87, & feq. for MEAN read MEANS.

P. 91. l 3 for *iniruity* read *iniquity*.

P. 92 l. 10 after *transfer* read *of*.

P 97. in the laft line, inftead of *1* read *it*.

P 126. l 2 for *us protecting* read *protecting us*:

P 134 l 5. add *Dan* ix 24, 48 (16)—l 13. for *are* read *is*

P 136 l 3 after *brought* read *in*—l 5 for *texts* r *text*.

P 144 at the bottom of the firft column, after *John* add iii 36.

P 151. l. 13. in the laft column, after *John* add xv 1.

P 153. l. 19 after *Gen* in the laft column, add xlix. 11. and after *Rev*. add i 5

P 185. at the bottom, for *bonds* read *a bond*.

is my hearty defire ; this is the end propofed by my labours to make *you* a partaker of our faith and joy *in thefe laft times.* For I cannot deny Chrift to be the *fupreme God,* *equal,* and of one *undivided* fubftance with the *Father,* and of courfe his offering to be divinely meritorious and fatisfactory for, and in the ftead of us ; neither can I deny them who *believe* their juftification already wrought out by Chrift, our *kindred God,* above 1700 years ago, and not *remaining* to be accomplifhed by any act *of* or *in* them *now,* to have a real and faving intereft in his *imputed* fonfhip, fufferings and obedience, and daily renovation of mind here, and in the end victory unto life eternal under his fhelter, when he fhall " fhake not this earth only, but alfo heaven" becaufe in *nothing terrified by our various adverfaries,* I am, by the grace of God, a lover, tho' a too *cold* one, of the *Lord*'s word, that teaches thefe fublime truths. And tho' I am afhamed of the poor defence they have received from me, I am not afhamed, as I have been called upon to do it, to bear *my teftimony* to their truth, and to fubfcribe myfelf, with my prayers to *God* for *your* acknowledgment of it, that you may be found in the *white* robes of the *Lamb,* S I R,

Your very ready Servant in the Lord,

London, Feb 28, 1756. HENRY LEE.

F I N I S.

Lightning Source UK Ltd.
Milton Keynes UK
UKHW030634080421
381649UK00005B/312

9 781170 173725